Why Don't Americans Vote?

Why Don't Americans Vote?

Causes and Consequences

Bridgett A. King and Kathleen Hale, Editors

ABC-CLIO™

An Imprint of ABC-CLIO, LLC
Santa Barbara, California • Denver, Colorado

Library of Congress Cataloging-in-Publication Data

Names: King, Bridgett A.
Title: Why don't Americans vote? : causes and consequences / Bridgett A. King and Kathleen Hale, Editors.
Description: Santa Barbara, California : ABC-CLIO, [2016] | Includes bibliographical references and index.
Identifiers: LCCN 2016011826 | ISBN 9781440841156 (hardcopy : alk. paper) | ISBN 9781440841163 (ebook)
Subjects: LCSH: Voting—United States. | Elections—United States. | United States—Politics and government.
Classification: LCC JK1976 .K56 2016 | DDC 324.973—dc23
LC record available at https://lccn.loc.gov/2016011826

ISBN: 978–1–4408–4115–6
EISBN: 978–1–4408–4116–3

20 19 18 17 16   1 2 3 4 5

This book is also available as an eBook.

ABC-CLIO
An Imprint of ABC-CLIO, LLC

ABC-CLIO, LLC
130 Cremona Drive, P.O. Box 1911
Santa Barbara, California 93116-1911
www.abc-clio.com

This book is printed on acid-free paper ∞

Manufactured in the United States of America

Dedicated in loving memory to Dorsey Ward.

Contents

Introduction: Why Don't Americans Vote? The History of the Franchise in the United States

Bridgett A. King

Concerns about voter turnout in the United States are not new. To the contrary, they date back to the late 19th and early 20th century. Prior to the election of 1896, voter turnout in the United States was typically high, frequently over 80 percent (Appendix A.1.). In the elections that followed the presidential election of 1896, however, voter turnout in the nation began to decrease. From the presidential election of 1896 to the presidential election of 1912, turnout dropped from almost 80 percent to less than 60 percent nationally. As with contemporary American elections, turnout was even lower in midterm elections during this period.

Potential explanations for this decline included disinterest, lack of party competition, and legal constraints. In response, considerations were given to compulsory voting measures and scholars began to study "get out the vote" (GOTV) campaigns targeting non-voters, who were disproportionately poor and working class. Turnout was also low among women, immigrants, and their children (Keyssar 2000, 185). Due to the influence of classist and partisan biases, however, the recognition of steadily declining turnout did not result in extensive proactive efforts to enfranchise more of the citizen population.

In the 21st century, concerns persist regarding low voter turnout. With few exceptions, turnout in American presidential elections hovers around 50–60 percent. In midterm elections, turnout is often lower than 50 percent (see Appendix A.1).

More than a century after concerns over voter turnout first emerged, politicians, pundits, and academics continue to attempt to understand why Americans do not exercise their right to vote in greater numbers. As with initial concerns over voter turnout, which produced various potential explanations and solutions, a variety of explanations and solutions have been proposed to explain the state of voter turnout in contemporary American politics. Although most policy solutions have addressed matters related to voter eligibility and access to registration and voting, other proposed solutions have focused on other potential factors, such as voter mobilization, lack of interest, and limited candidate options.

Over the course of American history, voting has been described as a right, privilege, and duty. Each of these terms prescribes a certain expectation regarding who should participate. For much of American history, the ability to participate in the franchise has been limited by legal restrictions. The right to vote as we know it today has changed and evolved over time, shaped by legislation in individual states, the U.S. Congress, and decisions by the U.S. Supreme Court.

VOTER ELIGIBILITY IN EARLY AMERICA

Prior to the founding of the nation, colonies determined their own suffrage laws. These laws traditionally stemmed from British tradition. From this period, perhaps the most notable voting provision was the restriction of voting to adult men who owned property. The necessity of property ownership was justified on two grounds. First, individuals who owned property were viewed as having a unique stake in society. Because of this, it was expected that they would not vote in subversive ways that would undermine their own best interest. Second, property owners were independent. Because they had the means to own land, they were not dependent upon or in debt to anyone and thus could make decisions independently, or at least, independent of influence. In colonies where economic opportunities were believed to be unbounded, anyone legally permitted to own land but who failed to acquire property was considered to be of questionable competence. The importance of having a stake in the colony or state in which one voted produced additional requirements for residency and citizenship. Finally, to ensure that those who were dependent were not allowed to vote, several colonies barred servants and paupers. Additionally, women were excluded because they were not believed to have the necessary intellectual and emotional capabilities to navigate the world of politics and policy.

Exclusion from and inclusion in the franchise also depended on social status. In the South, freedmen (African descendants or Amerindian descendants) were excluded, and in some states, participation was determined by religious affiliation. For example, in Massachusetts during the 17th century only members of the Congregational Church could vote.

In the 18th century, Catholics were disenfranchised in five states and Jews were similarly disenfranchised in four states. Variation in suffrage laws was also rooted in geography. In rural areas, the ability to participate was often determined by property ownership and residency; in larger cities, those granted political citizenship were often those who had commercial affairs within city limits rather than a residence. Thus, in many instances, only those who contributed to the municipality's finances were able to participate.

During America's earliest history, systems of voting varied from colony to colony as well as from city to county and ultimately from state to state. During this time, values varied about who had the right to participate in a democracy and these values influenced voting laws and practices. Across the 13 colonies, laws were being used to shape democracy in very different ways. As time progressed, some colonies became more lenient while others became more restrictive. Religious restrictions were lifted in the late 17th and early 18th centuries, cities began to allow land owners to vote as opposed to just those with commercial enterprises, and property requirements were reduced in Massachusetts and Virginia. In other colonies such as Pennsylvania, Rhode Island, and Virginia, the property requirements became more restrictive and severe. As time passed and the original 13 colonies became today's 50 states, legal variations governing access to the franchise continued to persist.

In the midst of the colonies' ongoing efforts to determine the rules providing for political participation, the American Revolution began. As a revolution that sought to secure both independence and representation, questions were raised regarding whether and to what extent rules that were adopted because of English tradition should be maintained. Lack of representation was one of the colonists' central grievances with the King of England; however, segments of the population would be excluded from the franchise with these rules, effectively denying representation.

Wealthy individuals wanted to restrict the expansion of the franchise to allow for their continued economic and social advantage. It was suggested that if the propertyless were allowed to vote, they would be a menace to a well-ordered community. Representation of these ineligibles was essentially virtual rather than actual; it was asserted that the interests of the propertyless, women, and children could be effectively represented by wise, fair-minded, wealthy white men. The importance of (financial) independence was emphasized to ensure votes would not be bought and sold. Interestingly, this argument coexisted with the assertion that people who did not own property should not vote because, if able to vote, they would have too much will of their own and, therefore, threaten the interests of property owners.

Poor, nonproperty-owning individuals objected to this state of affairs. They wanted to expand the franchise, ensuring they would have a say in setting the young nation's course. In favor of men who did not own property, it was argued that voting was a natural right that the state could not abridge except in the most severe cases. The notion of popular consent—the idea that "no man can be bound by law that he has not given his consent to, either by his person or legal representative"—was also invoked to support expansion of the franchise. As these arguments gained traction, the property ownership requirement was replaced with a taxpaying requirement. The original colonies (Maryland, Massachusetts, New York, Virginia, and North Carolina) were the first to eliminate their property requirements. Additionally, no state that entered the union after 1790 had provisions that included property ownership as a requirement to vote. By the 1850s, there were only two property requirements remaining; these pertained to foreign-born residents of Rhode Island and African Americans in New York (Keyssar 2000).

Following the American Revolution, there was no guaranteed right to vote included in the Constitution. What the Constitution does provide is a federalist system in which both the federal government and state governments operate as sovereign entities. The Tenth Amendment, stating that "The powers not delegated to the United States by the Constitution, nor prohibited by it to the States, are reserved to the States respectively, or to the people," effectively provided states with the authority over all issues not explicitly established within federal jurisdiction. This left states in the position to continue to make decisions regarding voter eligibility, requirements, and administrative procedures. As the population of the United States grew from less than 4 million in 1790 to more than 20 million in 1859 (Keyssar 2000), individual states began to focus on establishing qualifications and exclusions that would be consistent across the cities and townships within each state, and on administrative procedures related to voter registration and the act of voting itself.

Although as initially established, the qualifications for voting in local and state elections were not identical, by the mid-1800s suffrage laws in cities became identical to those of their states. This occurred because of two developments. First, the notion that city charters were inviolable deteriorated. Cities came to be viewed as creatures of the state rather than as sovereign entities. Second, the concept of state supremacy allowed state legislatures to set the rules for enfranchisement in the state and in municipalities.

As voting restrictions were loosened, the franchise opened to a whole host of people who had previously been classified as "undesirables" and they also had emerged as prominent fixtures in the nation's industrialization. These groups included women, free blacks, recent immigrants, poor whites, day laborers, and factory workers. Each of these groups has had a unique experience and struggle toward gaining full and complete access to the franchise. Although the franchise expanded with the founding of the United States and the removal of property ownership requirements, many states maintained the taxpaying requirement, established citizenship and residency requirements, and created tests for registration and voting. These stipulations served to curtail the political participation of the poor, women, minorities, and new immigrants. The franchise thus expanded only fitfully during this time.

PAUPERS, TRANSIENTS, AND FELONS

Although 60–70 percent of all white males could vote in 1790 (Keyssar 2000), states continually excluded specific groups of white males from the franchise. Those on the social margins or fringes who did not conform to the social norms of the time were not deemed worthy of the franchise. One group excluded was paupers, or men who received public relief from their communities or from the state. The exclusion of paupers resulted from constitutional provisions determined by the newly formed states, in contrast to the English legal legacies of property ownership and taxpaying requirements. The rationale for these laws was that, "men who accepted public support surrendered their independence and lost the capacity to function as a citizen" (Keyssar 2000, 49). Men who encountered misfortune were described as also having willingly surrendered their rights (Keyssar 2000, 49).

Felons were also excluded in many states. The exclusion of felons existed as a carryover from Roman law and English tradition. Disenfranchisement served as retribution for committing a crime and as a deterrent to future antisocial behavior. States began incorporating disenfranchisement provisions into their constitutions shortly after the founding of the Republic. In most cases, the disenfranchisement was permanent and applied to those who had committed felonies or infamous crimes.

Although the states eventually abolished property ownership and taxpaying requirements for enfranchisement, residency requirements were used to restrict access to the franchise to those who had a vested interest in the outcome of elections. Although there was little argument regarding the inclusion of residency restrictions, the period of time necessary to qualify as a resident was not as easily agreed upon. In the 1800s, the average residency requirement was one year in a state and three or six months in a county or township. Lengthy residency requirements were used to ensure migrant and transient populations were excluded from participating.

As political parties formed, they began to collectively assert positions regarding access to the franchise. These positions were often not based on ideologies about what was right, honorable, or moral, but rather on the perceived political support the parties would receive from particular groups of people. Although there was some consensus across parties regarding the exclusion of felons, the exclusion of transient populations and paupers was highly contestable and laden with partisan preference. The Federalists and the Whigs, for example, favored longer residency requirements because of a belief that the transient and the poor would be more likely to support Democratic and Republican candidates. The Democrats supported this notion as well, advocating for shorter residency requirements in order to enfranchise more of their supporters.

AFRICAN AMERICANS

Following the American Revolution and the founding of the nation, African Americans were enfranchised in North Carolina, Massachusetts, New York, Pennsylvania, Maryland, and Vermont. Very few states had laws that placed voting restrictions on African Americans. In 1790, only Virginia, Georgia, and South Carolina had formal restrictions. Prior to the start of the Civil War, five states in New England allowed African Americans to vote based on the same qualifications as whites. After the Civil War and the abolition of slavery by the Thirteenth Amendment (Appendix A.2) in 1865, there were 4 million new free black Americans in the United States. Some states that had previously allowed black Americans to vote at the initial founding (New Jersey, Maryland, Connecticut) began to limit access to the franchise to white men. Over time, other states began to formalize racial exclusions by adding 'white' to the language of their constitutions or through legislation limiting participation to white men (New York, Ohio, Indiana, Wisconsin). By 1855, only five states (Massachusetts, Vermont, New Hampshire, Maine, and Rhode Island) did not discriminate against African Americans; these states contained a very small portion of the free black population. In the South, ideas of black enfranchisement were continually viewed as contrary to structured and deeply rooted racism. Whites thus worked mightily to maintain or regain political, social, and economic control over the black population. In the North, racist beliefs from the 1840s persisted and were coupled with fears about massive African American migration.

The U.S. Supreme Court decision in *Dred Scott v. Sandford* in 1857 established the federal precedent that blacks, whether free or slave, could not be citizens and were not eligible for the full rights of citizenship including the right to vote. During the Civil War, several states and territories were actively engaged in trying to enfranchise blacks. Following the Civil War, the adoption of the Fourteenth Amendment in 1868 addressed citizenship rights and equal protection of the laws and extended certain political and civil rights to African Americans (see Appendix A.2). The amendment was bitterly contested particularly by southern secessionist states, which were forced to ratify it in order to regain representation in Congress.

The Fourteenth Amendment did not provide blacks with access to the franchise; however, several clauses influenced the national conversation in that direction. The Citizenship Clause overruled the *Dred Scott* decision and stated that black people were citizens and eligible to enjoy the full benefits of citizenship—including voting. The Privileges and Immunities Clause prohibited states from interfering with the privileges and immunities possessed by virtue of national citizenship. The Due Process Clause guaranteed the right to fair procedural and substantive due process. Lastly, the Equal Protection Clause was created largely in response to the lack of equal protection provided by law in states with so-called Black Codes that did not allow blacks to sue, give evidence, or be witnesses in legal proceedings. The Fourteenth Amendment also penalized states that denied the right to vote to all male citizens of age 21 by reducing the basis of representation accordingly (Reiman 1995, 5). Effectively, any state that denied the right to vote of its male citizens would have its representation in Congress reduced by the portion of male citizens who were denied the right to vote.

The Fifteenth Amendment, adopted in 1870, further extended the franchise by prohibiting states from denying access to the franchise solely based on race, color, or previous condition of servitude (Appendix A.2).

Following the passage of the Fourteenth and Fifteenth Amendments, Democrats from the southern states sought to solidify their hold on the region by modifying voting laws to exclude African Americans from the polls (Wood and Trivedi 2007). States in the South expanded their voting restrictions on the felon population. This included the extension of disenfranchisement laws to encompass a variety of crimes not previously included. At the same time, states expanded the criminal codes to punish offenses that they believed freedmen (former slaves) were most likely to commit, including vagrancy, petty larceny, miscegenation, bigamy, and receiving stolen goods (Ewald 2002, 1088–1089). Groundless charges were also easy to level against blacks, and many African Americans lost the franchise in this manner.

During the Jim Crow Era (1877 to mid-1960s), states enacted felon voting bans alongside constitution interpretation tests, literacy tests, and poll taxes that were all designed to keep blacks from voting. States also enacted grandfather clauses, which exempted from tests and taxes those whose grandfathers had been eligible to vote. These laws were often called Jim Crow Laws. The term "Jim Crow" refers to a racial epithet or slur that was used for blacks in the 1800s. Jim Crow Laws were legal barriers (including literacy tests, residency requirements, grandfather clauses, and poll taxes) employed by states that appeared to be race-neutral (because the laws did not discriminate based on race) but were designed to prevent African Americans from voting (Behrens 2004; Ewald 2002; Keyssar 2000). In Mississippi, after the state implemented Jim Crow

Laws in 1890, fewer than 9,000 of the 147,000 voting age African Americans were registered to vote. Similarly, in Louisiana, where more than 130,000 black voters had been registered in 1896, the adoption of Jim Crow Laws slashed the number of registered African American voters to 1,342 by 1904. In addition, despite the newfound voting eligibility, freedmen remained practically disenfranchised as a result of organized efforts to prevent them from voting.

WOMEN'S SUFFRAGE

At the founding of the United States, women comprised half of the population and represented the largest group of citizens excluded from the franchise. Although the Fourteenth and Fifteenth Amendments to the Constitution greatly expanded the franchise, the term "male" was expressly used throughout the amendments, excluding women regardless of race. The exclusion of women from political life had cultural roots that extended back to Europe. Even women who were perceived as intelligent adults were not treated as individuals but as members of families. Like paupers and nonproperty owners, they were viewed as lacking the requisite *independence* necessary to participate in politics.

The women's suffrage movement began in 1848 in Seneca Falls, New York, with the Declaration of Sentiments. The Declaration of Sentiments, drafted by Elizabeth Cady Stanton, was modeled after the Declaration of Independence and asserted, "All men and women are created equal; that they are endowed by their Creator with certain inalienable rights; that among these are life, liberty, and the pursuit of happiness." The declaration also listed a series of grievances including those related to the franchise stating, "He has never permitted her to exercise her inalienable right to the elective franchise," and "Having deprived her of this first right of a citizen, the elective franchise, thereby leaving her without representation in the halls of legislation, he has oppressed her on all sides."

The timing of the Seneca Falls Convention coincided with social changes regarding the role of women in the United States and the expansion of the franchise for other marginalized groups. Women were increasingly an integral part of the paid labor force, and conversations about the disenfranchisement of other groups (immigrants, African Americans, the propertyless, etc.) and universal suffrage created opportunities to discuss the enfranchisement of women. Prior to the passage of the Fifteenth Amendment, there was an expectation among the suffragists that prodemocratic sentiments would welcome women as well as African Americans into political life.

With the ratification of the Fourteenth Amendment in 1868 and its express guarantee of political rights to males, suffragettes and their political allies engaged in a vigorous campaign to promote universal suffrage and connect the causes of suffrage for women and African Americans.

In the midst of these campaigns, diverging strategies emerged among Republican abolitionist supporters. Concerned that the ability to enfranchise freedmen would be jeopardized by the combining of the two issues, some believed it best to first enfranchise African American men, and women second. The result was that many abolitionists and African Americans campaigned against women's suffrage and many feminists and supporters of women's suffrage demeaned the abilities and qualifications of African Americans for the franchise. With the 1870 ratification of the Fifteenth Amendment, which extended suffrage to African American men, the once unified causes of black male suffrage and women's suffrage were severed. Following this setback, the suffrage movement adopted several strategies. First, the National Women Suffrage Association (NWSA) pressured the federal government to grant women suffrage rights through a national organization controlled by women. Second, the NWSA attempted to convince individual state legislatures and constitutional conventions to grant women suffrage rights. This latter strategy was also utilized by the American Woman Suffrage Association (AWSA).

As momentum and support for the suffragettes' movement grew, the primary argument for women's suffrage remained the natural and universal rights perspective that was presented at the Seneca Falls Convention in 1848. Additionally, the suffragettes argued that women possessed certain qualities that would improve politics and governance. This argument, that women should be enfranchised not because they are just like men but because they are different from men, was embraced not only by suffragettes but also many male politicians. Other arguments also referenced the principle of "no taxation without representation" and touted the economic protections that enfranchisement would provide for an ever increasing number of female wage earners. In addition to pressure from suffragettes and their supports, the debate over whether to enfranchise women was also driven by the ideological and psychological resistance of men, the size of suffragette organizations and the pressure they could exert, and regional differences.

In 1890, AWSA and NWSA combined to form the National American Woman Suffrage Association (NAWSA). In 1915, NAWSA embarked on a national strategy to secure women's suffrage. The plan was to garner support for the Nineteenth Amendment by focusing on the 36 states most likely to support the ratification of a women's suffrage amendment. Additionally, more decisive political maneuvers were used. The Congressional Union, Women's Party, and National Women's Party began encouraging eligible women to vote against Democratic candidates who did not support suffrage. The National Women's Party picketed the White House, public demonstrations were held, money was raised, and state and national political leaders were lobbied.

When the nation entered World War I in 1917, the NAWSA used the war as an opportunity to demonstrate the ways that women could mobilize and contribute to the war effort. The NAWSA provided Americanization classes, distributed food, sold bonds and thrift stamps, knitted clothes, and provided gifts to soldiers and sailors (Keyssar 2000, 174). By 1918, 20 territories and states provided women with full enfranchisement, allowing them to vote in state and federal elections, 17 states allowed women to vote in presidential elections, and 14 states allowed women to vote in municipal elections. Additionally, 30 states and territories permitted women to vote in elections addressing issues that were perceived to be a woman's responsibility. Women were allowed to vote in municipal elections for local school boards, on issues affecting education, and on liquor license issues.

The NAWSA also provided political support to the Wilson administration. In January 1918, President Wilson announced support for a suffrage amendment. Following this announcement, the House of Representatives voted in favor of the Nineteenth Amendment. In 1919, after pressure from suffragettes, the Senate approved the measure. The constitutional amendment was quickly approved in many northeastern, midwestern, and western states, but opposition in the South was much stronger. In spite of this resistance, in August 1920, Tennessee became the 36th state to positively vote for the amendment, and consequently, the Nineteenth Amendment became law and women were fully enfranchised (Appendix A.2).

AMERICAN INDIANS AND IMMIGRANTS

During the antebellum period (approximately 1815 to 1860), matters of citizenship and racial identity affected not only blacks but also American Indians and immigrants. In assessing the right to vote for America's indigenous population, the racial identity of American Indians was called into question. States assessed the race of American Indians in a variety of ways. For example, Michigan determined that American Indians were in fact white because white simply was the opposite of black. Thus, to be classified as white, one essentially had to not be black (Keyssar 2000). Most states, however, determined that American Indians should not be excluded from participating, regardless of their racial classification, as long as they were "civilized," taxpaying, and assimilated into the dominant culture in the United States. Citizenship status also hindered American Indian enfranchisement. U.S. Supreme Court decisions rendered American Indian tribes as "domestic, independent nations." Consequently, Indians living in tribes were considered aliens even when born in United States. American Indians were provided a clear path to citizenship if they would leave their tribes and settle among whites. However, because they were not immigrants, they could not become citizens through the traditional process and could only become citizens by a treaty or a special act of Congress.

The pendulum of suffrage continually swung back and forth for noncitizens and the foreign born (individuals who were not citizens but often met residency requirements). In some states, foreign-born men who had not been naturalized by the federal government but who met property, taxpaying, and residency requirements were able to participate in elections. That said, continued concerns about the influence of immigrants often led states to limit enfranchisement by simultaneously increasing the requirements for citizenship and increasing the requirements for voting. Immigrants were often divided into two classes: settlers who typically brought with them some form of capital and workers who took jobs in manufacturing, transportation, and construction. Working-class immigrants, specifically the Irish, were often the target of ethnic antagonism. Justifications for excluding new immigrants from the franchise often centered around claims that immigrants had insufficient tutoring in American values and the workings of American democracy, that they were prone to selling their votes, and that enfranchisement would trigger mass naturalization (Keyssar 2000).

In order to protect themselves from the potential influx of undesirable foreign-born voters, many states changed their constitutions to limit voting to citizens only. However, in the latter half of the 1800s, states in the upper Midwest (Wisconsin, Michigan, Indiana, the Oregon Territory and the Minnesota Territory) opened the franchise to noncitizens who had lived in the United States for at least two years with the intention of becoming citizens. After the Civil War, a dozen more states in the South followed suit. Outside of the Northeast, noncitizen suffrage was commonplace. Federal intervention in suffrage laws also coincided with federal policy governing the circumstances under which new states could enter the Union. The Northwest Ordinance marked the first significant westward expansion of the United States and encompassed land between the Great Lakes and the Mississippi River; today that land includes Ohio, Indiana, Illinois, Michigan, Wisconsin, and Minnesota. The terms of the Northwest Ordinance enfranchised all free white men in the Northwest Territory who resided there and had paid taxes.

As with most attempts to expand or limit the franchise, these immigration issues also illustrate a clear and direct relationship between political parties and voter preferences. For example, the Know Nothing Party active during the 1840s and 1850s supported changes to federal policy that advocated extensive waiting periods before naturalization or permanent denial of citizenship to the foreign born. The Know Nothings also supported state-level proposals to tighten voter registration laws through literacy tests and long naturalization residency waiting periods (14 or 21 years) before a foreign-born male could vote. Policies were also suggested that would require naturalized citizens to wait 1, 5, 10, and even 21 years after becoming citizens before they were eligible to vote.

Although most of these provisions failed, concerns about electoral fraud and ballot box purity led four New England states to prohibit judges from naturalizing citizens. Concerns about immigration extended beyond the Northeast and Midwest. In the West, Oregon limited the vote to white males in order to prevent Chinese immigrants from voting. There were also anti-immigrant policy changes in the South. Georgia responded to a growing Irish working class within its borders by limiting the right to vote to white males with property. Dramatic changes also occurred in Massachusetts and Connecticut, which required immigrants to read the Constitution and write their own names before registration.

ELECTION ADMINISTRATION

Concerns about undesirable populations gaining the franchise also led to state administrative reforms. Voter registration was one specific focus. Although Massachusetts adopted a voter registration system in 1801, most states had no formal system for voter registration and no procedures to maintain an accurate list of registered voters in the early 19th century. Proponents of voter registration at the time—such as the Whigs, who believed that ineligible voters were casting ballots for their opponent Democrats—argued that the express goal of voter registration was to reduce fraud. Opponents of voter registration, however, suggested that the real goal of voter registration was to disenfranchise poor voters, as they would often be working rather than at home when assessors went door to door to register voters. In some states, voter registration was used explicitly by lawmakers as a partisan tool to exclude certain religious and ethnic groups from voting. In New York, for example, early voter registration proposals were designed to limit the participation of Irish Catholic immigrants and consequently reduce support for the Democratic Party.

Reforms were also made regarding the way ballots were cast. Prior to the American Revolution, voice voting was regularly used to determine voter preference and electoral outcomes. By the mid-19th century most votes were cast using paper ballots that contained the names of candidates. Although ballots could be written or printed, most of the ballots were printed. Ballots were not printed formally by a governmental agency, but were printed by political parties on paper in varying distinguishable colors. Partisan-colored ballots eliminated voter secrecy and eased the creation of counterfeit tickets. They also provided uninformed voters with an opportunity to vote for their preferred party ticket (Evans 1917). Between 1831 and 1881, objection to these conditions led 15 states to pass laws regulating the color of the paper and type of ink used to print the ballots. Although white was typically the color of paper specified by state law, parties began using different shades of white. Consequently, it was still possible to determine the party ticket that was voted. To address this latter issue, states like California and Oregon required ballots be printed on paper supplied by the secretary of state (Evans 1917). The failure of these new provisions to provide for voter secrecy led to vote buying, corruption, and intimidation.

To combat these issues, the concept of a secret ballot printed by the government was first introduced in the United States in 1888 in Louisville, Kentucky. Known as the Australian ballot, it was adopted in 39 states by 1896. The adoption of the Australian ballot led to several changes in election procedures: uniform ballots were printed and distributed by the federal government at taxpayer expense; candidates had to be nominated by a political party or a threshold number of voters in order to have their name printed on the ballot; the state was required to advertise the name of all individuals who were to appear on the ballot; and officers charged with the designation of polling locations were required to supply an appropriate number of voting booths (Evans 1917).

EARLY VOTING AND REGISTRATION REQUIREMENTS

Additional administrative efforts to limit the franchise included the adoption of poll taxes and literacy tests. Poll taxes were payments required by voters in order to register to vote. In many jurisdictions, voters were required to present a poll tax receipt at their polling location before they were allowed to vote. Those who could not present proof of payment were deemed ineligible to vote.

Between 1871 and 1902 poll taxes were adopted in Georgia, Florida, Alabama, Tennessee, Arkansas, Louisiana, Mississippi, North Carolina, South Carolina, Virginia, and Texas (Dowdy 2014). In 1877, Georgia instituted a cumulative poll tax requirement that required eligible men to pay back taxes for every year from the time they turned 21, or from the time that the law took effect. The value of the poll tax in the former confederate states varied from $1–$2 and was difficult, if not impossible, for poor black and white sharecroppers to pay. Thus, the implementation of poll taxes had a dramatic effect on voter registration and turnout. During the 1880 presidential election, Georgia was the only southern state with a poll tax in effect. Overall turnout in Georgia was more than 66 percent lower than other southern states. When compared to Florida, a state with the same percentage of African Americans, black turnout in Georgia was less than half the turnout in Florida (Kousser 1999).

Poll taxes were also in place in some northern and western states. For instance, California had a poll tax until 1914, when it was abolished through a popular referendum. Washington also had a poll tax until

1922, when it was abolished through initiative. Poll taxes in federal elections were banned nationally by the passage of the Twenty-Fourth Amendment in 1964 (Appendix A.2). However, it was not until the passage of the Voting Rights Act (VRA) in 1965 that poll taxes were banned in state and local elections.

Similar to poll taxes, literacy tests are most commonly associated with the Jim Crow South. But they were also used outside the South to exclude immigrants and the poor from the franchise. In northeastern states, concerns about immigrant voting led many states during their constitutional conventions to consider the implementation of literacy tests or English language literacy tests for potential voters. In the 1840s, New York, New Jersey, Indiana, Maryland, and Missouri considered the implementation of such measures. In the 1850s, Massachusetts and Connecticut adopted literacy tests, and support for such measures spread in the 1870s. The use of literacy tests to weed out ignorant voters was deemed by many to be much more palatable than restrictions related to paying taxes or voting waiting periods for the foreign born. Partisan and ethnic preferences directly affected views about literacy tests. Northern Democrats who counted on the urban poor as partisan supporters were strongly opposed to literacy tests. Politically organized ethnic groups also opposed literacy tests. Consequently, none were adopted in the Midwest, where large German and Scandinavian communities vehemently opposed English language literacy tests. In New Mexico, the sizable Spanish-speaking electorate included in the state's first constitution a provision prohibiting the restriction of the right to vote on account of inability to speak, read, or write English or Spanish. In spite of this, by the mid-1920s, 13 northern and western states disenfranchised illiterate citizens who otherwise qualified to vote (Keyssar 2000).

CONTEMPORARY FEDERAL POLICY INTERVENTIONS

Multiple pieces of federal legislation have been passed to standardize and create avenues of participation in the United States. In 1845, Congress passed a law designating the first Tuesday after the first Monday in November as Election Day. Often voters had to travel to the county seat in order to cast their ballot. Tuesday was selected as it gave rural voters a day to travel following the day of rest on Sunday. Congress also believed that November would be the most convenient month for farmers and citizens who lived in rural areas. Prior to the passage of this legislation, states could hold elections when they pleased as long as the elections were held during the period 34 days prior to the first Wednesday in December. Subsequent changes to the franchise included the passage of the Fourteenth, Fifteenth, Nineteenth, and Twenty-Fourth Amendments. The last constitutional change to the franchise occurred in 1971 with the ratification of the Twenty-Sixth Amendment that extended voting rights to individuals of age 18–20 (Appendix A.2).

In 1964, the Civil Rights Act was passed by Congress. The Civil Rights Act outlawed discrimination based on race, color, sex, religion, or national origin. Although the Civil Rights Act did not outlaw literacy tests and other mechanisms that were used to disenfranchise black voters in the South, the Civil Rights Act did include a provision that voter registration rules and procedures be applied equally to all races.

The Voting Rights Act (VRA) of 1965 directly addresses discriminatory registration and voting procedures. The VRA most profoundly impacted the voting rights of blacks because it forced states to comply with the Fifteenth Amendment to the U.S. Constitution, which had eliminated the right to deny access to vote solely based on race (Henderson 2006). Prior to the VRA, there was no federal guarantee of the right to vote. In turn, states reserved the right to preside over elections as they chose; because of discriminatory practices in many states, this approach did not favor black voters (Henderson 2006).

The primary purpose of the 1965 VRA was to establish a federal guarantee and eliminate policies in states, particularly those in the South, that impeded the right of blacks and other minorities to vote (Barker and Barker 1987). With the passage of the VRA, literary tests, poll taxes, and other obstacles to enfranchisement were eliminated (Barker and Barker 1987; Cain and Miller 1998). Immediately following the enactment of the VRA, there were dramatic increases in black registration and subsequently black voting (Henderson 1987). This increase in the number of black registered voters was most noticeable in the South. In Mississippi, the number of registered black voters increased from 28,500 in 1965 to 406,000 in 1984 (Colby 1986). In Louisiana, in 1964 blacks accounted for 13.7 percent of registered voters, by 1985 blacks accounted for 25.1 percent of registered voters (Wright 1986).

The general provisions against discrimination found in the VRA apply nationwide. However, the dramatic changes in registration that occurred in the South also were attributable to special VRA provisions that designated some states for additional federal oversight of election practices. These so-called covered jurisdictions were identified through a formula in the VRA, tied to the use of discriminatory voting practices. Initially, the designation applied to states that had a history of employing discriminatory tests, devices, or practices in voting (Cotrell 1986, 7–8). Covered jurisdictions (whether counties or entire states) were required to obtain federal review and approval of any changes related to voting laws or practices before implementing them; this review, known as preclearance, is contained in Section 5 of the VRA and was conducted either administratively through the U.S. Department of Justice or through the federal courts. Without preclearance, officials in the covered jurisdictions were not allowed to change any of their "election procedures until the proposed changes have been certified as not having the potential for significant interference with the right of Blacks to register and vote" (Wright 1986, 97). Although initial coverage was limited to states of the former confederate South, over time coverage extended to individual counties and townships in New York, South Dakota, California, Michigan, and New Hampshire. The VRA formula was ruled unconstitutional in 2013 (*Shelby County v. Holder*) in part because the coverage formula was based on information that was more than 40 years old and thus could not be used to address contemporary voting concerns. One of the primary concerns raised by voting advocates following *Shelby County v. Holder* was that states that were once covered by Section 5 would enact legislation that was discriminatory. In fact, in the wake of the *Shelby County v. Holder* decision, many of the states that had been previously subject to Section 5 moved quickly to amend their voting laws. These changes included tightening voter identification requirements, reducing early voting periods, and imposing new redistricting plans.

Additional federal voting legislation has been passed by Congress. The 1993 National Voter Registration Act (NVRA) and the 2002 Help America Vote Act (HAVA) have the express intention of securing access to the ballot for potentially marginalized citizens. As a voter registration convenience measure, NVRA requires states to provide individuals with the opportunity to register to vote at the same time they apply for a driver's license or seek to renew a driver's license and to offer voter registration opportunities at all offices that provide public assistance and all offices that provide state-funded programs primarily engaged in providing services to persons with disabilities. The connection to state agencies that regulate driver licenses gave the NVRA its popular name, "Motor Voter." Passed after the contentious and highly publicized outcome of the 2000 presidential election, HAVA established minimum federal election administration standards. These include standards for voter identification, provisional voting when identification or registration is uncertain, statewide electronic voter registration databases, and new electronic voting systems to address the shortcomings of the nation's aging voting equipment. Through HAVA the Election Assistance Commission (EAC) was established as an independent, bipartisan commission. The EAC serves as a national clearinghouse of information on election administration. The EAC is also charged with developing guidance to meet HAVA requirements including grants to the states to purchase new electronic voting equipment and adopting guidelines for certifying voting systems in a voluntary certification program.

In addition, HAVA further facilitates participation by voters with disabilities. Since 1965, the VRA has required election officials to allow voters who are blind or who have other disabilities to receive assistance from a person of the voter's choice. Additionally, the Voting Accessibility for the Elderly and Handicapped Act of 1984 requires accessible polling places in federal elections for elderly individuals and people with disabilities. Where no accessible location is available to serve as a polling place, voters must be provided an alternate means of voting on Election Day. HAVA requires jurisdictions responsible for conducting elections to provide at least one accessible voting system for persons with disabilities at each polling place in federal elections and to allow all voters to vote privately and independently.

FIFTY LABORATORIES OF DEMOCRACY

Although federal legislation has dramatically changed the landscape of American elections, states also continue to greatly influence what citizens experience when they make the decision to register and vote. Where federal interventions have not produced the desired electoral integrity or increases in registration and turnout, some states have created policies that provide greater access to registration and voting. For example, some states have extended voting and registration periods by adopting Election Day Voter Registration and early voting provisions. Other states allow some or all elections to be conducted by mail, allow individuals to request an absentee ballot without providing an excuse, and allow voters to establish permanent absentee voting status. In addition to the requirements of the NVRA and HAVA, many states have also implemented policies that specify more rigorous requirements for voter identification. These policies diffuse from state to state, creating a continually evolving electoral environment.

When trying to answer the question, "Why don't Americans vote?" it is important to remember that no one administrative rule, psychological orientation, or voting and registration policy can fully explain why an individual may not participate on Election Day. Understanding why Americans choose not to vote requires the consideration of a variety of factors that collectively lend themselves to low voter turnout in the United States. Each of the 20 essays that follow discusses one component of the American electoral system; together, these essays help answer the question, "Why don't Americans vote?"

FURTHER READING

Barker Jr., Twiley W., and Lucious Barker. 1987. "The Courts, Section 5 of the Voting Rights Act, and the Future of Black Politics." In *The New Black Politics: The Search for Political Power* (2nd ed.), edited by M. B. Preston, L. J. Henderson Jr., and P. L. Puryear, 59–75. White Plains, NY: Longman Inc.

Behrens, Angela. 2004. "Voting—Not Quite a Fundamental Right?" *Minnesota Law Review* 89: 231–245.

Cain, Bruce E., and Kenneth P. Miller. 1998. "Voting Rights Mismatch: The Challenge of Applying the Voting Rights Act to 'Other Minorities'." In *Voting Rights and Redistricting in the United States*, edited by M. E. Rush, 141–163. Westport, CT: Greenwood Publishing Group, Inc.

Colby, David C. 1986. "The Voting Rights Act and Black Registration in Mississippi." *Publius: The Journal of Federalism* 16: 123–137.

Cotrell, Charles L. 1986. "Assessing the Effects of the U.S. Voting Rights Act." *Publius: The Journal of Federalism* 16: 5–16.

Dowdy, Wayne. 2014. "Poll Taxes." In *Race and Racism in the United States*, edited by C. Gallagher and C. Lippard, 955–956. Santa Barbara, California: Greenwood.

Evans, Eldon C. 1917. *The History of the Australian Ballot System in the United States*. Doctoral dissertation.Chicago, IL: University of Chicago. Retrieved December 18, 2015 from https://archive.org/stream/ahistoryaustral00evangoog #page/n4/mode/2up.

Ewald, Alec C. 2002. " 'Civil Death': The Ideological Paradox of Criminal Disenfranchisement Law in the United States." *Wisconsin Law Review* 5: 1045–1138.

Henderson, Lenneal J. 1987. "Black Politics and American Political Elections." In *The New Black Politics: The Search for Political Power* (2nd ed.), edited by M. B. Preston, L. J. Henderson Jr., and P. L. Puryear, 3–27. White Plains, NY: Longman Inc.

Henderson, Wade. 2006. "Claiming our Democracy in the Covenant with Black America." In *The Covenant with Black America*, 123–142. Chicago, IL: Third World Press.

Keyssar, Alexander. 2000. *The Right to Vote: The Contested History of Democracy in the United States*. New York, NY: Basic Books.

Kousser, J. Morgan. 1999. "Poll Tax." In *The International Encyclopedia of Elections*, edited by Richard Rose, 208–209. Washington, DC: Congressional Quarterly, Inc.

McDonald, Michael. 2015. United States Elections Project. Retrieved December 18, 2015 from http://www.electproject.org/home.

Reiman, Jeffrey. 1995. *The Rich Get Richer and the Poor Get Prison* (4th ed.). Boston, MA: Allyn & Bacon.

Wood, Erika L., and Neema Trivedi. 2007. "The Modern-Day Poll Tax: How Economic Sanctions Block Access to the Polls." *Clearing House Review Journal of Poverty Law and Policy* 41 (1–2): 30–45.

Wright, Frederick. 1986. "The Voting Rights Act and Louisiana: Twenty Years of Enforcement." *Publius: The Journal of Federalism* 16: 97–108.

1

Declining Trust and Efficacy and Its Role in Political Participation

Megan M. Ruxton and Kyle L. Saunders

INTRODUCTION

For decades, political scientists have been trying to understand the puzzle of the individual-level act of voting and its reflection on the quality of American democracy. The individual costs to vote can be high: it takes time and effort for a person to register, find complete information about the election to guide his or her vote, and then actually cast a ballot. Among Americans who do choose to register to vote, the likelihood of voting is quite high. In fact, as a proportion of registered voters, the percentage is comparable to other advanced democracies. However, as a proportion of the overall population of legal age, Americans continue to vote at lower rates compared to many other countries.

From a purely economic/rational choice perspective, there is little rea-son for any given individual to vote, and yet, a good number of people still do so. One might assume that the most likely cause of voting is the possibility of having a direct influence on an election's outcome. However, American history has yet to present us with a major election won by a sin-gle vote, providing evidence that the chance that one person can sway the outcome of a race is incredibly small. In fact, a person is more likely to win the lottery or get hit by lightning than to cast the deciding vote in a federal election.

A particular and interesting irony is that it is in local elections with small constituencies where one vote can actually make a difference, even though these elections see a much smaller share of participation than federal elections, especially in "off-year" elections held in nonpresidential election years. However, when that unlikely scenario—a single vote having the potential to decide an important race—is not in place, what benefits other than potential influence are there? The civic satisfaction of exercising a basic right? The approval of others? In the face of high personal costs, why would reasonable people go to the effort to vote in the first place?

There are many answers to this question. One is that habit plays an important role in political behavior. Beyond that, there are some civic benefits that citizens are getting out of the act to offset those costs. Even so, in election cycle after election cycle, it has become apparent that many American voters are wondering about the benefits as well. The common story told in the media, political circles, and academia has often been that most Americans are uninterested in politics: they do not care, they do not believe their individual actions will make a difference, they do not know enough about political officeholders to hold them accountable for their records, and they do not trust those who are running for election.

On the face of things, this story seems to make sense. As with many stories, however, this one is far more complex than common discussions would have us believe. What so many political pundits and media outlets—and yes, academics—often forget is that the American public is notorious for not following the story quite as it is written.

INTEREST AND DISINTEREST

Interest in politics has been characterized by political scientist Van Deth (2000, 119) as the "potential readiness to participate" because of the strong impact it has on an individual's likelihood to participate in political activities, particularly voting (Lane 1959). This makes intuitive sense: when something requires the kind of time and effort that is necessary for voting in a way that actually reflects the voter's preference, there must be some motivating factor that compels a person to overcome those barriers.

There are several factors that can contribute to a person being interested or not, including age (Bennett 1986), strength of ideological/partisan identification (Miller and Rahn 2002), education (Campbell 1962), and levels of efficacy and trust (Bennett 1986; Rosenberg 1954). Although interest is generally stable throughout an individual's lifetime (Prior 2010), as individuals get older, they tend to become more interested in politics, until a certain point in their twilight years when interest wanes. Individuals with strong political preferences are more interested than those whose attitudes are more weakly developed, and unsurprisingly, individuals who strongly identify as part of a political party also show more interest than nonpartisans. Those who feel their political efforts have an effect on what happens in government and believe that government is responsive to the public (internal and external efficacy, as will be discussed below) also vote and actively participate more than those who do not see a similar relationship between their actions and the political sphere. Time, resources, and skills are also a prerequisite for interest, which is then more likely to translate into political action, far more so for those who are interested and knowledgeable than for those who are not (Delli Carpini and Keeter 1996; Verba, Schlozman, and Brady 1995).

The common theme that connects each of these characteristics with political interest is a sense of personal importance in the outcome of political activities, whether that comes with the age-related awareness of politics that comes from paying taxes, or the knowledge that a particular policy will impact the likelihood of maximizing personal political preferences. Separate from self-interest, research has found that interest in politics is a learned characteristic, picked up early in life, particularly from family. Though not quite an "inherited" trait, when children are taught early on that voting is the act of a good citizen, this is internalized so that even if they grow up not sharing the ideology or party preferences of their family, they are still more likely to maintain their level of interest and the motivation to be an active political participant (Verba, Schlozman, and Brady 1995).

This begs the question of why some individuals are interested, while others are not. Is it simply because they did not learn early on that everyone has a stake in politics regardless of age or strength of political preferences? What activates political interest in some parts of the population and not others? This is a question that has, until recently, rarely been addressed. Although we tend to know who has higher levels of interest, we do not fully know why that is, or conversely, why other individuals have so little interest in politics whatsoever. The answer to this puzzle lies in a complicated web of interweaving elements, but may partially be a matter of context that goes beyond demographics, attitudes, and socialization. Voter mobilization efforts to raise the public's overall level of interest typically produce small returns—more often than not, they are mobilizing (likely well-resourced and educated) individuals who are already interested and motivated to vote—but larger events can dampen or encourage interest on a broad scale. The Watergate scandal, the war in Vietnam, the terrorist attacks of September 11, 2001—all have served as triggers to the mass public, and for good or ill, have influenced the levels of interest in politics more generally and in a much larger way than could be accomplished by any campaign efforts (Shani 2009, unpublished doctoral dissertation).

So, the extent to which the public remains disinterested—and the numbers for that segment of the population typically remaining rather sizeable—continues to serve as a dampener to voter participation. However, this less participatory segment of the population is also consistently ignored by elected and campaigning politicians, mostly because of the disincentive candidates have to commit resources to individuals who will not participate. If American society made civic engagement of all citizens a priority, or at least made it easier to participate via easier voter registration methods, compulsory election holidays, and the like, the evidence seems to suggest increased levels of engagement are likely to result. Why? Because, as the attitude and socialization elements discussed above show, education can raise levels of interest, and as the importance of political decisions on the lives of individual citizens is activated into becoming part of a person's identity, the more interested they will become not only in the outcome but in participating in the process as well.

EFFICACY AND ALIENATION

As noted above, political efficacy relates to the relationship between the wants and needs of the public, and their ability to translate that into action through their elected representatives. When an individual feels confident in his or her ability to effectively participate and be heard by the political process, this is known as internal political efficacy. External political efficacy refers to an individual's feelings about the responsiveness of the political system to the public at large. Levels of both internal and external efficacy vary from person to person, and we can often tell how a person will choose to act, or not act, in the political system based on these levels.

According to Pollock III (1983), if a person has low levels of both internal and external efficacy, he or she is more likely to be withdrawn from politics in general and is therefore far less likely to vote or to get involved in a protest or other political behaviors. This appears to be true regardless of age or sex. It also appears true regardless of levels of education or income, though the effect of low internal and external efficacy is more substantial for lower levels of education. Conversely, if levels of internal and external efficacy are both high, those individuals are considered "complete participators," because the likelihood that they will vote or otherwise participate in politics is very high, and the very act itself, once committed, opens itself to the power of habit. Much like interest, efficacy can ebb and flow over a person's lifetime, but those who participate early in life are most likely to continue to do so as the years go by (Gerber, Green, and Shachar 2003). The process of voting, then, serves as a positive feedback loop in which the connection an individual sees between his or her vote and actions taken in elected government reinforces his or her feeling of having an impact, which in turn spurs him or her to continue to vote in subsequent elections; thus, it makes the individual a complete participator. Importantly, this feedback loop can be negative as well. If a person is unable to vote because of external constraints (such as literacy tests during the early 20th century or contemporary voter identification laws), this will lower the chances of voting in future elections as well as potentially limit intergenerational socialization to the act. Even if one does manage to vote, a perception of a wide discrepancy between an individual's interests and the actions being taken by government will similarly affect future decisions to vote, as it will seriously damage feelings of both internal and external efficacy, and possibly political trust as well.

Overall, those with high internal efficacy and low external efficacy—what amounts to feelings of alienation as a result of a system that does not respond to individuals—do not vote quite as much, but they do participate in other modes of political participation that are more closely connected to the political process, such as campaigning. For this combination of efficacy levels among the more highly educated, internal efficacy is a requirement for political activity, including voting. This seems to be the case because these individuals believe that their high levels of competency can overcome a lack of system responsiveness; this appears to be less of the case for those with lower levels of education. For the less educated, a low level of internal efficacy paired with a high level of external efficacy seems to be the catalyst for voting, with the belief being that the way the political system is structured will make up for a lack of individual competence.

Many things can impact individual levels of internal and external efficacy. Higher levels of education have been connected to higher perceptions of internal efficacy as well as increased social capital. According to Putnam (2001), these social capital factors include membership in community organizations, church membership, and interpersonal connections with other community members. External efficacy is often affected by contextual factors, such as the outcome of individual elections or promised policy changes (civil rights in the 1960s is an oft-cited factor), as well as perceptions of the processes and institutions of government, such as the effectiveness of the Electoral College or the actions of Congress.

Low levels of external efficacy are fairly common and characterize the portion of the electorate that feels alienated from the political process. Polling shows that more and more Americans do not believe they, as individuals, matter to the political process. As of 2008, polls conducted by the American National Election Studies and Gallup showed that 60 percent of Americans agreed with the statement "Public officials don't care much about what people like me think" and 49 percent agreed with the statement "People like me don't have any say in what the government does." When election time rolls around, these people do not believe the system offers candidates that give them a real choice—political polarization has pushed candidates to the extremes of the ideological poles, leaving those in the middle without an option. Some also believe that even if a candidate's message aligns with their own beliefs, little can be accomplished because the political system favors interests other than the public interest. As will be discussed, low perceptions of system responsiveness interact with levels of trust, which can sometimes push individuals away from the polls and also have some surprising reactions in the other direction.

TRUST AND CYNICISM

One of the difficulties in discussing the trust between citizens and government has been how to accurately define and measure this relationship. Trust is not a physical object to be measured with a ruler, but instead is an abstract concept that has to be constructed using various pieces of information on how individuals perceive the world around them. Because of this, scholars have debated how much individuals trust the government: whether it is the political institutions they find fault with when they lack trust, or the people who have been elected to govern within those institutions, and whether or not a lack of trust is the same as distrust, or even cynicism. This is not a debate easily settled, since none of these concepts share a common metric. However, what has commonly been agreed upon, in order to have a functioning democracy, is the need for people to generally trust their government to do the right thing (Warren 1999). Some cynicism is natural and is even a necessary part of a democracy—this is why the United States has a system of checks and balances between the three branches of the federal government, with two of these branches being chosen by the public, so that power is not concentrated in the hands of the few. Some call this a "healthy distrust" of those who have been given power and argue that what we see today is evidence of that. Others, however, believe we have become a nation of increasingly distrustful citizens and this is making it more and more difficult for the country to progress (Hetherington 2005).

Figure 1.1 depicts levels of public trust in government from 1958 to 2014—recorded responses to national surveys conducted throughout that period. The percentages reported in this graphic are the percentage of survey respondents who state that they "trust the government in Washington" "always" or "most of the time."

Looking at data from survey sources such as the Pew Research Center and Gallup, we can see the proportion of Americans who believe the government does the right thing most or all of the time has dropped precipitously since the beginning of the post–World War II years. Increases occurred when citizens were "spurred to action" such as after the 9/11 terrorist attacks, but subsequently returned to a lower and lower equilibrium.

Figure 1.1
Public Trust in Government: 1958–2014

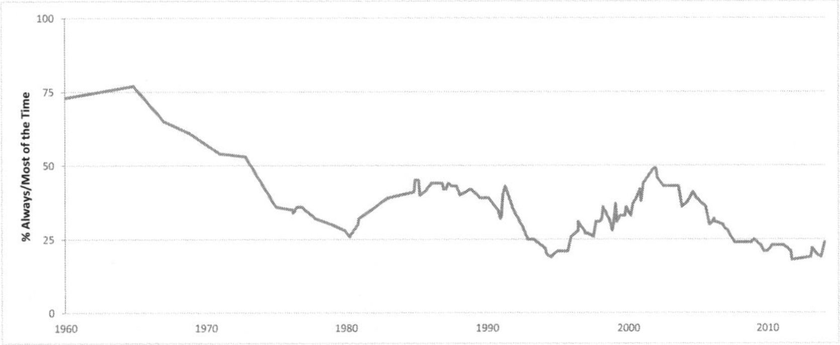

Source: Pew Research Center, http://www.people-press.org/2014/11/13/public-trust-in-government/, see a more interactive graphic and other details on political trust via this link.

Some attribute the decline in trust to the political upheaval that came with various wars and scandals in the highest levels of government: the Korean War during the 1950s, President Nixon resigning in disgrace, the Vietnam War, the Iran-Contra affair during the Reagan presidency, and the wars in Afghanistan and Iraq in the early years of the 21st century. Scholars in the 1950s who suggested "controversiality" (Rosenberg 1954) as the reason for declining participation may have been mistaking disappointment in the results of the system as a withdrawal from controversy. Conversely, rather than distrust coming from what the government *has* done, there is also the possibility that distrust is the result of what the government *has not* done. The U.S. government has taken on increasingly complex problems in the past several decades—civil rights and the environment, in particular—and once the low-hanging fruit had been plucked with ambitious legislation and promises of definitive solutions, reality set in and the nation collectively realized that legislation could not provide an easy answer for the problems the nation faced (Hetherington 2005).

Regardless of the underlying cause, distrust has been highlighted as a major roadblock to progress on the issues that continue to challenge the American political system. Without trust, politicians are increasingly faced with a public that is suspicious and sometimes even hostile about new legislation and policy, particularly anything that comes with a high public price tag. This leads to the question of political participation, and in particular, voting. If the public does not trust politicians as far as they can throw them, do they abstain completely? Although the rapid decline in political trust often plays a leading role in the story of an uninterested public, to the best of our knowledge, the decline in the recent past has not resulted in non-voters.

Overall, distrust alone seems to have little to no influence on the decision of whether or not to vote. Distrust, however, does have a related
impact on the decision of *who to vote for*. Social scientists have found that
distrust can actually serve as a motivator, a "throw the rascals out" men-
tality, where individuals vote for candidates representing the party currently out of power, or in some cases, a third party or political outsider
candidate who has drummed up enough momentum to be well known
(e.g., Ralph Nader, Ross Perot, or most recently, Donald Trump; Hetherington 2005; Sigelman et al. 1985). There are many reasons to be concerned
with a distrustful public, but so far we have no reason to believe it has a
major negative effect on voter turnout, and may actually improve mobilization. In fact, a lack of trust can actually serve as a motivator for black
Americans in particular, improving the chances of political participation
for a demographic that historically has been underrepresented in terms
of voter turnout. Regardless of other influencing factors such as age,
education, or income, an individual with low levels of trust who is black
is far more likely to vote than a white person with similar levels of trust.
All things being equal, why does race matter when it comes to trust and
voting?

The answer brings us back to efficacy. When trust is low, it is most
likely that external efficacy will also be low—a government that is unresponsive to a person is not a government that person is likely to trust.
Black Americans have consistently shown lower levels of trust and lower
levels of external efficacy, though levels of internal efficacy vary based on
age, education, and income. However, regardless of feelings of personal
political competence, distrustful blacks are much more likely to vote than
white voters with the same characteristics. This is because of an additional
concept: group efficacy (Mangum 2003). Studies have shown that despite
feelings of personal inefficacy, black citizens vote more often because of
a strong group consciousness, an identification as one part of a larger
group that can affect change en masse in a way that the individual never
could acting alone. The 2008 election of Barack Obama to the White House
serves as an important illustration of this. Mobilization efforts of the
Democratic Party bear much of the credit for black voters turning out at
unprecedented levels for this federal election; it is also true that the presence of the first black candidate for a major American political party
ignited this group consciousness in a way that had never been seen before
in a federal election.

CONCLUSION

In an era of increased ideological polarization and increased inequality
between the haves and the have-nots with regard to resources, education,
free time, and income, we must look past the traditional research that

demonstrates that these relatively invariant factors are significant predictors of political activity. Instead, we should look to identify and understand factors that increase the level of interest in politics among the American electorate. As noted above, this starts in youth with a quality civic education that can sustain the interest necessary for individuals to be interested in a complex topic like politics. From the research side, we need to develop a much better understanding of the ebbs and flows of the psychological motivations of the electorate and their relationship to political interest, as well as a better understanding of the factors that contribute to increasing political trust, with eyes toward the effects of good, transparent governance and the promotion of a governmental system that begins to remove the inequities that continue to disempower so many American citizens.

FURTHER READING

Bennett, Stephen E. 1986. *Apathy in America, 1960–1984: Causes and Consequences of Citizen Political Indifference*. Dobbs Ferry, NY: Transnational Publishers.

Campbell, Angus. 1962. "The Passive Citizen." *Acta Sociologica* 6: 9–21.

Delli Carpini, Michael X., and Scott Keeter. 1996. *What Americans Know about Politics and Why It Matters*. New Haven, CT: Yale University Press.

Gerber, Alan S., Green, Donald P., and Ron Shachar. 2003. "Voting May Be Habit-Forming: Evidence from a Randomized Field Experiment." *American Journal of Political Science* 47: 540–550.

Hetherington, Marc. 2005. *Why Trust Matters: Declining Political Trust and the Demise of American Liberalism*. Princeton, NJ: Princeton University Press.

Lane, Robert E. 1959. *Political Life: Why People Get Involved in Politics*. Glencoe, IL: Free Press.

Mangum, Maurice. 2003. "Psychological Involvement and Black Voter Turnout." *Political Research Quarterly* 56: 41–48.

Milbrath, Lester W., and M. L. Goel. 1977. *Political Participation: How and Why Do People Get Involved in Politics?* Washington, DC: University Press of America.

Miller, Joanne, and Wendy M. Rahn. 2002. "Identity-based Thoughts, Feelings and Actions: How Being Influences Doing." Unpublished manuscript. Minneapolis: University of Minnesota.

Pollock III, Phillip H. 1983. "The Participatory Consequences of Internal and External Political Efficacy: A Research Note." *The Western Political Quarterly* 36: 400–409.

Prior, Markus. 2010. "You've Either Got It or You Don't? The Stability of Political Interest over the Life Cycle." *Journal of Politics* 72: 747–766.

Putnam, Robert D. 2001. *Bowling Alone*. New York, NY: Simon and Schuster.

Rosenberg, Morris. 1954. "Some Determinants of Political Apathy." *Public Opinion Quarterly* 18: 349–366.

Shani, Danielle. 2009. *On the Origins of Political Interest*. Unpublished doctoral dissertation. Princeton, NJ: Princeton University.

Sigelman, Lee, Roeder, Phillip W., Jewell, Malcolm E., and Michal A. Baer. 1985. "Voting and Nonvoting: A Multi-Election Perspective." *American Journal of Political Science* 29: 749–765.

Southwell, Priscilla L., and Kevin D. Perch. 2003. "Political Cynicism and the Mobilization of Black Voters." *Social Science Quarterly* 84: 906–917.

Van Deth, Jan W. 2000. "Interesting but Irrelevant: Social Capital and the Saliency of Politics in Western Europe." *European Journal of Political Research* 37: 115–147.

Verba, Sidney, Schlozman, Kay L., and Henry E. Brady. 1995. *Voice and Equality: Civic Voluntarism in American Politics.* Cambridge, MA: Harvard University Press.

Warren, Mark E. 1999. *Democracy and Trust.* Cambridge, UK: Cambridge University Press.

Wolfinger, Raymond E., and Steven J. Rosenstone. 1980. *Who Votes?* New Haven, CT: Yale University Press.

2

Qualifying to Vote: Voter Registration Requirements

Gayle Alberda

Voting in the United States is a two-stage process. A potential voter must first register before he or she is eligible to cast a ballot. In order for an individual to register, he or she must meet certain voter qualifications, which vary greatly from state to state. Registration rules are important because they are the key that unlocks the voting process for citizens. Without being registered, a citizen cannot vote.

The federal and state governments share the responsibility of elections in the United States. The U.S. Constitution sets the date for federal offices (the president and Congress). At the same time, the Constitution grants states the authority to determine the time, place, and manner of elections. Interestingly, and of significance to this chapter, at the nation's founding, the U.S. Constitution did not grant individuals voting rights. Voter qualifications were left to the states, which produced a variety of laws varying from state to state.

In the nation's formative years, many states adopted laws that systematically excluded women, American Indians, and blacks from the electorate. Common voter qualifications during this time included being white and owning real property, such as land. The rationale behind this requirement was that individuals who owned real property had a stake in community affairs and possessed an independence that warranted a say in government affairs (Keyssar 2000). In 1792, Delaware became the first state to eliminate the property requirement. The last state to abolish the property requirement was Virginia in 1850. These changes created universal white male suffrage and expanded the electorate to include thousands of newly enfranchised voters.

The removal of the property requirement promoted the adoption of residency requirements among the states. On average, an individual would have to reside in a state for one year before being eligible to vote (Keyssar 2000). Residency requirements are still used today by the states. This form of registration requirement is discussed in more detail later in this chapter.

Although white men were able to enjoy suffrage, blacks, women, and American Indians were still denied access to the ballot. Free black men in early America often did not meet the property requirements to vote and slaves could not vote. Most states barred black men, including free black men, from the ballot box. By 1855 there were only five states that did not disenfranchise blacks: Massachusetts, Vermont, New Hampshire, Maine, and Rhode Island (Keyssar 2000). In *Dred Scott v. Sanford* (1857), the Supreme Court ruled that blacks, free or slaves, were not citizens. It was not until the ratification of the Fifteenth Amendment in 1870 that black men gained the right to vote.

After Reconstruction ended in the late 1870s, however, many southern states enacted laws that had the effect of disenfranchising black voters. For instance, in 1890, Tennessee adopted the poll tax. Eligible voters had to pay the poll tax before they could vote. The tax was often beyond the income of black men. Literacy tests were also used to exclude blacks from voting. A potential voter had to pass a literacy test in order to qualify to vote. According to Keyssar (2000), 50 percent of black men were illiterate. Louisiana adopted the grandfather clause in 1898, which denied blacks the right to vote unless their grandfathers could vote in 1867. These laws had a severe impact on the number of blacks registered to vote. According to the Smithsonian National Museum of American History, in Mississippi, fewer than 9,000 of the 147,000 eligible black voters were registered after 1890. In 1889, Louisiana had more than 130,000 black registered voters; this number dwindled to 1,342 by 1904. The Supreme Court ruled the grandfather clause unconstitutional in *Guinn v. U.S.* (1915). However, poll taxes remained constitutional until the ratification of the Twenty-Fourth Amendment in 1964 made poll taxes unconstitutional. The passage of the Voting Rights Act of 1965 prohibited literacy tests as a prerequisite to vote.

In early America, states also established coverture laws, which treated a husband and wife as one legal entity upon marriage. These laws, in essence, extinguished the wife's separate legal existence; because she was *covered* under her husband, she did not need voting rights. Over time, the gender prerequisite to voter registration disappeared. Wyoming was the first state to grant women suffrage in 1869. While other states followed Wyoming, in 1875, women were set back when the U.S. Supreme Court ruled that citizenship did not confer suffrage to women (*Minor v. Happersett*). This decision allowed each state to determine whether women were allowed to vote. In 1920, the Nineteenth Amendment was ratified granting women the right to vote. In 1924, American Indians were fully enfranchised.

The Constitution was amended again in 1971 to expand voting rights to 18-year-olds through the Twenty-Sixth Amendment. Prior to that time, states could determine age requirements. Many states had the voting age set at 21. Although the Voting Rights Act of 1965 established 18 as the voting age for both state and federal elections, in 1970 the Supreme Court ruled that Congress could regulate the voting age for federal elections but not for state elections, (see *Oregon v. Mitchell*). Consequently, the Twenty-Sixth Amendment was proposed and ratified.

Many federal and state policy decisions regarding voting and registration are based on the assumption that there are costs associated with the acts of registration and voting. These costs not only include actual monetary costs for travel and fees for obtaining required documents, but also include barriers such as time and other resources needed to travel to particular locations where registration and/or voting occur, and time to obtain required documents. If the barriers or costs to registration can be reduced or eliminated, the number of citizens who register and vote should increase. The two-stage process of voting in the United States suggests that consideration be given to motivations for voters at each stage of the process; factors that might motivate individuals to register may be different than those that prompt them to vote.

The National Voter Registration Act (NVRA) is a key example of a federal law that was enacted with the purpose of reducing the costs of registration. Passed by Congress in 1993, the NVRA requires states to offer potential voters an array of different avenues to register including mail-in registration, agency-based registration, and registration when renewing a driver's license. The central anticipation after the passage of the NVRA was that voter turnout would increase since the costs of registration were decreased. In a study of the NRVA, Martinez and Hill (1999) found that registration increased, but not turnout. Others, however, found that registration increased among groups traditionally less likely to register (Brown and Wedeking 2006; Hill 2003; Rugeley and Jackson 2009). Although the NVRA created additional opportunities for registration and expanded the potential electorate, it has not increased turnout in American elections. Beyond the requirements of the NVRA, several states have implemented additional policy reforms aimed at reducing the costs of voter registration. These laws affect *when* and *how* a person can register to vote.

RESIDENCY REQUIREMENTS

An individual must be a legal resident of the state in which he or she wishes to register and vote. Like many election rules, the requirements for legal residency are established by the states and vary from state to state. In the early 1960s, 38 states required at least one year of residency before an individual could register to vote (Wolfinger and Rosenstone 1980). When Congress passed the 1970 amendments to the 1965 Voting Rights Act, it created a 30-day residency requirement for presidential elections (Rosenstone and Wolfinger 1978; Wolfinger and Rosenstone 1980). Shortly thereafter, in 1972, the U.S. Supreme Court ruled Tennessee's one-year residency requirement unconstitutional (*Dunn v. Blumstein*). Although the Court did not impose a new residency requirement in this decision, it did imply that a 30-day residency requirement for any election was sufficient. Although state residency requirements continue to vary, today all states have a residency requirement that is 30 days or less.

Residency requirements often affect those who are more transient. When an individual moves, he or she generally needs to re-register in order to vote. There are exceptions. In Oregon and California, for example, individuals are automatically re-registered when they change their address on their driver's license or state ID card. "The requirement that citizens must register anew after each change in residence constitutes a key stumbling block in the trip to the polls" (Squire, Wolfinger, and Glass 1987, 45). Individuals who move must obtain information on voter registration requirements, meet residency requirements, and actually re-register. The costs are high for movers because they are often unfamiliar with their new area. Those who move, regardless of distance, have lower voter turnout than those who do not move (Highton 2000; Wolfinger and Rosenstone 1980). One policy that reduces the burden of registration for voters is statewide registration portability. Statewide registration portability allows individuals who move anywhere within a state to transfer their registration. Registration portability increases voter turnout by 2.4 percentage points; however, movers are still less likely to vote even when these policies are available (McDonald 2009a).

REGISTRATION DEADLINES, SAME-DAY AND ELECTION-DAY REGISTRATION

States often require eligible voters to register to vote prior to Election Day. These registration deadlines are also known as closing dates. Citizens living in states with closing dates who fail to register by the given date are prohibited from voting. With the exception of North Dakota, which does not require registration, and those states that allow for registration on

Election Day, most closing dates are 10–30 days prior to Election Day. Table 2.1 illustrates the variety of registration deadlines found among the states.

Table 2.1
States' Registration Deadlines

Registration Deadline	State	
No registration deadline	North Dakota	
Same Day Registration or Election Day Registration	California	
	Colorado	
	Connecticut	
	Hawaii*	
	Idaho	
	Illinois	
	Iowa	
	Maine	
	Minnesota	
	Montana	
	New Hampshire	
	Vermont	
	Wisconsin	
	Wyoming	
1–15 days prior to Election Day	Alabama	
	South Dakota	
	Utah	
	Virginia	
	Washington	
16–30 days prior to Election Day	Alaska	Nevada
	Arizona	New Jersey
	Arkansas	New Mexico
	Delaware	New York
	Florida	North Carolina
	Georgia	Ohio
	Indiana	Oklahoma
	Kansas	Oregon**
	Kentucky	Pennsylvania
	Louisiana	Rhode Island
	Maryland	South Carolina
	Massachusetts	Tennessee
	Michigan	Texas
	Mississippi	West Virginia
	Missouri	
	Nebraska	

*Hawaii will implement in 2018.
**Oregon passed automatic registration in 2015.
Sources: Secretary of State Offices, USA.gov, and National Conference of State Legislatures.

The costs of voting are higher for citizens residing in states that require registration prior to Election Day. For instance, individuals must be aware of the registration deadline, locate the registration office, and take the time to make the special trip to the registration office to register.

Registration deadline dates that are further from Election Day have a negative effect on registration and voter turnout because they often occur before the campaign has built momentum (Rosenstone and Hansen 1993; Wolfinger and Rosenstone 1980). Wolfinger and Rosenstone (1980) find that deadlines that are 30 days before Election Day decrease the likelihood of voting by 3–9 percent. Further, deadlines that are closer to Election Day appear to increase voter registration *and* turnout (Vonnahme 2012).

States have taken two general policy approaches to easing the registration process by either easing or eliminating closing dates. Same Day Registration (SDR) permits a voter to register and vote on the same day *prior to* Election Day. Election Day Voter Registration (EDVR) allows voters to both register and vote *on* Election Day. These two approaches are similar as they both offer a one-stop shop that allows individuals to register and vote simultaneously. If potential voters can incur the costs of registration and voting at the same time, and do so closer to Election Day when campaign momentum is higher, the perceived benefit of voting may be greater. This should have a positive effect on turnout as the costs are decreased and the perceived benefits are increased.

Both SDR and EDVR have been shown to increase voter turnout. Rhine (1996) found a positive relationship between SDR and voter turnout and estimated an increase in turnout between 10 and 14 percent. EDVR has a positive impact on voter turnout in both midterm and presidential elections (Brians and Grofman 2001; Burden et al. 2009; Fenster 1994; Knack 1995). Voter turnout in midterm elections increased by 6 percent (Fenster 1994), while turnout in presidential elections increased by 3–7 percent (Brians and Grofman 2001; Knack 1995). It is estimated that a national EDVR law would increase turnout by 5 percent in presidential elections (Fenster 1994).

Similar to portable voter registration, EDVR also has the capacity to offset the cost of registration among movers and new residents (Knack and White 2000; Larocca and Klemanski 2011). These findings support the hypothesis that low turnout among movers is due to the burden of re-registering to vote (Squire, Wolfinger, and Glass 1987). EDVR also has a positive effect on voter turnout among younger populations (Knack and White 2000).

AGE REQUIREMENTS AND PRE-REGISTRATION

In many states, an individual must be 18 years of age in order to register to vote. However, some states have implemented pre-registration laws. Pre-registration is an election procedure that allows individuals under the age of 18 to register to vote. Although able to register prior to the age of 18, those who pre-register are not eligible to cast a ballot until they are 18 years old.

Pre-registration policies vary among the states. Some states allow 16-year-olds to register, some allow 17-year-olds to register, and yet some have no specific age limit for pre-registration (National Conference of State Legislatures, n.d.). Overall, 21 states and the District of Columbia, have adopted pre-registration laws (National Conference of State Legislatures, n.d.). Table 2.2 denotes which states have adopted some form of pre-registration. Of these, the most common approach is to permit pre-registration of 17-year-olds.

Table 2.2
States with Pre-Registration Laws

Pre-registration	State
16-year-olds	California
	Colorado
	Delaware
	District of Columbia
	Florida
	Hawaii
	Louisiana
	Maryland
	Rhode Island
17-year-olds	California
	Colorado
	Delaware
	District of Columbia
	Florida
	Georgia
	Hawaii
	Iowa
	Louisiana
	Maine
	Maryland
	Missouri
	Nebraska
	Oregon
	Rhode Island
	Texas
	West Virginia
18 by or on Election Day	Kansas
	Minnesota
	Nevada
	Wyoming

Source: National Conference of State Legislatures.

The goal of pre-registration laws is to increase registration and voter turnout among younger voters, who are often non-voters. According to the U.S. Census Bureau, in the 2012 election, the turnout rate for voters aged 18–24 was 38 percent. In the same election, the turnout rate for voters aged 25–44 was 49.5 percent, 69.7 percent for those aged 45–64, and 63.4 percent for those aged 65 and older. Not surprisingly, pre-registration programs have increased the number of registered voters, especially during even-numbered election years (McDonald 2009b). Individuals who pre-registered before turning 18 were more likely to vote than those who registered after turning 18, with the largest increase occurring in presidential elections (McDonald 2009b).

AUTOMATIC REGISTRATION

In the United States, eligible voters must opt in, meaning the individual is responsible for registering to vote. Other countries, particularly those in Europe, have automatic registration where the government automatically registers eligible voters (Piven and Cloward 2000). Countries with automatic registration have higher turnout rates. Powell (1986) asserts that automatic registration could raise turnout in American elections by 14 percentage points.

Oregon is the first state to adopt an automatic registration process. The new automatic registration law went into effect in January 2016. When an eligible voter in Oregon renews or applies for a driver's license or state ID, he or she will automatically be registered to vote. Under Oregon's automatic registration process, eligible voters receive a postcard via mail. The postcard allows the eligible voter to affiliate with a political party, opt out, or do nothing. If an eligible voter does not want to vote, he or she signs the postcard and returns it via mail. This removes the eligible voter from the system. If an eligible voter does nothing, he or she is automatically registered to vote.

Oregon's approach eases the burden of registration on the individual by transferring that burden to the government. Intuitively, we could expect the new law to increase the number of registered voters. According to the Oregon secretary of state, there are approximately 800,000 eligible voters in Oregon who are not registered to vote; the new law is expected to bring half of them into the electorate.

More recently, California legislators proposed a similar policy. Like Oregon's law, California's automatic registration law registers anyone who is 18 years of age or older and has a driver's license, unless he or she opts out. Supporters of the bill hope it leads to higher turnout. In the 2014 general election, turnout was only 42 percent across the state, and in the Los Angles local municipal election held in March 2015, turnout was only about 10 percent. The California bill became effective on January 1, 2016; however, complete implementation will depend at least in part on regulations yet to be developed by the Department of Motor Vehicles.

CONCLUSION

Registering to vote can be a significant barrier to the voting booth. Potential voters must navigate bureaucratic red tape in order to register. Often the costs associated with registration are not equal for everyone (Wolfinger and Rosenstone 1980). Many citizens either cannot overcome the barriers or opt not to overcome them. Lessening the burden associated with registration expands the pool of eligible voters and, in some cases, boosts turnout.

It should be noted that simply because an individual is registered does not mean he or she will turn out on Election Day. Motivation and engagement play a large role in an individual's choice to register to vote (Lloyd 2001). A disinterested individual who is registered will not necessarily turn out to vote (Brown and Wedeking 2006; Lloyd 2001). There are likely different dynamics that encourage eligible voters to register versus vote. For example, partisan intensity and political efficacy have been shown to influence registration (Timpone 1998). Once registered, campaigns and political parties can motivate registered voters to actually cast a ballot (Berinsky 2005; Jackson 1996; Timpone 1998).

Overall there is no easy solution. Each registration law impacts the process of registration and the eligible voter differently. Nevertheless, the first step to increasing voter turnout is to have eligible voters registered. States could adopt policies that remind eligible voters to register. Individuals who received a reminder after downloading a voter registration form increased their registration rates by four percentage points (Bennion and Nickerson 2011). Additionally, campus voter registration programs have shown promise of increasing both registration and turnout among young adults. Students who registered to vote through campus-based partisan voter registration drives were more likely to vote, especially during a period of early voting (Ulbig and Waggener 2011). Programs that help recent movers re-register would also be beneficial.

For registration and turnout to increase, it is essential that states craft policies that address both when and how a person can register. In doing so, these laws may have a significant positive impact on both registration and turnout.

FURTHER READING

Bennion, Elizabeth, and David Nickerson. 2011. "The Costs of Convenience: An Experiment Showing E-Mail Outreach Decreases Voter Registration." *Political Research Quarterly* 64: 858–869.

Berinsky, Adam J. 2005. "The Perverse Consequence of Electoral Reform in the United States." *American Politics Research* 33: 471–491.

Brians, Craig L., and Bernard Grofman. 2001. "Election Day Registration's Effects on U.S. Voter Turnout." *Social Science Quarterly* 82: 170–183.

Brown, Robert D., and Justin Wedeking. 2006. "People Who Have Their Tickets but Do Not Use Them: Motor Voter, Registration, and Turnout Revisited." *American Politics Research* 34: 479–504.

Burden, Barry C., Canon, David T., Mayer, Kenneth R., and Donald P. Moynihan. 2009. "The Effects of Early Voting, Election Day Registration, and Same Day Registration in the 2008 Election." Report presented to Pew Charitable Trust on December 21, 2009. http://www.pewtrusts.org/~/media/legacy/uploadedfiles/pcs_assets/2009/uwisconsin1pdf.pdf.

Fenster, Mark J. 1994. "The Impact of Allowing Day of Registration Voting on Turnout in U.S. Elections from 1960–1992." *American Politics Quarterly* 22: 74–87.

Highton, Benjamin. 2000. "Residential Mobility, Community, and Electoral Participation." *Political Behavior* 22: 109–120.

Highton, Benjamin. 2004. "Voter Registration and Turnout in the United States." *Perspectives on Politics* 2: 507–515.

Hill, David. 2003. "A Two-Step Approach to Assessing Composition Effects of the Nation Voter Registration Act." *Electoral Studies* 22: 703–720.

Jackson, Robert. 1996. "A Reassessment of Voter Mobilization." *Political Research Quarterly* 49: 441–449.

Keyssar, Alexander. 2000. *The Right to Vote: The Contested History of Democracy in the United States.* New York, NY: Basic Books.

Knack, Stephen. 1995. "Does 'Motor Voter' Work? Evidence from State-Level Data." *Journal of Politics* 57: 796–811.

Knack, Stephen, and James White. 2000. "Election-Day Registration and Turnout Inequality." *Political Behavior* 22: 29–44.

Larocca, Roger, and John Klemanski. 2011. "U.S. State Election Reform and Turnout in Presidential Elections." *State Politics and Policy Quarterly* 11: 76–101.

Lloyd, Randall. 2001. "Voter Registration Reconsidered: Putting First Things First Is Not Enough." *American Politics Research* 29: 649–664.

Martinez, Michael, and David Hill. 1999. "Did Motor Voter Work?" *American Politics Quarterly* 27: 296–315.

McDonald, Michael. 2009a. "Portable Voter Registration." *Political Behavior* 30: 491–501.

McDonald, Michael. 2009b. "Voter Preregistration Programs." Retrieved March 29, 2016 from http://www.cses.org/plancom/2009Toronto/CSES_2009Toronto_McDonald.pdf.

National Conference of State Legislatures. n.d.. http://www.ncsl.org/.

Piven, Frances S., and Richard Cloward. 2000. *Why Americans Still Don't Vote: And Why Politicians Want It That Way.* Boston, MA: Beacon Press.

Powell, G. Bingham. 1986. "American Voter Turnout in Comparative Perspective." *American Political Science Review* 80: 17–43.

Rhine, Staci. 1996. "An Analysis of the Impact of Registration Factors on Turnout in 1992." *Political Behavior* 18: 171–185.

Rosenstone, Steven, and John. M. Hansen. 1993. *Mobilization, Participation, and American Democracy.* New York, NY: Longman.

Rosenstone, Steven, and Raymond Wolfinger. 1978. "The Effect of Registration Laws on Voter Turnout." *American Political Science Review* 72: 22–45.

Rugeley, Cynthia, and Robert Jackson. 2009. "Getting on the Rolls: Analyzing the Effects of Lowered Barriers on Voter Registration." *State Politics and Policy Quarterly* 9: 56–78.

Squire, Peverill, Wolfinger, Raymond, and David P. Glass. 1987. "Residential Mobility and Voter Turnout." *American Political Science Review* 81: 45–66.

Timpone, Richard. 1998. "Structure, Behavior, and Voter Turnout in the United States." *American Political Science Review* 92: 145–158.

U.S. Census Bureau. 2014. Young-Adult Voting: An Analysis of Presidential Elections, 1964–2012.

Ulbig, Stacy, and Tamara Waggener. 2011. "Getting Registered and Getting to the Polls: The Impact of Voter Registration Strategy and Information Provisions on Turnout of College Students." *Political Science and Politics* 44: 544–551.

Vonnahme, Greg. 2012. "Registration Deadlines and Turnout in Context." *Political Behavior* 34: 765–779.

Wolfinger, Raymond, and Steven Rosenstone. 1980. *Who Votes?* New Haven, CT: Yale University Press.

3

Digitizing Democracy: Online Voter Registration

Krysha Gregorowicz and Thad E. Hall

Many American citizens do not find politics to be interesting or relevant to their lives; therefore, they do not bother to register to vote or cast a ballot in democratic elections. People who do participate in elections generally turn out because they are partisans who want to support their "team," or because they perceive expressive or intrinsic benefits to this form of political participation (Abramowitz 2010; Aldrich 1993; Verba, Schlozman, and Brady 1995). Voters may be motivated because they feel a sense of civic duty, enjoy politics as a form of entertainment, are emotionally aroused by the campaign, or receive social benefits through the act of participation (Delli Carpini and Keeter 1997; Tetlock 1985; Valentino et al. 2011; Verba and Nie 1972). Indeed, political interest, or the lack thereof, was among the strongest predictors of political participation in 2008; nearly 40 percent of non-voters in the U.S. Census Bureau's Current Population Survey (CPS), 2008 Voting and Registration Supplement, reported that a lack of interest was their primary reason for not participating, and nearly half of those who were unregistered explained that they lacked interest in the election or politics more generally.

The census data illustrates one of the complexities of American elections: individuals have to register to vote, obtain the information necessary to make an informed voting decision, and then finally get to the polls. Historically, registering to vote in the United States has not been easy; voter registration has often been used as a means of disenfranchising certain groups of voters. As Keyssar (2000) notes, in the 1800s and early 1900s, voter registration was often used to disenfranchise urban voters, members of the political party out of power, and members of racial and ethnic minority communities. For example, Keyssar (2000, 123–128) provides illustrations of Republicans in New Jersey requiring men to register to vote in person on the Thursday before an election and of Jews in New York City being discriminated against when voter registration dates were set for the Jewish Sabbath and Yom Kippur. From the late 1800s up until the 1960s, registration laws were used to discriminate against blacks and poor southerners through the implementation of poll taxes, which had to be paid prior to registering to vote in some states and jurisdictions.

Research conducted after the passage of the Voting Rights Act of 1965 found that registration requirements remain among the most significant institutional barriers to voting (Erikson 1981; Rosenstone and Wolfinger 1978). If registration is among the primary direct cost barriers to voting, then reducing the burden of registration should boost turnout among those citizens most sensitive to this cost. Using a variety of methodological approaches, researchers have consistently found at least a modest increase in turnout associated with the relaxation of registration requirements (Ansolabehere and Konisky 2006; Highton 1997; Rosenstone and Hansen 1993; Wolfinger and Rosenstone 1980).

The more stringent barriers a state puts in place, the lower its participation rates will be. Eliminating prior registration altogether, as occurs in states with Election Day Voter Registration, has been estimated to boost turnout by approximately seven percentage points. The greatest beneficiaries of this reform have been those with a high school diploma or less, and lower- and middle-income citizens (Brians and Grofman 2001). Keep in mind that "even unlikely registrants are relatively frequent voters when they do register" (Erikson 1981, 271). Across the socioeconomic spectrum, turnout rates are quite high among those who have overcome the institutional hurdle of registration. For over a decade, turnout rates among the voting eligible citizen population have hovered around 60 percent in presidential elections, but turnout consistently exceeds 85 percent among those who are registered to vote. Consider, for example, that the CPS Voting and Registration Supplement typically finds that only about half of the youngest, poorest, and least educated members of the voting age citizen population register to vote, but more than three-quarters of those who do register go on to cast a ballot. This is evidence that sociodemographic biases in the composition of the electorate are at least in part a function of systematic differences in rates of voter registration.

ONLINE VOTER REGISTRATION

Those states that do not provide for Election Day Voter Registration cite a number of reasons for their position, including the need to produce a final voter roster prior to the election. To facilitate registration, though, many states have adopted online voter registration in an effort to leverage modern technology and make voter registration more convenient. Rather than requiring citizens to return paper copies of completed registration forms to state or local election officials, online registration systems allow potential voters in a given state to submit new registration applications or updates to existing voter registrations using a special registration portal. These systems connect electronic voter databases to motor vehicle or other state records' databases so that registration information can be validated and electronically-stored signatures can be transferred.

In 2002, Arizona became the first state to implement an online system for voter registration. Online registration has rapidly become more widespread. By 2012, 15 states allowed voters to register online. According to the data from the National Conference of State Legislatures, as of December 2015 there were 28 states and the District of Columbia that either had online voter registration or were in the process of implementing such systems. These states are shown in Table 3.1 along with the year of implementation.

Table 3.1
States with Online Voter Registration

State	Year Implemented	State	Year Implemented
Arizona	2002	Minnesota	2013
California	2012	Missouri*	2014
Colorado	2010	Nebraska	2015
Connecticut	2014	Nevada	2012
Delaware	2014	New Mexico	Under development
District of Columbia	2015	New York	2011
Florida	Under development	Oklahoma	Under development
Georgia	2014	Oregon	2010
Hawaii	2015	Pennsylvania	2015
Illinois	2014	South Carolina	2012
Indiana	2010	Utah	2010
Kansas	2009	Virginia	2013
Louisiana	2010	Washington	2008
Maryland	2012	West Virginia	2015
Massachusetts	2015		

*Registrations in Missouri have to be done on a touch screen device that allows a person to sign the registration application electronically.
Source: National Conference of State Legislatures (as of October 6, 2015).

Many scholars have expressed skepticism that reforms to voter registration will have the intended effect of boosting turnout and creating a more democratically representative electorate. They note that the registration process has already been simplified through reforms mandated by the National Voter Registration Act of 1993. For these scholars, allowing individuals to register to vote at a state department of motor vehicles dramatically lowered the costs of registration, so any marginal further reduction in costs created by new reforms may be negligible both in size and effect (Highton 2004). Additionally, many convenience reforms similar to online voter registration have been found to primarily make voting easier for those already predisposed to turn out (Berinsky 2005). These reforms rarely mobilize those less predisposed to vote. However, Street et al. (2015) found that people tend to search for registration information in the month prior to an election, when many state deadlines for registration have already passed.

Emerging research suggests that online voter registration does have the potential to stimulate turnout among some populations who face higher direct costs of registration and voting. Pellissier (2015) found that online registration created a small initial boost in registration and turnout immediately after the policy reform was introduced and a greater increase in registration and turnout in the years that followed. Further, the availability of online registration was particularly influential for young citizens and those who had recently moved—clear target audiences for this registration reform. It is possible that online voter registration might actually change the composition of the electorate; some changes could be sufficient to alter election outcomes (Pellissier 2015).

ONLINE REGISTRATION AND VOTING

The CPS Voting and Registration Supplement can be used to examine the relationship between online voter registration and the propensity to register and vote. Specifically, we estimate the probability that various demographic subpopulations will register to vote and turn out to vote, given that the state they live in does or does not allow online voter registration. We build upon existing research related to the probability that individuals will register to vote and turn out to vote. In these models, political participation has been found to be related to both individual resources and skills, and institutional factors in the electoral environment (Rosenstone and Hansen 1993; Rosenstone and Wolfinger 1978; Verba, Schlozman, and Brady 1995). Specifically, factors such as household income, age, educational attainment, race, ethnicity, home ownership, and employment status are related to whether a person will vote. Individuals who are older, better educated, own their homes, and are employed are more likely to vote. Historically, members of minority populations were less likely to vote compared to whites; however, black voter turnout during the elections involving Barack Obama has equaled or exceeded the turnout among whites. In addition, residential mobility—whether a person has lived at his or her current residence for two years or less—is also related to the likelihood a person will have registered or voted. The institutional factors that have been found to influence registration and voting decisions include whether a state has Election Day Voter Registration, no-excuse absentee voting, early voting, and vote by mail, as reported by the National Conference of State Legislatures.

The question of interest here is whether a state having online voter registration will affect the registration and voting rates overall or among particular sociodemographic subgroups. The examinations of registration and turnout include interactions between the demographic variables and the availability of online registration. These will show whether the effect of online voter registration on turnout or voting varies across demographic subpopulations. It is also important to control for variation in state political culture and for election type, both of which are done here. If proponents of online registration are correct and online voter registration reduces the costs of voting and makes participation more accessible for those with relatively limited resources, then the relationship between these demographic variables and participation should be weaker when online voter registration is available. That is, advocates argue that online registration makes participation easier for citizens with limited income, education, and other socioeconomic resources, who might otherwise be deterred from voting because they find the process of voter registration too burdensome. If this is the case, then registration and voting should be less strongly correlated with income, education, and other relevant resource variables in states where online voter registration is available. In the models of registration and voting, coefficients on the interactions between online registration and resource variables that have the opposite sign of the coefficient on the resource variable alone indicate that online registration lessens the participatory benefit of a particular resource.

After analyzing the impact of online voter registration on the propensity to register and to vote, it is clear that online voter registration does have a positive impact on the likelihood that an individual will both register and vote. The results of a multivariate analysis testing the likelihood an individual will register or vote can be found in Appendix A.8. As expected, regardless of whether a state has online registration or not, older, wealthier, and more educated citizens register and vote at much higher rates than their less privileged counterparts. Likewise, having recently moved or being a member of certain racial or ethnic groups decreases the likelihood of registering to vote or voting.

By itself, the availability of online voter registration in a given election cycle has a small, marginally significant positive effect on the overall probability of registering to vote, but no discernable effect on turnout. All things being equal, if a state has online voter registration, a one percentage point increase in the rate of voter registration is to be expected. Predicted turnout rates are roughly equivalent with or without online voter registration.

Critically, online voter registration changes the relationship between the stable, individual level resources (education, income, etc.) and political participation. In particular, online voter registration weakens the relationship between these individual resources and political participation. When online voter registration is available, those at the lowest levels of household income and education are more likely to register to vote, and the gap in registration and voter turnout between these groups decreases.

Figure 3.1 shows the predicted gaps in registration and turnout between those at the highest and lowest levels of income and education by the availability of online voter registration. Overall, there is a seven percentage point gap in voter registration between those at the lowest and highest household income levels. The availability of online voter registration decreases this gap to six percentage points, increasing the propensity to register by one percentage point for those in the two lowest income brackets. Further, the turnout gap between the wealthiest and poorest citizens decreases by almost 2 percent, from 12 percentage points to 10 percentage points, when online voter registration is available.

Figure 3.1
Online Voter Registration and Registration and Turnout Gaps between the Highest and Lowest Income and Education Groups

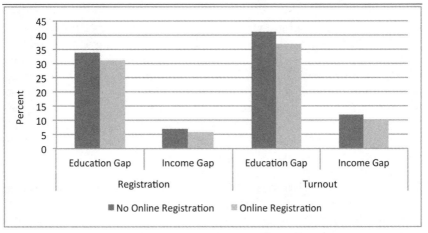

Source: The Current Population Survey Voting and Registration Supplement, 2008, 2010, 2012, and 2014.

Online voter registration also weakens the effect of education on political participation. Those with less than a high school education are two percentage points more likely to register when they can do so online. Online voter registration is also associated with a 1 percentage point increase in the propensity for those with only a high school degree to register to vote. Overall, the gap in voter registration between those at the highest and lowest levels of education decreases by 3 percentage points (from 34 percent to 31 percent) when online voter registration is available. Similarly, this convenience voting reform decreases the turnout gap associated with varying levels of education. Overall, those with the highest levels of education are twice as likely to vote as the least educated citizens, 82 percent versus 41 percent, respectively. The availability of online voter registration reduces this gap by four percentage points.

CONCLUSION

Online voter registration has the potential to boost registration and turnout among some traditionally underrepresented groups. For those with the lowest levels of income and education, the availability of online voter registration increases the propensity to register and decreases the gap in turnout relative to more educated and affluent citizens. Though this change has a seemingly small magnitude, such small changes can still be important in the election context, especially if implemented broadly: a 1 percent change in voting rates in a presidential election means approximately 1.3 million additional votes. Because online voter registration reduces the direct costs of registration, which are most salient for underrepresented groups, it has the potential to create a more democratically representative electorate.

Further, beyond its effects on voters, online registration has significant benefits for election administration, providing a relatively low-cost way to reduce the burden on local election officials. According to a survey conducted by the Pew Charitable Trusts in 2015 of officials from the 20 states offering online registration in 2014, the average cost to build an online voter registration system was approximately $250,000, with the total costs ranging from zero in two states that built these systems internally to a total estimated cost of $1.8 million for California's online registration system. These relatively low-cost systems created a significant reduction in paperwork and time required for data entry, and greatly improved the accuracy of voter registration rolls. California estimated cost savings of $2.34 per online registration and $2.5 million overall factoring in per-registration processing and mailing costs. Further, these systems allow individuals to verify that their registration information is correct and jurisdictions can more efficiently cross-reference data, potentially resulting in fewer registration-related problems on Election Day.

FURTHER READING

Abramowitz, Alan I. 2010. *The Disappearing Center: Engaged Citizens, Polarization, and American Democracy*. New Haven, CT: Yale University Press.

Aldrich, John H. 1993. "Rational Choice and Turnout." *American Journal of Political Science*: 37 (1): 246–278.

Ansolabehere, Stephen, and David M. Konisky. 2006. "The Introduction of Voter Registration and Its Effect on Turnout." *Political Analysis* 14: 83–100.

Berinsky, Adam J. 2005. "The Perverse Consequences of Electoral Reform in the United States." *American Politics Research* 33: 471–491.

Brians, Craig L., and Bernard Grofman. 2001. "Election Day Registration's Effect on U.S. Voter Turnout." *Social Science Quarterly* 82: 170–183.

Delli Carpini, Michael X., and Scott Keeter. 1997. *What Americans Know about Politics and Why It Matters*. New Haven, CT: Yale University Press.

Erikson, Robert S. 1981. "Why Do People Vote? Because They Are Registered." *American Politics Research* 9: 259–276.

Highton, Benjamin. 1997. "Easy Registration and Voter Turnout." *The Journal of Politics* 59: 565–575.

Highton, Benjamin. 2004. "Voter Registration and Turnout in the United States." *Perspectives on Politics* 2: 507–515.

Keyssar, Alexander. 2000. *The Right to Vote: The Contested History of Democracy in America*. New York, NY: Basic Books.

Pellissier, Allyson L. 2015. *At Your Convenience: Facilitating Voting and Registration*. Doctoral dissertation, California Institute of Technology.

Rosenstone, Steven J., and John M. Hansen. 1993. *Mobilization, Participation, and Democracy in America*. New York, NY: Macmillan.

Rosenstone, Steven J., and Raymond E. Wolfinger. 1978. "The Effect of Registration Laws on Voter Turnout." *American Political Science Review* 72: 22–45.

Street, Alex, Murray, Thomas A., Blitzer, John, and Rajan S. Patel. 2015. "Estimating Voter Registration Deadline Effects with Web Search Data." *Political Analysis*: 23 (2): 225–241.

Tetlock, Philip E. 1985. "Accountability: The Neglected Social Context of Judgment and Choice." *Research in Organizational Behavior* 7: 297–332.

Valentino, Nicholas A., Brader, Ted, Greonendyk, Eric W., Gregorowicz, Krysha, and Vincent L. Hutchings. 2011. "Election Night's Alright For Fighting: The Role of Emotions in Political Participation." *The Journal of Politics* 73: 156–170.

Verba, Sidney, and Norman H. Nie. 1972. *Participation in America*. New York, NY: Harper & Row.

Verba, Sidney, Schlozman, Kay L., and Henry E. Brady. 1995. *Voice and Equality: Civic Voluntarism in American Politics*. Vol. 4. Cambridge, MA: Harvard University Press.

Wolfinger, Raymond E., and Steven J. Rosenstone. 1980. *Who Votes?* Vol. 22. New Haven, CT: Yale University Press.

4

Political Citizenship: Whether and Why College Students Vote

Jodi Benenson, Margaret Brower, and Nancy L. Thomas

Each election season, news analysts, politicians, and researchers lament low voter turnout, particularly among young people. In fact, young people, including those in college, vote at rates far lower than those of older Americans. Some commentators suggest young people are apathetic about doing their civic duty. Others point to barriers to voting for young people, such as restrictive voter identification laws or inconvenient or hostile local voting conditions. And others defend young non-voters as having made a conscious choice, citing polls and studies that document American frustration with the electoral system and distrust of politicians.

Whatever the reasons for their decision, the low rate of voting by college students has a definite impact on American democracy. Over 18 million people attend colleges or universities every year, enough to influence election results and shape public policy. Voting offers college students an opportunity to be involved with policy making and society more broadly and may be a gateway to other forms of civic engagement. Democracy works best when all Americans have the opportunity and motivation to participate and influence the policies and governance structures that affect their daily lives. Simply stated, college student voting matters.

UNDERSTANDING COLLEGE STUDENT VOTING RATES

Perhaps surprisingly, measuring college student voting rates is not a simple undertaking. The federal government does not calculate an "official" voting rate (Leighley and Nagler 2013, 18), the percent of eligible voters who actually vote. Because of the rapidly changing population in the United States due to relocations, births, and deaths, determining the number of eligible voters is arduous. Moreover, voting records are collected and maintained at the state and local level. Until recently, this decentralized system resulted in challenging inconsistencies in the way voting records were collected, maintained, and reported. With technological advances, accuracy at the local and state level is improving, but this is a relatively recent development.

The most commonly-cited and reliable measures of voting rates are based on individual responses to national surveys such as the U.S. Census Bureau's Current Population Survey (CPS) Voting and Registration Supplement. Typical CPS datasets include well over 100,000 individuals, and college students are represented by thousands of observations (Richman and Pate 2010). Similarly, the American National Election Study is a biennial survey of 1,000–2,000 U.S. citizens and is conducted before and after every presidential election. Although the self-reported nature of these voting data are not without limitations, such as social desirability bias (the natural inclination for people to answer questions the way they believe they should), these surveys have been the best source of voting data to date.

The CPS has provided the data most widely used to understand the characteristics of American voters. For 30 years, voter turnout for all Americans in presidential elections has held steady at around 60 percent, but young people consistently vote at lower rates. For instance, during the 2012 election, only 45 percent of 18–29-year-olds voted (Center for Information and Research on Civic Learning and Engagement 2013). In the midterm elections of 2014, only 19.9 percent of 18–29-year-olds and 17.1 percent of 18–24-year-olds voted, making 2014 the lowest youth turnout in 40 years (Center for Information and Research on Civic Learning and Engagement 2015).

Many of the attributes of likely voters are widely accepted. Women vote at higher rates than men. Among different racial and ethnic groups, African Americans and whites vote at the highest rates, and Latino/as and Asian Americans vote at the lowest rates (Center for Information and Research on Civic Learning and Engagement 2013). Wealthier Americans vote at higher rates than less affluent Americans (Leighley and Nagler 2013). One of the most widely accepted characteristics of voters is the level of educational attainment. The more educated people are, the more likely they are to vote (Verba, Schlozman, and Brady 1995). Arguably, education improves students' political knowledge and cognitive skills, providing students with confidence in their voting choices. However, traditional theories about likely voters may not align with the unique characteristics of college students (Niemi and Hanmer 2010). For instance, students attending college far away from home have the option of choosing between voting locally and voting absentee in their home jurisdictions, a factor not relevant to all population groups. More research is needed to understand the voting behavior of college students across different types of higher education institutions.

THE NATIONAL STUDY OF LEARNING, VOTING, AND ENGAGEMENT

The National Study of Learning, Voting, and Engagement (NSLVE) database offers the first objective measure of U.S. college and university student voter registration and voting rates and the opportunity to explore these for the 2012 and 2014 elections. The database contains information about whether a student registered to vote, where a student is registered (e.g., in-state, out-of-state), and whether a student voted. In 2012, NSLVE institutions reported that an average of 69.2 percent of eligible college students were registered to vote.

The NSLVE database is created by matching publicly available local and state voting records with student enrollment lists from nearly 700 colleges and universities nationally (data is currently available for 689 colleges and universities). Representing 48 states, these institutions reflect all institutional types (e.g., community colleges, liberal arts colleges), missions (e.g., religiously affiliated institutions, public research universities), student populations, and geographic locations. These data are obtained by merging public voting records and student enrollment lists submitted by individual institutions to the National Student Clearinghouse, a repository of up-to-date enrollment lists from nearly all of the degree-granting institutions in the United States. The resulting database contains 2012 and 2014 voter registration and voting records broken down by student characteristics (e.g., age, student field of study) and institutional characteristics (e.g., public or private institution, size of institution); however, information that identifies individual students has been removed.

Of those who registered, NSLVE institutions report that an average of 68.7 percent of students were also voters. Thus, the average voting rate across these institutions was 46.9 percent. Although NSLVE institutions do not constitute a representative sample of higher education institutions in the United States, these colleges and universities do serve nearly 7 million students, which is approximately one-third of the student population in 2012.

An examination of these registration and voting rates shows differences across types of institutions. As seen in Figure 4.1, the average

Figure 4.1
Average Voting Rate by Type of Institution: 2012 U.S. Election

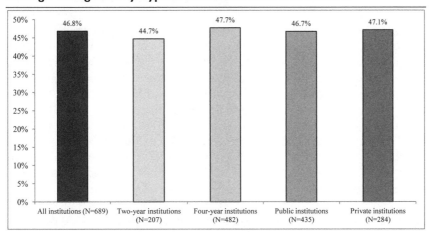

Source: The National Study of Learning, Voting, and Engagement database.

student voting rate for all institutions is 46.8 percent. Two-year institutions have a lower average student voting rate of 44.7 percent compared to four-year institutions, which have a higher voting rate of 47.7 percent. There is a small difference in the average voting rates between students enrolled in public institutions (46.7 percent) and private institutions (47.1 percent). These differences support earlier research that suggests that student voter turnout is influenced by institutional characteristics, such as whether a student attends a two- or four-year institution (Lopez and Brown 2006).

WHY COLLEGE STUDENTS DO NOT VOTE

Apathy, or inertia, is often identified as a primary reason why young people do not vote. However, according to the 2007 report of the Center for Information and Research on Civic Learning and Engagement, *Millennials Talk Politics: A Study of College Student Political Engagement*, college students are not apathetic (Kiesa et al. 2007). In fact, some studies indicate that Millennials (born after 1980, roughly) are more civically active than the prior Generation Xers (born 1960–1980, roughly). Yet Millenials remain ambivalent about formal politics, do not view voting as an effective way to change society, and dislike the "all talk, no action" of politicians, whom they view as out of touch with the needs of young people and everyday people (Kiesa et al. 2007). Public issues are often viewed by students as so daunting that they cannot envision how to make a difference. Millennials also do not trust news sources or politicians and have difficulty sorting through information and identifying reliable facts.

In this way, college students' views are similar to the historically high numbers of Americans who lack trust in U.S. government (Pew Research Center 2014).

College students are also not *asked* to vote. As first-time voters, college students are not listed in voting databases, which makes it difficult to locate them for purposes of encouraging registration or voting. College students are also more challenging to locate because their residence can change when they enroll in college (Niemi and Hanmer 2010). Contact by political parties is strongly associated with higher voter turnout (Niemi and Hanmer 2010), and over the past 10 years, mobilization efforts by political parties have been strategically targeted to reach *likely* voters. If college students are not considered likely voters because they lack a voting history or they change residence, they then miss out on opportunities for contacts designed to engage them in the election process.

Over one-third of the registered students in the NSLVE database do not go on to vote. Several factors could account for this significant drop-off. For students who choose to vote in their hometowns and attend college far from home, they may not mail the absentee ballot on time or at all. Voting locations might be located far from campus, and students may not have a way to get there. Or students may feel unprepared to choose among candidates. Changes in voter identification requirements can deter student voters, and local voting officials can impose non-statutory barriers to student voting (Kiesa 2015). These deterrents can significantly reduce student voter turnout.

PROMOTING STUDENT POLITICAL ENGAGEMENT

Research shows that when students acquire basic civic knowledge, they are more likely to participate in other political activities such as voting (Hillygus 2005). Colleges and universities have long been tasked with responsibility for educating students for civic participation and social responsibility. Yet in recent years, questions have been raised about how committed higher education is to that role. In 2012, a National Task Force on Civic Learning and Democratic Engagement issued a report calling upon higher education to strengthen education *for democracy* (Musil 2012), yet many institutions avoid political conflict and student activism. Colleges and universities are uniquely situated to engage students in public problem solving and the political process through one or more of the following strategies intended to promote college student political engagement.

Teach College Students the Fundamentals of Democracy

At the college level, this knowledge should be both nuanced and sophisticated. All students, not just those who choose to study relevant disciplines such as political science or public administration, need to grapple with tensions inherent in applying democratic principles and practices. For example, students should consider the extent to which the representative U.S. system of government reflects the values and opinions of the diverse constituencies in the United States. All college graduates should know the history of civil rights movements and how diverse immigrant populations shape American public life.

Help Students Navigate Barriers to Voting

Students should also understand the barriers and challenges that are unique to them as a voting population. These barriers include laws such as restrictive voter identification requirements and changes in Same Day Registration. Kiesa (2015) discusses additional non-statutory challenges that are unique to their location on a college campus. These subtle barriers to voting that students should understand include—but are not limited to—voting booth location, student identification restrictions, and the misplacement of registration materials.

Create a Campus Climate That Values Diversity and Complexity

Educators know that learning experiences are richer and more transformative when they provoke a student to question their worldview or get students out of their "comfort zones." Yet, political opinions tend to align with personal characteristics, such as age, socioeconomic status, party affiliation, religion, gender, and race/ethnicity. Like most people, students tend to gravitate to communities of people who share their values and perspectives. These are "comfortable" communities where relationships form more easily. Students who interact with diverse peers also participate in more political campus activities and have more political interest (Gurin, Nagda, and Lopez 2004). Colleges and universities can create learning environments that value and nurture student diversity and allow for discussions that help them examine issues from multiple perspectives. Although these diverse environments may be challenging, conflict should be treated as a learning opportunity, not an interaction to be avoided.

Engage Students in Controversial Issue Discussions

Talking politics in settings that encourage respect and candor increases students' political skills and interests (Beaumont 2011). The classroom is an ideal setting where students can discuss current events and public problems; talking politics can also happen in dormitories, cafeterias, and at special events. It is important that faculty be prepared to lead discussions on popular topics, establish ground rules for the conversation, and carve out time to hear all perspectives on an issue. Similarly, colleges and universities should support campus-wide training in dialogue and deliberation across differences of social identity and ideology. Colleges and universities should invest in these processes to ensure that no one on campus is avoiding political conversations because they are difficult.

Teach Students the Public Relevance of Each Discipline

Students should understand the social, economic, and policy implications of the field they choose to study in college. To incorporate public relevance into the curriculum, faculty can connect learning (e.g., basic science principles) with public policy (e.g., regulations on stem cell research). Higher education institutions can also create hands-on learning experiences (e.g., engineering students build a house for a community organization such as Habitat for Humanity) that incorporate opportunities to discuss relevant social and political factors related to this experience (e.g., causes of homelessness).

Support Opportunities for Students to Practice Democratic Engagement

Debate teams, ethics bowls, mock trials, residential theme houses or first-year experiences, Model UN, and other simulations can provide students with opportunities to think critically about issues and develop skills to analyze, frame, discuss, and collectively resolve public problems. Student government offers another opportunity for students to develop their leadership skills and to gain political savvy. Colleges and universities should also provide students with authentic opportunities and actual authority to play a role in institutional governance. Students can serve on institutional committees, run offices, and even manage critical functions such as the bookstore. Giving students real responsibility facilitates learning for political leadership.

Provide Opportunities for Community Engagement

Service-learning and other forms of interactive learning can shift student attitudes in favor of political participation, as long as students also learn the social, economic, and policy dimensions of the service experience. Community-based research projects, particularly case studies on public problems, can also be valuable learning experiences. Colleges and universities need to teach students *how* to talk about public concerns and politics in ways that are respectful but forthright. Students should also be offered internships with elected officials and political offices, campaigns, and organizations.

Teach Social Responsibility

Students need to understand that in a democracy, a system of self-rule, a case can be made that ineffective governance is a reflection of ineffective citizen engagement. Of course, it is not always that simple, particularly in a system plagued by excessive campaign donations and spending and special interest policy making. Nonetheless, students can make a difference if they understand their responsibilities. Colleges and universities must create and foster opportunities for them to develop this awareness and initiative.

Address Inequality in Civic Learning Opportunities

American colleges and universities have historically selected and served a privileged class, a pattern that persists. White students are concentrated in the nation's 468 most well-funded, selective four-year colleges and universities, while students of color are more concentrated in the 3,250 least well-funded, open-access two- and four-year institutions (Carnevale and Strohl 2013). The 82 most selective institutions annually spend up to $27,900 per student, whereas open-access institutions spend as little as $6,000 per student (Carnevale and Strohl 2013). Highly resourced institutions are more able to provide students with opportunities to engage politically (e.g., paid internships). Students enrolled in lower-resourced institutions are often juggling jobs and families and may not have the time for political engagement beyond the classroom. For these reasons, political learning needs to be embedded in the curriculum, making political experiences available to *all* students.

CONCLUSION

Disengagement among young people, college students in particular, has significant implications for policy making. Although political officials and federal, state, and local governments should be responsive to the preferences and needs of all citizens, they are far more responsive to *voters* than non-voters. Because voters are traditionally older, wealthier, and more conservative, policies reflect their interests more than those of college students, particularly about which programs should be funded and other decisions about how government dollars are distributed (Leighley and Nagler 2013). In other words, when young people do not vote, their needs and interests are not always reflected in policy decisions and the voting calculus alone does not provide an incentive to include them. This problem perpetuates a cycle of disengagement: college students are disillusioned by politicians and government because they feel their interests are ignored, and politicians undervalue young non-voters because they seem disinterested and do not vote.

Voting is a basic and important civic act that college students value. Cultivating citizens for responsible civic engagement is a central purpose of U.S. higher education. Colleges and universities can provide students with democratic learning experiences through intentional programming consistent with the above recommendations. It is through these experiences that we can increase commitment to solving the problems of the 21st-century American democracy.

FURTHER READING

Beaumont, Elizabeth. 2011. "Promoting Political Agency, Addressing Political Inequality: A Multilevel Model of Internal Political Efficacy." *The Journal of Politics* 73: 216–231.

Carnevale, Anthony P., and Jeff Strohl. 2013. "Separate and Unequal: How Higher Education Reinforces the Intergenerational Reproduction of White Racial Privilege." Retrieved March 30, 2016 from https://cew.georgetown.edu/wp-content/uploads/2014/11/SeparateUnequal.FR_pdf.

Center for Information and Research on Civic Learning and Engagement (CIRCLE). 2013. "The Youth Vote in 2012." Medford, MA: Tufts University. Retrieved March 30, 2016 from http://www.civicyouth.org/wp-content/uploads/2013/05/CIRCLE_2013FS_outhVoting2012FINAL.pdf.

Center for Information and Research on Civic Learning and Engagement (CIRCLE). 2015. "2014 Youth Turnout and Youth Registration Rates Lowest Ever Recorded; Changes Essential in 2016." Medford, MA: Tufts University Jonathan M. Tisch College of Civic Life. Retrieved March 30, 2016 from http://www.civicyouth.org/2014-youth-turnout-and-youth-registration-rates-lowest-ever-recorded-changes-essential-in-2016.

Gurin, Patricia, Nagda, Biren R. A., and Gretchen E. Lopez. 2004. "The Benefits of Diversity in Education for Democratic Citizenship." *Journal of Social Issues* 60: 17–34.

Hillygus, D. Sunshine. 2005. "The Missing Link: Exploring the Relationship between Higher Education and Political Engagement." *Political Behavior* 27: 25–47.

Kiesa, Abby, Orlowski, Alexander P., Levine, Peter, Both, Deborah, Kirby, Emily H., Lopez, Mark H., and Karlo B. Marcelo. 2007. "Millennials Talk Politics: A Study of College Student Political Engagement." Center for Information and Research on Civic Learning and Engagement (CIRCLE). Retrieved March 30, 2016 from http://www.civicyouth.org/PopUps/CSTP.pdf.

Kiesa, Abby. 2015. "Democracy Matters: Addressing Non-Statutory Barriers to Voting Guide." Institute for Democracy and Higher Education, Tufts University. Retrieved from http://activecitizen.tufts.edu/wp-content/uploads/IDHE-Non-Statutory-Barriers-to-College-Student-Voting.pdf.

Leighley, Jan E., and Jonathan Nagler. 2013. *Who Votes Now? Demographics, Issues, Inequality, and Turnout in the United States*. Princeton, NJ: Princeton University Press.

Lopez, Mark H., and Benjamin Brown. 2006. "Civic Engagement among 2-Year and 4-Year College Students. Fact Sheet." Center for Information and Research on Civic Learning and Engagement (CIRCLE), University of

Maryland. Retrieved from http://www.civicyouth.org/PopUps/FactSheets/FS06_comm_coll.pdf.

Musil, Caryn. M. 2012. "A "National Call to Action" from the National Task Force on Civic Learning and Democratic Engagement." *Civic Provocations* 1: 69–74. Retrieved from https://www.aacu.org/sites/default/files/files/CLDE/CivicProvocations.pdf.

Nie, Norman H., Junn, Jane, and Kenneth Stehlik-Barry. 1996. *Education and Democratic Citizenship in America*. Chicago, IL: University of Chicago Press.

Niemi, Richard G., and Michael J. Hanmer. 2010. "Voter Turnout among College Students: New Data and a Rethinking of Traditional Theories." *Social Science Quarterly* 91: 301–323.

Pew Research Center. 2014. "Public Trust in Government: 1958–2014." Retrieved from http://www.people-press.org/2014/11/13/public-trust-in-government.

Richman, Jesse, and Andrew Pate. 2010. "Can the College Vote Turn Out?: Evidence from the U.S. States, 2000–08." *State Politics & Policy Quarterly* 10: 51–68.

Verba, Sidney, Schlozman, Kay L., and Henry E. Brady. 1995. *Voice and Equality: Civic Voluntarism in American Politics*. Vol. 4. Cambridge, MA: Harvard University Press.

5

Nonprofit Voter Registration and the Limitations on Nonprofit Advocacy

Kelly Krawczyk

Nonprofits and community-based agencies have the potential to play a huge role in remedying inequities in voter registration. Because many nonprofits serve marginalized populations that are less likely to register to vote on their own, these organizations are well positioned to engage in voter registration efforts that target these underrepresented groups (LeRoux 2011). From a legislative standpoint, the passage of the 1993 National Voter Registration Act (NVRA) paved the way for nonprofits to facilitate voter registration on behalf of their constituents. Yet, research indicates that nonprofits and other community-based organizations do not regularly or actively engage in advocacy and get out the vote activities that extend to voter registration drives. Why not? If nonprofits have the potential to engage in voter registration activities, why do they rarely do so? What prevents these organizations from facilitating voter registration on behalf of their stakeholders? Several barriers have been identified that hinder nonprofit organizations from engaging in voter registration activities. Nonprofits may refrain from engaging in voter registration due to restrictive state laws, prohibitive and unclear federal laws, lack of necessary or sufficient resources and expertise to successfully engage in voter registration, and fear that advocacy activities such as voter registration will adversely affect their relationship with government funders.

INEQUITIES IN VOTER REGISTRATION

At least 51 million Americans, or about 25 percent of the eligible voting population, are not registered to vote (Pew Charitable Trusts 2012). A large share of those missing from voter rolls are members of underrepresented and marginalized groups, including the poor, undereducated, disabled, and minorities. This underrepresentation of millions of eligible voters is, in part, the result of a voter registration system that places the responsibility for registration on citizens. The voter registration process often burdens individuals and is complex and inefficient. One mechanism that has been successful in reducing the burden of the registration system and in reducing some of the imbalance in voter registration is the voter registration drive. Voter registration drives have added millions of voters to the rolls over the past few decades and have been particularly successful in targeting underrepresented groups. Nonprofits and community-based agencies can be effective vehicles for implementing voter registration drives, offering assistance to voters who might not otherwise be able to register successfully on their own or who are more likely to register only after personal encouragement from a community member. These methods lead to greater registration and increased participation: voters are more likely to cast a ballot if they have registered through community-based efforts.

THE POTENTIAL ROLE OF NONPROFITS IN VOTER REGISTRATION

Nonprofits play an important role in promoting civic engagement and helping to strengthen democracy (Putnam 2007; Skopol 2003). Nonprofits function as "civic intermediaries" that link their clients to the political environment, which makes them well suited to promote participation by underrepresented groups (LeRoux 2007, 411). One way nonprofits function as civic intermediaries is by conducting nonpartisan voter engagement activities, which are also referred to as "get out the vote" (GOTV) activities. GOTV activities encompass a wide range of voter education, voter assistance, and voter registration activities. These activities include providing nonpartisan information to voters about candidates, conducting voter registration drives, helping voters locate their polling places, and offering voters transportation to their polling places on Election Day. Piven and Cloward (1988) focused on the important role nonprofits could play in voter registration. They proposed that citizens should be able to register to vote in community agencies and nonprofit organizations, including those that provide social services in the areas of health, housing, welfare, and unemployment. Because these social services are increasingly delivered outside public agency settings and instead by nonprofit organizations acting as partners with government, nonprofits are especially well positioned to facilitate voter registration on behalf of their constituents. Piven and Cloward's ideas are captured in the 1993 NVRA, which attempts to reduce disparities in voter registration rates by race, income, age, and disability.

THE 1993 NATIONAL VOTER REGISTRATION ACT (NVRA)

In the United States, voter registration is the responsibility of the individual. However, government can act to make the registration process easier or more difficult, and this has an effect on voter turnout. A significant amount of research suggests voter registration is a substantial barrier to voting. In fact, turnout is approximately 7–10 percentage points higher in states with reduced barriers to voter registration (Ansolabehere and Konisky 2006). This is because citizens weigh the benefits of voting against the costs, and higher costs of participation result in lower participation rates. For some people, voting is not a priority, and a small obstacle like registration may keep them from participating. Others do not think to register until the final weeks of an election, when many voter registration deadlines have already passed. Still others complain of errors in the registration system that prevent them from voting (Ansolabehere and Konisky 2006).

One way the federal government tried to simplify and improve the voter registration process was through the passage of the 1993 NVRA. The NVRA requires states to implement procedures that reduce the burden of voter registration, in order to open the gateway for increased voting. In essence, the NVRA attempts to make voter registration easier by eliminating the necessity of a special trip to register, eliminating that cost of registration.

The NVRA contains four specific provisions designed to increase voter registration and facilitate higher turnout in any state that does not allow Election Day Voter Registration (Highton and Wolfinger 1998). The NVRA mandates that states must establish both mail-in and agency-based voter registration programs, and it also ends the practice of removing (purging) registered voters from the voter rolls simply because they did not vote. The key feature of the NVRA is a provision known as "Motor Voter." This provision states that voter registration must be an integral part of the application for a motor vehicle driver's license. A single form can be used for both voter registration and a motor vehicle driver's license application. If two separate forms are used, the voter registration form must be supplied as part of the application process for a motor vehicle license.

The "Motor Voter" provision of the NVRA is also important for non-profit organizations, because it provides the enabling legislation for non-profits to engage in voter registration efforts (Independent Sector 2004). The "Motor Voter" provision does not simply encourage nongovernmental organizations to register their clients to vote, but it in fact requires any agency receiving state funding to provide these opportunities to their clients. Any office of a state-funded program that is primarily engaged in providing services to people with disabilities must provide all program applicants with voter registration forms, assist them in completing these forms, and pass on the completed forms to the appropriate state official. Some nonprofits go even further by providing additional forms of voter education, assistance, and encouragement (LeRoux 2011, 567).

The NVRA is intended to make the voter registration process more accessible for citizens that are underrepresented in the political process. More than 15 years have elapsed since this legislation was passed, however, and a number of factors continue to inhibit the effectiveness of the NVRA, specifically related to the ability of nonprofit organizations to carry out voter registration activities.

STATE LAWS RESTRICT THE VOTER REGISTRATION ACTIVITIES OF NONPROFITS

There is substantial variation in state law regulating voter registration. Many states have acted to reduce the costs and barriers related to voter registration, making the process easier and more accessible. Some states, however, have passed laws that actually restrict the ability of community-based and nonprofit organizations to engage in voter registration. Supporters of these restrictive laws argue voter registration drives are susceptible to fraud and voter registration should be made more difficult in order to protect the right to vote. However, these restrictions reduce the likelihood that nonprofits will engage in voter registration.

States that regulate voter registration drives usually do so in four main ways: 1) using official volunteer systems, 2) requiring state training programs, 3) implementing strict registration and reporting mandates, and 4) applying voter registration return deadlines with penalties and fines for missed deadlines (Kasden 2012). Table 5.1 provides a summary of the state laws that restrict voter registration in each of these four categories.

The "Motor Voter" provision of the NVRA eliminated the requirement that individuals who wish to engage in voter registration, including individuals in nonprofits, petition to become certified "deputy registrars" that are officially allowed to register voters. However, some states still maintain a certification process for volunteers, if only on an optional basis. The state rules governing this certification process tend to vary widely

Table 5.1
State Laws Restricting Voter Registration Activities of Nonprofit and Community-Based Organizations

State	Official Volunteer Systems	Training Programs	State Registration and Reporting Mandates	Return Deadlines and Penalties
Alabama				
Alaska				
Arizona				
Arkansas				✓
California	*	*	✓	✓
Colorado		✓	✓	✓
Connecticut				
Delaware	*	*	✓	*
Florida			✓	✓
Georgia	*	*		✓
Hawaii				
Idaho				
Illinois	*	◇		*
Indiana				✓
Iowa				✓
Kansas				
Kentucky				✓
Louisiana	*			✓
Maine	*			✓
Maryland	*	◇		✓
Massachusetts				
Michigan				
Minnesota				✓
Mississippi				
Missouri	*		✓	✓
Montana				
Nebraska	*	◇		
Nevada	*		✓	✓
New Hampshire				
New Jersey				
New Mexico		✓	✓	✓
New York				
North Carolina				
North Dakota				
Ohio				✓
Oklahoma				
Oregon				✓
Pennsylvania				
Rhode Island				

Table 5.1 (Continued)

South Carolina				
South Dakota				✓
Tennessee				
Texas	✓	✓	✓	✓
Utah				
Vermont				
Virginia				✓
Washington				✓
West Virginia	*	◊		✓
Wisconsin	*	◊		✓
Wyoming				

Source: 2012 Brennan Center Report on State Restrictions on Voter Registration Drives.
Key:
✓ = Yes
* = Optional or varies
◊ = Official volunteers

and can be confusing, leading some nonprofits to mistakenly believe certification is a requirement, or that it confers some sort of special status. In addition, some states require a state-sponsored training program for all individuals and organizations that conduct voter registration. Yet these state-sponsored training programs are sometimes difficult to access, occurring infrequently or only in centralized locations.

Another recent trend that restricts the activities of nonprofits engaged in voter registration is the imposition of extensive registration and reporting requirements on volunteers or employees. A nonprofit may have to pre-register and provide a large amount of information about their organization and their plans to engage in voter registration activities. They may also be required to submit extensive disclosure information about their voter registration activities and provide tracking of the registration forms. In some cases, states place limits on the number of forms that can be requested by an organization. These requirements can be burdensome and intimidating to small, community-based nonprofits, effectively curtailing their ability to engage in voter registration.

Some states have adopted regulations that impose strict and even unrealistic deadlines for submitting completed voter registration forms. Typically, states require voter registration drives to return applications periodically. The deadline for nonprofits to return forms ranges from 2 to 30 days prior to an election, with most states having a deadline of around 10 days. Although most nonprofits can meet the longer deadlines, shorter deadlines make it very difficult for a nonprofit to complete voter registration drives. And because people pay more attention to an election as it gets closer (Green and Gerber 2004), including nonprofit leaders who are busy with the day-to-day activities of running their organizations, nonprofits may not be concerned with voter registration activities until the election is on the immediate horizon. Nonprofits in states with very conservative voter registration deadlines may miss the window for carrying out voter registration activities. Regardless of deadlines, in states that assess heavy fines and even criminal charges for failing to meet the deadlines, nonprofit organizations and their employees and volunteers are less inclined to become involved in voter registration.

Given the multitude of state laws regulating voter registration activities and the potentially stiff penalties for mistakes, nonprofit leaders may find state regulations difficult to navigate and avoid voter registration activities if they are located in a state with these sorts of laws. In fact, there is substantial evidence that nonprofit leaders base their decisions to register voters on the presence or absence of these restrictive state laws governing third party voter registration activities, and the presence of restrictive laws suppresses the voter registration activities of nonprofits (LeRoux 2011, 568). In states that have conservative voter registration deadlines, strict deadlines for submission of completed voter registration forms, heavy fines or criminal charges for failure to meet deadlines, and limits or charges for voter registration forms, nonprofits are less likely to engage in voter registration.

INTERNAL REVENUE SERVICE CODE RESTRICTS THE VOTER REGISTRATION ACTIVITIES OF NONPROFITS

The nonprofit sector encompasses a wide range of organizations, including those involved in the arts, health care, human services, education, environment, social justice, religion, and philanthropy. In fact, there are 27 types of nonprofits defined in the Internal Revenue Service (IRS) code (Salamon 1995, 8). By far, the most common type of nonprofit is the public charity, also known as a 501(c)(3). The public charity or 501 (c)(3) offers the dual advantages of tax exemption and tax deductibility. Public charities are exempt from paying federal income tax, and individuals who donate to a 501(c)(3) can claim a deduction from their federal income taxes. However, with these tax advantages come limitations. The government has the right to set rules as to how money can be spent by these and other nonprofits, and to set limitations on their political activities. In fact, one of the main ways of regulating nonprofits is through the lobbying provision of the IRS code applicable to 501(c)(3) organizations, which limits the amount of political advocacy activity that public charity nonprofits can engage in.

In some ways, federal law encourages nonprofits to promote civic engagement. Internal Revenue Service Rule 78-248, 1978-1 allows nonprofit organizations with a 501(c)(3) designation to engage in a wide variety of advocacy activities, including GOTV activities such as providing information on voter registration deadlines, providing nonpartisan candidate information, offering information on ballot measures, assisting voters in locating polling places, helping them fill out a sample ballot, and engaging in any other nonpartisan activity intended to increase voter turnout (LeRoux 2007). Public charity nonprofits are also allowed to hold forums, sponsor debates, register voters, publish analyses of election issues, and engage in other nonpartisan endeavors. Yet these nonprofits find this part of the IRS code confusing and generally avoid these activities because they believe they may run into trouble with the IRS if they are active in the electoral arena (Berry 2005). The IRS requirements for public charities—and the nonprofit community's perception of these—are especially important given that public charity profits are the direct service providers for many public programs directed at groups also underrepresented in the electorate.

Other aspects of federal law act to inhibit civic engagement by nonprofits and their constituents. The IRS regulations governing the political advocacy activities of nonprofits explicitly prohibit charitable organizations from participating in political campaigns, endorsing or opposing a candidate for political office, making campaign contributions, and engaging in any other form of partisan political activity. Through IRS law on public charities, the federal government restrains participation in the policymaking process by these nonprofits, their boards, their members, and their clients. Yet, at the same time, these nonprofits are charged by their stakeholders with mobilizing and representing their clients, who are often the poor and the disadvantaged, in order to provide them with a voice in the political system.

NONPROFITS LACK THE EXPERTISE AND RESOURCES TO ENGAGE IN VOTER REGISTRATION

As we can see from the previous discussion, state and federal laws governing the advocacy and civic engagement activities of public charity nonprofits are complex and difficult to interpret. This sometimes results in misunderstanding and even fear on the part of nonprofit executives regarding the regulatory standards they must abide by. Many executive directors in these nonprofit organizations are misinformed about what they can and cannot do under the law. Nonprofits may falsely believe they cannot engage in any sort of advocacy activities at all or they risk losing their tax-exempt status (Berry 2005; Chaves, Stephens, and Galaskiewicz 2004). Lack of relevant staff expertise and concerns about violating the law often keep this significant portion of the nonprofit sector out of the political arena altogether.

The research findings of scholar Jeffrey Berry illuminate these issues. Nonprofit leaders who were interviewed for Berry's study on nonprofit advocacy indicated that advocacy activities such as voter registration are not part of their mission. In some ways this makes sense, as nonprofit leaders note that they simply do not have the resources to engage in advocacy. Yet Berry's interviews reveal that part of the reluctance to engage in advocacy is also due to fear of the IRS and misunderstanding of the law (Berry 2005).

Overall, nonprofits may have little incentive to engage in voter registration activities, given that such activities are often beyond the scope of their missions or the services they provide. In addition, many nonprofits do not have sufficient resources—time, money, or staff—to implement new voter registration programs. In an environment of severe resource constraints, it is often all that nonprofits can do to execute programs that serve their clients and fulfill their missions.

GOVERNMENT FUNDING CAN INHIBIT NONPROFITS' VOTER REGISTRATION ACTIVITIES

Many nonprofit organizations depend on government funding to survive. This financial dependence has increased in recent decades as more government-funded services are delivered through grants and contracts with nonprofit organizations and in particular by public charities. Increased government support for nonprofits raises questions about the impact of this support on nonprofits' political activity, however. What is the relationship between government funding and civic engagement and advocacy activities in nonprofit organizations? Do nonprofits that receive government funding engage in these activities as actively as those nonprofit organizations that do not receive government support?

While there is some research that indicates government funding may cause nonprofits to become more active in advocacy (Berry and Arons 2003; LeRoux 2007), other studies find government funding may in fact reduce nonprofit advocacy activity (Clarke 2000). Nonprofits may be reluctant to mobilize clients because they fear unfavorable consequences such as loss of government support, both political and financial (LeRoux 2007, 413). This relationship between nonprofit organizations and government illustrates the theory of resource dependence. Resource dependence suggests that nonprofits who are reliant on government funding for support may be reluctant to engage in advocacy activities, because they do not want to be viewed as "biting the hand that feeds them" by becoming involved in politics.

The complex regulatory environment facing nonprofits that receive government funds may also produce a negative relationship between government funding and nonprofit advocacy activity, and a relationship in which all manner of advocacy is negatively affected, not just activity that directly challenges the funder. As mentioned previously, there are legal limits on the extent to which 501(c)(3) nonprofit organizations can engage in political advocacy. Some activities, such as supporting or opposing candidates running for office, are completely prohibited. Other activities, such as lobbying, are permitted as long as they are not a "substantial" part of an organization's activities. Still other activities, such as public education or voter registration, may be pursued without limits. And the regulatory situation is even more complex for nonprofit organizations receiving government funds (Chaves, Stephens, and Galaskiewicz 2004), which means there is less incentive for nonprofits to engage in advocacy activities, even those such as voter registration, which are without legal limitation.

FURTHER READING

Ansolabehere, Stephen, and David M. Konisky. 2006. "The Introduction of Voter Registration and Its Effect on Turnout." *Political Analysis* 14: 83–100.

Berry, Jeffrey M. 2005. "Nonprofits and Civic Engagement." *Public Administration Review* 65 (5): 568–578.

Berry, Jeffery M., and David F. Arons. 2003. *A Voice for Nonprofits*. Washington, DC: Brookings Institution Press.

Chaves, Mark, Stephens, Laura, and Joseph Galaskiewicz. 2004. "Does Government Funding Suppress Nonprofits' Political Activity?" *American Sociological Review* 69 (2): 292–316.

Clarke, Susan E. 2000. "Governance Tasks and Nonprofit Organizations." In *Nonprofits in Urban America*, edited by R. C. Hula, and C. Jackson-Elmore, 199–221. Westport, CT: Quorum.

Green, Donald P., and Alan S. Gerber. 2004. *Get Out the Vote*. Washington, DC: Brookings Institution Press.

Highton, Benjamin, and Raymond E. Wolfinger. 1998. "Estimating the Effects of the National Voter Registration Act of 1993." *Political Behavior* 20 (2): 79–104.

Independent Sector. 2004. "Nonprofit Advocacy and Lobbying." Retrieved June 30, 2015 from www.independentsector.org.

Kasden, Diana. 2012. "State Restrictions on Voter Registration Drives." Brennan Center for Justice, New York University Center for Justice. Retrieved June 30, 2015 from https://www.brennancenter.org/sites/default/files/legacy/publications/State%20Restrictions%20on%20Voter%20Registration%20Drives.pdf.

LeRoux, Kelly. 2007. "Nonprofits as Civic Intermediaries: The Role of Community-Based Organizations in Promoting Political Participation." *Urban Affairs Review* 42 (3): 410–422.

LeRoux, Kelly. 2011. "Examining Implementation of the National Voter Registration Act by Nonprofit Organizations: An Institutional Explanation." *Policy Studies Journal* 39 (4): 565–589.

Pew Charitable Trusts. 2012. "Inaccurate, Costly, and Inefficient." Retrieved June 29, 2015 from http://www.pewstates.org/research/reports/inaccurate-costly-and-inefficient-85899378437Pew 2012.

Piven, Francis F., and Richard A. Cloward. 1988. "National Voter Registration Reform: How It Might Be Won." *P.S. Political Science and Politics* 21 (4): 868–875.

Putnam, Robert D. 2007. "E Pluribus Unum: Diversity and Community in the Twenty-First Century: The 2006 Johan Skytte Prize Lecture." *Scandinavian Political Studies* 30(2): 137–174.

Salamon, Lester M. 1995. *Partners in Public Service: Government-Nonprofit Relations in the Modern Welfare State.* Baltimore, MD: Johns Hopkins University Press.

Skopol, Theda. 2003. *Diminished Democracy: From Membership to Management in American Civic Life.* Norman: University of Oklahoma Press.

6

Why Bother? Apathy in the American Electorate

Anne M. Cizmar

In a democratic society, the will of the people is meant to influence the policies created and implemented by elected officials. Without citizen input, the government cannot truly be one "of the people, for the people." Yet, many Americans abstain from voting in elections. One important reason for low voter turnout in the United States is voter apathy. Apathy can occur for a number of reasons, including low levels of political efficacy and a lack of contact with campaigns and candidates. Additionally, theories of voter turnout argue that apathetic voters often do not see the benefits of voting and therefore stay home on Election Day.

THE ROLE OF APATHY IN VOTER ABSTENTION

Existing research indicates that people who have low levels of political efficacy—both internal and external—will be less likely to vote. Internal political efficacy is the feeling that a person understands government and is politically aware enough to participate in politics. External political efficacy is the belief that the government is responsive to the needs and opinions of citizens. When people have low levels of either internal or external political efficacy, they are generally more apathetic about politics.

People who are less politically efficacious do not believe that they know enough about politics to participate, or that the government will listen to people like them. As a result, they are less likely to participate in politics because they do not see a point in participation.

Voters also may abstain because it is considered "irrational" to vote. The rationality-based theory of voting, first described by Downs (1957), argues that we can think of humans as rational actors. As rational actors, people will weigh the costs and benefits of any action they take to determine whether it is in their self-interest. When the benefits outweigh the costs, people will take action. When the costs outweigh the benefits, they will abstain. When applying this idea of rational cost-benefit analysis to voting, the payoffs from voting may be too small to persuade many Americans to give up their time to go to the polls. Proponents of this theory argue that the costs of voting are not outweighed by the benefits of voting.

THE "COSTS" OF VOTING

The "costs" of voting are many. Although participating in elections does not require monetary payment, voting requires voters to take time away from work or family obligations to go to the polls. Conflicting schedules may increase the costs of voting for many people who find it difficult to make it to the polls on Election Day. American election laws also place many requirements on individuals with regards to voting. Voter registration regulations vary from state to state and require individuals to ensure that they are properly registered in advance of the election, which can be confusing to some voters, and requires that they engage in a two-step voting process. Other requirements, such as voter identification laws and absentee ballot requirements, may add to the costs of voting that some experience.

In addition to scheduling conflicts and legal barriers to voting, people also must have enough information to vote. They must know when the election will occur and have some sense of the candidates or issues in order to make a decision for whom to cast a ballot. Obtaining this information is also not free of cost as it requires potential voters to focus on politics rather than work, family, leisure activities, or many other things that may require their attention.

Learning about the candidates and elections not only requires time away from other activities, but also requires cognitive effort as well. In order to cast a vote, potential voters need to make a choice about who to vote for in the election. This requires voters to sift through a plethora of information about the candidates, issues, and parties in the elections. Once they know who the candidates are and what the issues are in the election, they then need to make a choice by comparing their own political vision to those of the candidates.

There are potentially many costs of voting while, at the same time, the benefits are often considered to be low. Realistically speaking, a single vote is unlikely to impact an election, especially for the presidency or other national level office. When millions of votes are cast in an election, there is a very small chance that an individual's vote will matter, lessening the perceived utility of voting. Therefore, many rational people weigh the costs and benefits of voting and actually forgo voting on Election Day. This calculus of voting can lead to voter apathy—the costs can be high while the perceived benefits of participation are low—tipping the scales in favor of abstention. The costs of voting relative to the benefits of voting are so high, actually, that Downs's theory is unable to explain why people vote. Voting would actually be irrational for almost all people given this cost-benefit analysis. Yet, millions of people participate in every election.

In order to explain why people do so, Riker and Ordeshook (1968) added the concept of "duty" to the voting calculus. They argue that people who have a strong sense of duty to participate in democratic elections, as elections are important to maintain the health of our political system, will be more likely to vote. We see that people who are more interested in politics, who care deeply about the election outcome, or who have a profound sense of duty to maintain our democracy, are more likely to vote. For people interested in politics, their voting calculus will indicate they should go to the polls. Yet these are exactly the beliefs and behavior that people who have low levels of efficacy do not have, meaning they will stay home on Election Day. People who are apathetic about politics have a different voting calculus. When they have low levels of political efficacy, they do not believe they can affect government. As a result, their sense of duty to participate in elections, because it is a socially desirable action, is lower. For apathetic voters, the costs of voting outweigh the benefits and they stay home on Election Day.

A simplified version of the voting calculus formula by Riker and Ordeshook (1968) is as follows: the probability of voting is equal to $B-C+D$. In this formula, B stands for the benefits of voting (the benefit of one candidate winning over the other), C stands for the costs of voting (including the time and effort spent, and all the costs previously discussed), and D stands for the sense duty or civic benefit from voting. The benefits of voting (B and D together) must outweigh the costs of voting in order for citizens to participate on Election Day. Even if the $B-C$ portion of the equation is negative (meaning the costs outweigh the benefits, as is the case for most voters), citizens that have a strong sense of duty (a large value on the D term) and who believe the election is important will be able to overcome the costs. Apathetic voters will not turn out to vote because the costs are too high, but those who care deeply about the election will vote.

The importance of voter apathy on determining voter turnout can be seen when comparing midterm election years to presidential election years. Presidential elections are a national event, with all American voters invited to participate in the election. Presidential elections are the elections that receive the most media attention, have the most money spent on them, and feature the longest campaigns. Voter turnout in presidential elections is also regularly 15 percentage points to 20 percentage points higher than in midterm election years, when the only federal elections are ones to fill seats in the U.S. Congress. In the 2012 presidential election, for example, the voting eligible population (VEP) turnout was 58 percent and the voting age turnout (VAP) was 53.6 percent. By comparison, the VEP and VAP turnouts in the 2010 midterm elections were 41 percent and 37.8 percent, respectively (McDonald 2015). There are a number of reasons why voter turnout tends to be lower in midterm elections, but generally these elections receive less media and public attention than the presidential elections. Members of Congress are seeking election from a congressional district or a state. As such, there are hundreds of congressional races taking place at once. Each electoral competition for Congress is based in a small geographic region, and few will receive national attention. Fewer people pay attention to these races, and this lack of campaign information can impact voters.

PUBLIC OPINION DATA ON VOTER APATHY

In addition to data about aggregate voting trends (voter turnout rates for the United States as a whole), public opinion data from individual respondents help shed light on the role of apathy in low voter turnout as well. The 2012 Current Population Survey (CPS) Voting and Registration Supplement File is a recognized source of information about voting behavior in the United States. The survey has a large respondent pool of more than 100,000 respondents and includes the sociodemographic characteristics of respondents as well as a specific question about why people abstain from voting. Specifically addressing non-voters, the CPS asks people why they failed to vote using the question "What was the main reason (you/name) did not vote?" The survey provides a number of response options for people answering the question, many of which relate back to factors political science scholars have argued cause low voter turnout rates. The survey respondents could give any of the following responses as the main reason they did not vote: 1) Illness or disability (own or family's); 2) Out of town or away from home; 3) Forgot to vote (or send in absentee ballot); 4) Not interested, felt my vote would not make a difference; 5) Too busy, conflicting work or school schedule; 6) Transportation problems; 7) Did not like candidates or campaign issues; 8) Registration problems (i.e., did not receive absentee ballot, not registered in current location); 9) Bad weather conditions; 10) Inconvenient hours, polling place or hours or lines too long; 11) Other.

Some of these response options relate to electoral policy barriers such as registration problems and long lines at polling locations. Other response options tap into personal situations that prevent people from exercising their right to vote such as transportation problems or illness or disability. Two of these response options tie into political apathy. One response that indicates political apathy is respondents' choice not to vote because of lack of interest or because their vote would not make a difference. These people indicate that they are apathetic about politics and have low levels of external political efficacy. The other response indicating political apathy is respondents' choice not to vote because they did not like the candidates or campaign issues. These people are expressing political apathy created specifically by the election itself. Rather than low levels of political efficacy, which is a general belief that politics is not responsive to the public, these people find this particular election and its candidates and campaign issues to be unpersuasive.

The responses to the voting abstention question are displayed in Table 6.1. The percentages reflect the percent of respondents who did not vote for each reason. As Table 6.1 shows, more than 16 percent of people who responded to the survey cited lack of interest as the primary reason they abstained from voting. Another 13 percent reported they did not vote because of dislike of the candidates or campaign issues. Voter apathy—lack of interest in the election itself or toward the candidates and campaigns in particular—accounts for nearly 30 percent of voter abstention.

Table 6.1
Self-Reported Reasons for Abstention

Reason	Respondent Percentage (percent)
Too busy; conflicting schedule	19.42
Not interested; felt vote would not matter	**16.24**
Illness or disability	14.57
Did not like candidates or campaign issues	**13.32**
Other	11.08
Out of town	9.32
Registration problems	5.33
Forgot to vote	3.86
Transportation problems	3.45
Inconvenient hours	2.72
Bad weather conditions	0.69
Total percentage:	100

N = 7,936

Source: 2012 CPS Voter and Registration Supplement File.

Only two responses were more popular: potential voters were too busy to vote, or that they were prevented from voting due to a disability or illness of their own or another.

EXAMINING CHARACTERISTICS OF POLITICALLY APATHETIC CITIZENS

Certain demographic characteristics are associated with those more likely to say that they did not vote because of apathy. Previous research has shown income, age, education, race, region of residence, and gender can affect voting behavior in the U.S. electorate. Table 6.2 presents the results of an analysis of whether voter apathy is related to these demographic characteristics, and if so, whether that relationship is either positive or negative. The table shows the categories of each of these demographic characteristics as found in the CPS data and the results of their comparison to the two questions from the CPS survey that indicate voter apathy.

In Table 6.2, income is measured in 16 categories ranging from less than $5,000 at the lowest category to $150,000 or more at the highest category. Age is measured in years from 18 years old to 85 and older. Education is measured in five categories—less than high school, high school diploma/GED, some college/associate's degree, bachelor's degree, or a graduate degree. Race is measured as two categories—white and non-white, which includes blacks, Hispanics, Asians, and others. Region of residence is measured as southern residence or other region of residence. Gender is captured as male and female. For the comparison of demographic characteristics composed of two categories (race, region, and gender), the likelihood (predicted probability) presented reflects the comparison between both categories of each characteristic. For the demographic characteristics that consist of three or more categories (income, age, and education), the highest category is compared against the lowest category on each demographic characteristic. For example, in the case of income, the analysis compares the wealthiest respondents against the poorest respondents (see Appendix A.3 for the results of the full statistical model).

The results with asterisks indicate that one category of that characteristic is meaningfully different and that the results are not due to random chance. Several groups are more likely to report that they abstained from voting because of lack of interest in the elections or a feeling that their vote would not matter. There is a 19 percent probability that 18-year-old citizens said they did not vote because of lack of interest in the elections, as compared to only 12 percent for adults in the over 84 age range, controlling for the other sociodemographic characteristics. The 85+ group is

Table 6.2
Predicted Probability of Voter Apathy across Demographics

	Lack of Interest			Did Not Like Candidates		
	Minimum	Maximum	Difference	Minimum	Maximum	Difference
Income	<$5,000 0.148	$150,000+ 0.172	0.024	<$5,000 0.117	$150,000+ 0.145	0.028
Age	18 0.193	85+ 0.122	−0.071*	18 0.115	85+ 0.151	0.036
Education	<HS 0.194	College+ 0.122	−0.072*	<HS 0.144	College+ 0.118	−0.026
Race	Nonwhite 0.131	White 0.168	0.037*	Nonwhite 0.067	White 0.144	0.077*
Region	Non-South 0.163	South 0.160	−0.003	Non-South 0.138	South 0.124	−0.014
Gender	Male 0.175	Female 0.150	−0.025*	Male 0.146	Female 0.122	−0.024*

*p < 0.05

Note: Predicted probabilities are computed from the model that is presented in Appendix A.3, while holding all other variables at their observed values. Standard errors for the predicted probabilities are computed using the delta method.

seven percentage points less likely to say they abstained due to a lack of interest as compared to 18-year-olds. Similar findings hold based on level of education. Those with less than a high school diploma have a 19 percent probability of abstention due to lack of interest in the campaigns, controlling for the other sociodemographic characteristics. Those with at least a college degree have a 12 percent probability of abstention due to lack of interest, meaning they are seven percentage points less likely to cite lack of interest as the reason for abstention, even when considering the other sociodemographic characteristics.

There are also differences in voter apathy responses based on race and gender. Whites have a 17 percent chance of responding that they did not vote because of a lack of interest, as compared to 13 percent for nonwhites (including blacks, Hispanics, Asians, and others), controlling for the other variables. Whites are nearly 4 percent more likely to cite lack of interest as the reason for not voting. Men are also more likely to abstain because of lack of interest in the elections, with a probability of nearly 18 percent compared to 15 percent for women, controlling for the other sociodemographic factors.

When it comes to voter apathy due to dislike of candidates or campaign issues, responses again differ based on race and gender. Whites and males are more likely to abstain from voting because they do not like the candidates or campaign issues. Whites have a 14 percent probability of citing dislike of the candidates as the reason for abstention, and men have a probability of nearly 15 percent, controlling for the other variables. This is compared to a less than 7 percent chance of nonwhites saying they did not vote based on dislike of the candidates and a 12 percent chance of females abstaining because of candidate dislike. The predicted probabilities from the model results indicate men have a two percentage point higher probability of abstention due to candidate dislike than women, and whites have a nearly eight percentage point higher probability of abstention due to candidate dislike than others.

Income and region of residence (whether the potential voters live in the South or another region) have no effect on the probability of citing apathy as the reason for abstention. Variations in age and education level lead to different probabilities of reporting that lack of interest in the campaign is the primary reason for abstention. Sex and race impact the probabilities of abstention due to both lack of interest in the campaign and dislike of the candidates. Whites and men are more likely to abstain from voting because of apathy about the elections.

FURTHER READING

Downs, Anthony. 1957. *An Economic Theory of Democracy.* New York, NY: Harper and Row.

Hanmer, Michael J. 2009. *Discount Voting: Voter Registration Reforms and Their Effects*. Cambridge, England: Cambridge University Press.

McDonald, Michael P. 2015. "Voter Turnout." United States Elections Project. Retrieved December 18, 2015 from http://www.electproject.org/home/voter-turnout/voter-turnout-data.

Pew Research Center. 2014. "The Party of Nonvoters." http://www.people-press.org/files/2014/10/10-31-14-Party-of-Nonvoters-release.pdf.

Putnam, Robert D. 2001. *Bowling Alone: The Collapse and Revival of American Community.* New York, NY: Simon and Schuster.

Riker, William H., and Peter C. Ordeshook. 1968. "A Theory of the Calculus of Voting." *American Political Science Review* 62: 25–42.

Saad, Lydia. 2014. "Voters, Especially Independents, Lack Interest in Election." Gallup Inc. http://www.gallup.com/poll/179147/voters-especially-independents-lack-interest-election.aspx.

U.S. Department of Commerce, Bureau of the Census, 2012 Current Population Survey: Voter Supplement File (computer files). Washington, DC: U.S. Department of Commerce, Bureau of the Census (producer).

Verba, Sidney, Schlozman, Kay L., and Henry E. Brady. 1995. *Voice and Equality: Civic Voluntarism in American Politics*. Vol. 4. Cambridge, MA: Harvard University Press.

7

It's Not Convenient: Early and Weekend Voting

Keith Smith and Dari Sylvester-Tran

Early and weekend voting are reforms aimed at providing more options for busy people to go vote. Early and weekend voting were created as a way of decreasing the "costs" of voting by improving the convenience of voting, specifically with regard to the timing of elections. States expanded access to early voting through the 1980s and 1990s, but the politicization of voting rules, largely by the Republican Party, has led to a retrenchment in recent years. To date, analysis of early voting policies does not demonstrate that these policies consistently increase voter turnout in every situation; however, there are cases in which positive gains have occurred. Although early and weekend voting have some overlap in the way they are applied, there are some distinctions that require us to elaborate on each separately.

EARLY VOTING ACROSS THE STATES

According to the Presidential Commission on Election Administration, in 2012, of the 47 million people who cast a ballot in some way other than at a polling place on Election Day, about 18.5 million did so using early in-person voting (2014, 54). The U.S. Election Assistance Commission (EAC) reports that roughly 11 percent of all voters cast their ballot using early voting in the 2014 midterm elections (2014, 1), a small uptick from 2012 when 9 percent of voters did so (2013, 1).

Early and weekend voting, however, are not available to every registrant in the United States. Figure 7.1 shows the states that allow registrants to cast their ballot for any reason prior to an Election Day, either through early in-person voting or by casting an in-person absentee ballot. Twenty states (shown in dark gray), plus the District of Columbia, have formal early voting processes that allow registrants to cast their ballots either at their local registrar's office or at a publically available voting center (e.g., at a school or a mall). Voting in these states may take place during regular business hours, or it may take place later in the evening or on the weekend.

An additional 13 states (designated with stripes), allow in-person absentee voting, where registrants can cast an absentee ballot before an election in their registrar's office *without* needing to provide a reason (or, an excuse) for doing so. States without any shading offer neither early in-person voting nor in-person absentee voting. Some of these states, such as Virginia, allow registrants to cast an absentee ballot in person before an election, but registrants must justify—often with documentation—their need to do so. Unlike early in-person voting, in-person absentee voting is generally restricted to regular business hours during the workweek. In practice, as will become clear, there is little functional difference between one state's early in-person voting and another state's in-person absentee voting.

Western states are the most likely to offer extensive early voting opportunities, and eastern states (especially in New England) are the least likely to do so. In addition to the shaded states shown in Figure 7.1, Washington, Oregon, and Colorado hold all-mail elections, so registrants in these three states likewise have an extended time period within which to cast their ballots. Washington and Colorado also require each county to have at least one voting center available for in-person voting 15 (Colorado) and 18 (Washington) days before an election.

Hidden within Figure 7.1, however, is a great deal of variation in registrants' opportunities to cast an early ballot. Some states allow early voting well before an election. Wyoming and Vermont, for example, allow registrants to cast their ballots as soon as they become available. Registrants in these states can have as many as 45 days within which to vote. In contrast, other states offer a very narrow window for early voting. Oklahoma, for example, allows early voting from 8 a.m. to 6 p.m. the Friday and Monday before any election. If it is a federal or state election, registrants can also vote from 8 a.m. to 1 p.m. the Saturday before the election.

On average, states begin offering early voting 22 days before an election, although registrants may not have all 22 days available to cast their ballots. Not all states, for example, allow voters to cast their ballots on the weekend. Of the 33 states that allow some form of early voting, only

Figure 7.1
State Early Voting Policies, 2015

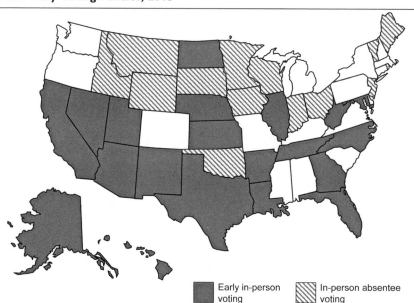

Early in-person voting

In-person absentee voting

Source: National Conference of State Legislatures, http://ncsl.org/research/elections-and-campaigns/absentee-and-early-voting.aspx.

22 allow voters the opportunity to cast their ballot on the weekend—18 states require Saturday voting; the other 4 leave the choice up to the local registrars. Only nine states allow Sunday voting. Similarly, although about half of the states allow voters to cast early ballots through the day before an election, the remaining states cut off early voting at some point the week before the election (most often that Friday or Saturday). As a result, registrants have, on average, 19 days of early voting available to them.

Voter usage of early in-person voting also varies considerably according to the EAC's Election Administration and Voting Survey (2014, 198–199). The states with the highest rates of early in-person voting in 2014 were Nevada (48 percent of all voters), Texas (45 percent), Tennessee (43 percent), New Mexico (41 percent), Arkansas (40 percent), North Carolina (37 percent), Georgia (33 percent), Florida (22 percent), and West Virginia (21 percent). At the other end of the scale, just 1.4 percent of Vermont voters used early in-person voting.

WHY EARLY VOTING?

Federal election law requires that all elections for federal office (president, House of Representatives, and the U.S. Senate) take place on the first Tuesday after the first Monday in November. The practice of holding federal elections on this particular Tuesday dates to the pre-Civil War period in U.S. political history. As the nation grew, and communication across the country became quicker, the tradition of letting states set their own dates for the presidential election became problematic. Critics worried that states voting earlier in the election period would influence the outcome in those voting later. In 1845, Congress decided to consolidate the date of the presidential election and mandate when states select their presidential electors. The federal voting day was expanded further in 1875 to include all House elections and again in 1914 to include Senate elections.

Why a Tuesday, though? Tuesday fit the pattern of cultural life as it existed at that time. Sunday was not an option for voting as many states were still governed by so-called blue laws, which restricted work on the Christian Sabbath. Given the travel time required for would-be voters to get to their county seat to cast their ballots, voting on Mondays would require people to travel on Sunday. Wednesdays were market days in many areas, and the rest of the week was needed for work. So Tuesday it was. If need be, people could travel on Monday with time to be back at the market on Wednesday.

Why the first Tuesday after the first Monday in November, then? The Electoral College "meets" on the first Wednesday of December to elect the president (actually, the electors gather in their respective state capitals and cast their ballots there), and federal election law required that the electors be selected no later than 34 days before the Electoral College met. Thus, in choosing a national, presidential Election Day, Congress needed to find a day that allowed all states to pick their electors within the necessary time frame. The first Tuesday after the first Monday in November always fit that criterion.

Although elections held on the first Tuesday after the first Monday in November were well timed in the early history of America (when it was an agrarian nation), this directive is now anachronistic and, in the eyes of many, problematic. Tuesday is now the middle of the workweek, and most people no longer have the ability to take a whole day off to go vote. Indeed, not every state provides protection for registrants who want to take time off from work to vote, and some only do so if there is insufficient time before or after work for someone to make it to the polls. Arizona, for example, requires that there be at least three consecutive hours between when the polls open and the beginning of a work shift or three hours between when a shift ends and the polls close. Utah provides two hours at the beginning or end of a work shift for voting. Idaho and New Jersey make no such provisions. Even if a state guarantees that someone cannot be fired for taking time to vote, the person may not be paid for the time they use doing so. Holding a national election on a Tuesday, therefore, imposes significant, direct costs on a large number of voters.

Early voting was created in response to the inconvenience of Tuesday voting in modern American society. Riker and Ordeshook (1968) illustrate the choice to vote as a calculation balancing the benefits of voting with its costs for a given voter. Their famous equation posits that $R = PB-C+D$, where R is the likelihood of voting, P is the probability that the voter's ballot will be decisive, B is the benefit that accrues to the voter from his or her preferred choice winning instead of the alternative, C is the set of costs incurred by the voter in voting, and D is the set of intrinsic benefits the voter receives from the act of voting. If the costs of voting are less than the benefits (i.e., $C < PB+D$), the person will vote. If the costs of voting are greater (i.e., $C > PB+D$), however, then the person will not vote.

In order to decrease the costs of voting, potentially increasing the probability of voting, states implemented measures that would make voting less costly by allowing more flexibility in the timing of election voting. In the late 1970s and early 1980s, following California's lead, states began experimenting with no-excuse absentee ballots, whereby individuals could request a ballot, without the need for an approved reason, that would allow them to cast a vote by mail or at approved locations as long as it was returned by Election Day (Fortier 2006; Gronke, Galanes-Rosenbaum, and Miller 2007). By the 1980s, Oregon established itself as a pioneer in the use of vote by mail, and in 1998, voters approved a fully mail-based election system by statewide referendum. The 1990s saw expansions of early voting in states such as Nevada, New Mexico, Oklahoma, Tennessee, and Texas. Similar to absentee or mail voting, early voting allowed for votes to be cast in advance of Election Day; in contrast to these other methods, the early voting act would need to take place at an officially designated location such as a polling place, satellite voting center, or county clerk's office (Fortier 2006).

Just as early voting reforms were implemented as a way to remove barriers and increase convenience for those who were unable or unwilling to vote on a Tuesday, weekend voting reforms have also centered around increasing the convenience of voting by offering more flexibility in Election Day scheduling. Although federal law mandates that congressional and presidential elections are held on the first Tuesday after the first Monday in November, the scheduling of subnational elections is not mandated by federal law. States such as Louisiana and Texas have opted to schedule certain state and local elections on Saturdays (Jenkins 2012). Other states such as North Carolina and Ohio that previously offered measures to expand the time frame for elections via early and/or weekend voting have retrenched, passing laws to rescind or decrease those time frames (Harvard Law Review 2015). This retrenchment has been amplified in the aftermath of the U.S. Supreme Court decision in *Shelby County v. Holder* (2013), which rendered unconstitutional the 1965 Voting Rights Act requirement for prior federal review and approval of election law changes in some jurisdictions.

Congress has considered legislation expanding federal elections to weekends. For example, in 2013, legislation was proposed to eliminate Tuesday Election Days and switch to a Saturday and Sunday in November; however, the bill died in Congress. Generally, such proposals have been met with strong opposition from election administrators throughout the states. The main reasons cited for opposition were increased administrative costs and increased workload in offering weekend elections pertaining to election logistics such as poll worker training and locating viable polling places that would be available for additional time periods (Jenkins 2012). Furthermore, the scant research that has been conducted on weekend voting seems to provide no evidence of a voter turnout increase that would justify the additional costs and burdens of offering such elections.

EFFECTS OF EARLY VOTING

In theory, increasing the time span for voters to cast ballots beyond a single day would lower the costs associated with voting, by increasing the convenience of voting. Nevertheless in practice, research has not borne consistent evidence of significant improvements in turnout. Some slight increases in turnout as a result of early voting measures have been found, but these effects tend to come with an asterisk. For instance, in a study of early voting that had just been implemented in Texas, Richardson and Neeley (1996) cautiously advised that expansions of early voting could improve turnout overall, contingent on other factors such as the type of ballot used and the type of election. Nevertheless, by 2001, the same authors find evidence that early voting turnout increases were largely based on enabling larger numbers of predisposed voters to turn out on a day other than Election Day rather than mobilizing previously nonvoting citizens (Neeley and Richardson 2001). Stein and Garcia-Monet (1997) found a 0.07 percent increase in turnout for every 1 percent increase in percentage of votes cast early, though their findings were based on a single election in Texas.

In contrast, authors such as Stein, Leighley, and Owens (2005) do not find increases in turnout as a result of early voting reforms. Others find limited increases that wane over time (Giammo and Brox 2010). Finally, when implemented as a stand-alone provision without accompanying convenience provisions (e.g., such as relaxed registration deadlines or same-day registration), Burden et al. (2014) and Larocca and Klemanski (2011) found evidence that early voting actually decreased voting turnout. Authors attribute the decline to a diffusion of voting urgency or salience and mobilization efforts that seem to accompany an extended time frame for voting.

SUBGROUP EFFECTS

Several studies have found evidence that distinct segments of the population are likely to take advantage of early voting opportunities. Gronke and Toffey (2008) find that early voters tend to have attained higher levels of education, are older, and more politically knowledgeable. Nevertheless, other research has pointed to increasing reliance on early voting by populations of color. For example, a 2008 study of Florida voters found that, among African Americans who voted, the majority cast early votes and they comprised a larger overall proportion of the early voter electorate than of the Election Day electorate (Herron and Smith 2012). The Department of Justice data confirmed that in North Carolina, 70 percent of African Americans who voted in 2008 cast their votes early and mostly on weekends (Weiser and Opsal 2014). It is too early to tell if these effects owe mainly to the fact that these elections were historic for electing and re-electing the first African American president, consequently drawing more and better informed black voters.

To the extent that early voting aims at bringing previously low-probability voting marginalized populations into the voting pool, increased voter stratification could result as pre-inclined voters simply turn out more often (Berinsky 2005; Neeley and Richardson 2001).

POTENTIAL NON-TURNOUT BENEFITS

The evidence suggests that there is a limited, though generally positive, impact on turnout rates from early in-person voting and in-person absentee voting. These reforms may offer other benefits for election administration that may indirectly affect voters' experiences at the polls and may make the concept worth pursuing. In one study, state and local election officials from nine states identified the following set of advantages related to early in-person voting: 1) it reduces stress on the voting system on Election Day, which can then (2) reduce the time registrants spend waiting in line, (3) improve poll worker performance, (4) allow more opportunity to detect and correct registration and technical errors, and therefore (5) it can provide greater access and voter satisfaction (Kasdan 2013). Even if early in-person voting does not significantly improve voter turnout, it has the potential to improve the efficiency and effectiveness of how elections in the United States happen.

THE GROWING POLITICIZATION OF EARLY VOTING

Early and weekend voting practices have become part of what Hasen (2012) calls the "voting wars"—the increasingly partisan conflict over voting rules as a means of contesting elections. Partisans of both stripes now believe that early voting helps Democrats (or at least groups of voters that tend to vote Democratic). As a result, a number of states, particularly those controlled by Republicans and with a growing Democratic or minority voter base (Bentelle and O'Brien 2013), have begun reducing the number of days and hours available for early voting. Since 2010 alone, eight states have done so (Weiser and Opsal 2014). For example, in 2013, North Carolina reduced its number of early voting days from 17 to 10. In 2014, Wisconsin reduced its number of early voting days and eliminated night and weekend early voting, and Ohio likewise shortened its window for early voting. (The other states are Florida, Georgia, Nebraska, Tennessee, and West Virginia.) Many of these changes have been met by lawsuits from democratically aligned groups seeking to prevent them from taking effect.

Similarly, efforts to expand early and weekend voting have been met by opposition from Republicans. For example, in 2014, efforts in Georgia to expand early voting on Sundays were met with opposition amidst complaints that such an extension would benefit the Democratic Party due to a large mobilization of church-going African Americans. Thus, despite the potential (albeit small) positive impact of early in-person voting on U.S. elections, the politicization of this concept makes it unlikely that this reform alternative will expand for some time.

FURTHER READING

Bentelle, Keith G., and Erin E. O'Brien. 2013. "Jim Crow 2.0? Why States Consider and Adopt Restrictive Voter Access Policies." *Perspectives on Politics* 11: 1088–1116.

Berinsky, Adam J. 2005. "The Perverse Consequences of Electoral Reform in the United States." *American Politics Research* 33: 471–491.

Burden, Barry C., Canon, David T., Mayer, Kenneth R., and Donald P. Moynihan. 2014. "Election Laws, Mobilization, and Turnout: The Unanticipated Consequences of Election Reform." *American Journal of Political Science* 58: 95–109.

Fortier, John C. 2006. *Absentee and Early Voting: Trends, Promises, and Perils.* Washington, DC: AEI Press.

Giammo, Joseph D., and Brian J. Brox. 2010. "Reducing the Costs of Participation: Are States Getting a Return on Early Voting?" *Political Research Quarterly* 63: 295–303.

Gronke, Paul, and Daniel K. Toffey. 2008. "The Psychological and Institutional Determinants of Early Voting." *Journal of Social Issues* 64: 503–524.

Gronke, Paul, Galanes-Rosenbaum, Eva, and Peter A. Miller. 2007. "Early Voting and Turnout." *PS: Political Science and Politics* 40: 639–645.

Harvard Law Review (HLR). 2015. "It's about Time (Place and Manner): Why and How Congress Must Act to Protect Access to Early Voting." *Harvard Law Review* 128: 1228. LexisNexis Academic: Law Reviews. Retrieved July 13,

2015 from http://harvardlawreview.org/2015/02/its-about-time-place-and-manner-why-and-how-congress-must-act-to-protect-access-to-early-voting/.

Hasen, Richard L. 2012. *The Voting Wars.* New Haven, CT: Yale University Press.

Herron, Michael C., and Daniel A. Smith. 2012. "Souls to the Polls: Early Voting in Florida in the Shadow of House Bill 1355." *Election Law Journal* 11: 331–347.

Jenkins Jr., William O. 2012. "Elections: Views on Implementing Federal Elections on a Weekend (GAO-12-69)." Washington, DC: Government Accountability Office. http://www.gao.gov/assets/590/587621.pdf.

Kasdan, Diana. 2013. "Early Voting: What Works." Brennan Center for Justice, New York University School of Law. Retrieved June 20, 2015 from https://www.brennancenter.org/sites/default/files/publications/VotingReport_Web.pdf.

Larocca, Roger, and John S. Klemanski. 2011. "U.S. State Election Reform and Turnout in Presidential Elections." *State Politics and Policy Quarterly* 11: 76–101.

Neeley, Grant W., and Lilliard E. Richardson Jr. 2001. "Who Is Early Voting? An Individual Level Examination." *The Social Science Journal* 38: 381–392.

Presidential Commission on Election Administration. 2014. The American Voting Experience: Report and Recommendations. https://www.supportthevoter.gov/files/2014/01/Amer-Voting-Exper-final-draft-01-09-14-508.pdf.

Richardson Jr., Lilliard E., and Grant W. Neeley. 1996. "The Impact of Early Voting on Turnout: The 1994 Elections in Tennessee." *State and Local Government Review* 28: 173–179.

Riker, William H., and Peter C. Ordeshook. 1968. "A Theory of the Calculus of Voting." *The American Political Science Review* 62: 25–42.

Stein, Robert M., Leighley, Jan, and Christopher Owens. 2005. "Who Votes, Who Doesn't, Why and, What Can Be Done?" A Report to the Federal Commission on Electoral Reform. http://www.verifiedvoting.org/wp-content/uploads/downloads/stein.pdf.

Stein, Robert M., and Patricia A. Garcia-Monet. 1997. "Voting Early but Not Often." *Social Science Quarterly* 78: 657–671.

U.S. Election Assistance Commission. 2013. "2012 Election Administration and Voting Survey: A Summary of Key Findings." http://www.eac.gov/assets/1/Page/990-050%20EAC%20VoterSurvey_508Compliant.pdf.

U.S. Election Assistance Commission. 2014. "The 2014 EAC Election Administration and Voting Survey Comprehensive Report." http://www.eac.gov/assets/1/Page/2014_EAC_EAVS_Comprehensive_Report_508_Compliant.pdf.

Weiser, Wendy, and Erik Opsal. 2014. "The State of Voting in 2014." Brennan Center for Justice, Retrieved June 27, 2015 from http://www.brennancenter.org/analysis/state-voting-2014.

8

It's Not Convenient: Absentee Voting and the Federal Write-In Absentee Ballot

Thad E. Hall, Krysha Gregorowicz, and Leah Alley

Anyone who has voted at a voting precinct understands the significant time commitment that can be required in order to cast a vote. In an age where simplification and convenience are becoming more attainable via technology, people are looking for more convenient and time-saving ways to vote than the traditional method of casting a ballot in person at a polling precinct (Alvarez and Hall 2004; Gronke et al. 2008). Many have found this convenience through voting absentee.

Efforts to promote absentee voting, and convenience voting more broadly, have existed for more than 150 years. First developed out of the need to ease voting for military personnel during the Civil War, absentee voting remained an option for people in the military in the 20th century (Alvarez, Hall, and Roberts 2007; Keyssar 2000; Patterson and Caldeira 1985). Eligibility for absentee voting slowly expanded to cover the needs of other populations. People with illnesses and disabilities, the elderly, and groups with limited or a complete lack of access to their polling precinct and voting materials were brought into the absentee voting population.

The past four decades have been a time of extensive growth for absentee voting due to the liberalization of voting laws. Historically, only people who were ill, disabled, or traveling on Election Day were allowed to vote with an absentee ballot. In 1978, however, California became the first state to allow absentee voting to be available to any registered voter, with no excuse for not voting on Election Day required (Patterson and Caldeira 1985). In California, this liberalization of the absentee voting laws greatly changed the way in which people vote.In the 1978 general election, 4.41 percent of Californians voted via absentee ballot but by the 2012 general election, 39.8 percent of Californians were voting absentee.

In Oregon and Washington, all elections are now held using only absentee voting. Oregon began exploring all vote-by-mail (VBM) elections in 1981, adopting it as an option for local elections and then expanded the law in 1987 for use in special elections as well (Gronke and Miller 2012). In 1993 and 1995, Oregon held statewide special elections using the all VBM format. However, it was not until 1995/1996 that the state utilized all VBM in a major election. All VBM was utilized statewide in a December 1995 primary election and a January 1996 general election when a special election had to be held to fill the seat of Senator Bob Packwood, who had resigned from office. These were the first federal elections in the United States to be conducted entirely by mail. For various reasons, the Oregon legislature was unable to pass legislation that would have expanded VBM to all elections. However, Oregonians led a successful drive to place an initiative on the 1998 general election ballot that would have all primary and general elections conducted using the VBM process. The initiative passed with 69.4 percent of the vote; since then, all elections in Oregon have been conducted by mail.

Today, 27 states plus the District of Columbia allow all registered voters to vote using VBM without an excuse and, in 17 states, eligible voters can automatically receive an absentee ballot for future elections by joining a permanent absentee voting list. Two states—Oregon and Washington—use only VBM, and Colorado has a hybrid system that combines VBM with vote centers. If a Colorado voter wishes to vote in person at a vote center, which are open for 8 to 15 days prior to the election (depending on the type of election being held), the voter has to surrender his or her absentee ballot at the polling place in order to vote (NCSL 2015a).

WHO BENEFITS FROM ABSENTEE VOTING

Absentee voting should make it easier to vote; after all, the ballot arrives at the voter's home and the voter can return the ballot at his or her convenience. However, scholars debate whether voting reforms increase overall turnout, or are simply being utilized by voters who would otherwise vote anyways via a traditional trip to their local voting booth (Berinski 2005; Gronke, Galanes-Rosenbaum, and Miller 2007; Gronke et al. 2008). It is clear that, once it is offered, the public does like to use absentee voting. Over the past 15 years, there has been an upward trend in the use of absentee voting in the United States. In the 2000 presidential election, 14 percent of votes were cast absentee (U.S. Census 2002). By 2012, that number had increased to 16.6 percent and, in the 2014 general election, 17.5 percent of votes were absentee ballots (EAC EAVS 2012).

Berinsky (2005) reviews the research on convenience voting—including absentee voting—and finds that reforms that are sold as benefitting the general population actually tend to benefit habitual voters. Those who use absentee voting tend to already be active voters, and "levels of political engagement currently follow, rather than cross, demographic divisions in the electorate." As a result, reforms designed to make the electorate more representative may actually magnify the existing socioeconomic gap in the electorate (Berinsky 2005, 472).

Research by Karp and Banducci (2001) bears this out. Although absentee voting reforms should be lowering the costs for all voters, including the less educated and those from lower socioeconomic and minority populations, absentee voting is primarily used by the most engaged voters. Karp and Banducci found that the primary users of absentee voting are older, more educated, and more politically active voters. Liberal absentee voting laws are also related to a slight increase in turnout for students and the disabled, but no increase in voting was seen for minorities.

SERVING NEW VOTERS OR SERVING HABITUAL ONES BETTER

In general, the question of whether absentee voting has the potential to affect overall voter turnout is considered to be very important. As noted above, just because people use absentee voting does not mean that it is boosting turnout; it may be simply that existing voters are voting using a different mode. In order to increase voter turnout, the introduction of absentee voting would need to occur in a way where habitual voters were retained and participation by non-voters increased. A study by Berinsky, Burns, and Traugott (2001) found that introducing voting by mail will not by itself bring new voters into the voting fold when it is introduced. However, they did find that it can effectively retain habitual voters, who now have an even easier time doing something they would do anyway. In addition, when new voters do start using VBM, they are likely to continue voting after this initial introduction.

The focus on turnout as a rationale for the introduction of or expansion of absentee voting can miss several of the key benefits of absentee voting for election officials and voters alike. One of these benefits is that, by having many votes cast prior to the election, election officials can relieve some pressure on polling places to serve as many voters on Election Day. This is important because, for election officials, Election Day is a difficult management problem because they have to delegate control of the election to poll workers, almost all of whom are temporary workers (volunteers, essentially), who receive limited training prior to the election (Alvarez and Hall 2006). Absentee voting is a process that election officials can control by incorporating it into standard election office operations; the ballots can be sent out and processed upon return by permanent election staff. Absentee voting can make Election Day voting more manageable if there are fewer voters to serve on that day. Having more than one mode of voting also provides redundancies to the system. Should there be a problem early in the election process, having another mode of voting can ensure that the entire election works more effectively.

Another benefit is that absentee voting helps election officials serve their core clientele—partisans who are older, well educated—in ways that they want to be served. If voting is thought of as a service provided to customers, the people who vote absentee are the core customer base. Thought of this way, absentee voting and other forms of convenience voting are beneficial because they are allowing election officials to provide better service to those who are a key voting constituency. In this context, absentee voting is like any other multimodal service provision; anyone can use any mode and the variation in mode will allow wide varieties of individuals to participate in the way that works best for them.

ABSENTEE VOTING AND THE MILITARY

Although discussions of absentee voting often center on how it affects turnout and who uses this mode of voting, it is important to remember that absentee voting was originally used to serve—and continues to be critical to serving—military personnel. For military personnel, there is often no option other than to vote absentee. The election of 1864 brought absentee voting and early voting to the North, when Union soldiers were allowed to vote using these methods. The military was organized by state regiments at the time; thus, military personnel could vote by having the polls brought to them by state election officials and other soldiers voted by proxy, with a family member voting for them (Alvarez and Hall 2004; Alvarez, Hall, and Roberts 2007).

World Wars I and II brought to the fore problems with serving the needs of military personnel when they are stationed far from home. Getting registration materials and voting materials from an election official to a voter and then back to the election official when the voter is an ocean away can take quite a long time. This ballot transit time problem was recognized by Congress when it passed the Solider Voting Act of 1942. This law was intended to help military personnel vote from the European and Pacific theaters of World War II. After the continued difficulties military personnel faced voting in the Korean War, Congress passed the Federal Voting Assistance Act of 1955. Each of these laws was intended to improve the voting experience for military voters but, with states remaining in charge of elections, it remained difficult in many states for military personnel to register and vote.

Congress enacted the Uniformed and Overseas Citizens Absentee Voting Act (UOCAVA) of 1986 to better address the voting needs of members of the uniformed services—the military branches, Coast Guard, and merchant marines—and their family members and overseas citizens (Huefner 2013). Among other things, UOCAVA mandated that covered citizens be able to register and vote in federal elections, and it established the Federal Post Card Application (FPCA) and the Federal Write-in Absentee Ballot (FWAB).

The FPCA is both a registration and ballot request form that can be used by those covered under UOCAVA, and the FWAB is a backup ballot for general elections in the event that a voter covered by UOCAVA has an issue receiving a ballot from his or her home state (Huefner 2013). The goal of the FPCA is to simplify the process of registering to vote and then requesting a ballot—something that could be two separate steps prior to UOCAVA. The FWAB is a write-in ballot for UOCAVA voters who have not received their traditional ballot in a timely manner. The voter can write in the name of the candidate or the name of the party for the federal offices on the ballot that they would like to vote and send this ballot in lieu of the official absentee ballot.

It was not until the passage of the Military and Overseas Voter Empowerment (MOVE) Act in 2009 that states were finally given a deadline for distributing absentee ballots to UOCAVA voters (Huefner 2013). Under this law, all states must send out absentee ballots to UOCAVA voters 45 days prior to the general election. States must also be able to distribute ballots electronically to a UOCAVA voter that requests electronic blank ballot delivery (Huefner 2013).

These online transmission methods vary in their level of development and ease of use from state to state. On one hand, Alaska and Arizona have developed their own systems for ballots to be directly uploaded and printed from the Internet (NCSL 2015b). Other states have a much less user-friendly process that involves the voter contacting local election officials in order to have a ballot delivered via e-mail. The latter can become time-consuming and complicated depending on the degree of organization of local departments and officials. To simplify and speed up the process of absentee voting for military personnel, many have suggested that UOCAVA voters be allowed to vote absentee using Internet voting (Alvarez and Hall 2004). An entirely online voting system for military service members would mean fewer issues in sending and receiving ballots on both ends. Security concerns related to this technology, however, have deterred large-scale implementation of Internet voting as either impractical or unfeasible.

Internet voting is not yet available but electronic blank ballot delivery is available, and UOCAVA voters can access the FWAB online, print it out, and submit it through the mail. The Federal Voting Assistance Program (FVAP), the agency in charge of implementation of UOCAVA and the MOVE Act, recommends that if a UOCAVA voter requested an absentee ballot but has not received it within 30 days of the election, submission of the FWAB is an alternative. It is mandated that the FWAB be an accepted ballot for federal elections in all states, but different states have different requirements for its submission and processing. Although the FWAB was designed as an "emergency" ballot for use by those who have not received their requested ballot in time, a few states now allow submission of the FWAB when an FPCA is not on file.

One of the biggest problems associated with the FWAB is voter awareness. Many voters are not aware that the FWAB is an option for voting. Unless the voter knows of the availability of the FVAP online FWAB voting tool, the voter would have to contact his or her state or local election official in order to receive the form and receive a list of candidates for each position. Data from the 2012 FVAP Post-Election Voting Surveys of Active Duty Military and Military Spouses show that difficulty of FWAB use may contribute to continued low usage rates—only 25 percent of active duty military who said they did not receive their requested absentee ballot reported using the FWAB in the 2012 election. Low awareness of the FWAB, demonstrated by the 16 percent of military spouses who reported they were not aware that the FWAB was available to them, is a key reason why many military voters and their families do not use it. In addition, FWAB rejection rates are relatively high. In 2012, approximately 25 percent of FWABs were rejected, with voter confusion cited as a major contributor (FVAP 2012). States have different requirements for FWAB usage, and in jurisdictions where having an FPCA on file is a requirement, some voters are still submitting only the FWAB.

It is not yet clear whether the changes mandated by UOCAVA and the MOVE Act are actually resulting in more votes by UOCAVA voters. In the 2000 election, one-third of military personnel and 20 percent of other overseas citizens who did not vote reported that they were not able to do so either because they did not receive their ballot in enough time to return it, or they did not receive a ballot at all (Alvarez, Hall, and Roberts 2007). A decade later, many of the ballots distributed by states to UOCAVA voters are never returned, and an even smaller portion of these are actually counted. Figure 8.1 shows outcomes for absentee ballots transmitted to UOCAVA voters during the 2012 and 2014 general elections (DMDC 2013, 2015; EAC EAVS 2012, 2014).

In the 2012 general election, states sent more than 1 million ballots to eligible UOCAVA voters; fewer than 70,000 of those ballots were returned and less than 60 percent were counted as part of election totals. During the

Figure 8.1
Transmitted UOCAVA Ballot Outcomes by Election Year (2012 and 2014)

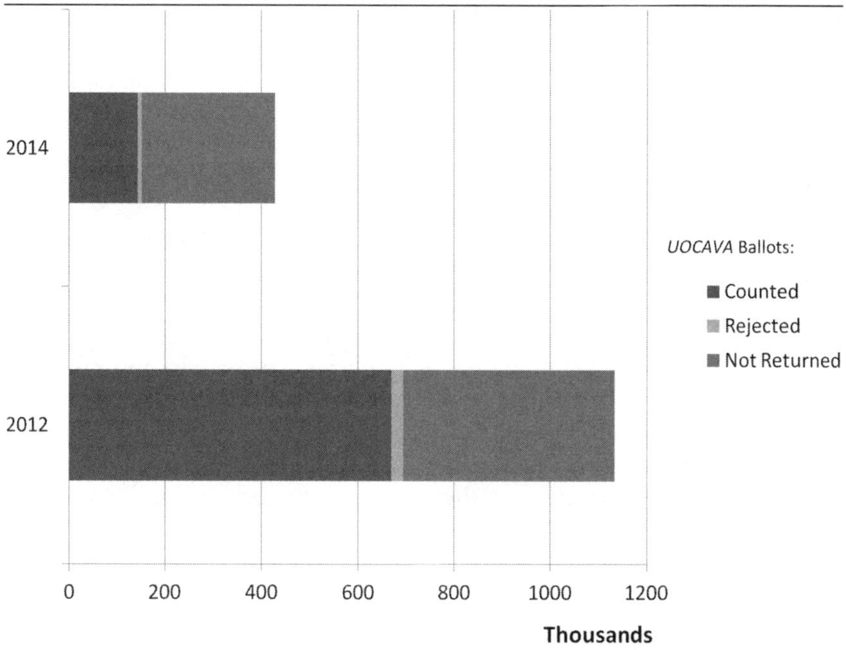

Source: The U.S. Election Assistance Commission Election Administration and Voting Survey.

2014 midterm election, nearly 65 percent of ballots sent to UOCAVA voters were never returned, and less than a third of transmitted ballots were ultimately counted (DMDC 2015). These results underscore the necessity of developing more efficient systems for both distributing and receiving ballots from military and other UOCAVA voters. Absentee voting is a necessity for military personnel and their family members, and while it has seen many changes in the past three decades, there is still room for improvement in the absentee voting process for military voters.

CONCLUSION

As past research has shown, cost to the individual is a major barrier to voter participation (Piven and Cloward 2000), and these costs are higher for certain groups, such as military personnel, persons with disabilities, and the elderly. At its conception, the purpose of absentee voting was to increase turnout by extending the vote to military personnel who were absent from their precinct on Election Day. In recent years, reforms in favor of liberalizing absentee voting laws have become popular in response to the notion that many non-voters do not vote because they do not have the time. In states like California and New Jersey, any voter can obtain permanent absentee voter status and receive an absentee ballot for every election, automatically, no matter where he or she is. These trends demonstrate a shift in the utility of absentee voting, from a means of increasing voter participation in populations for whom it is especially difficult to vote to a means of simplifying the voting process for everybody.

Although current absentee voting reforms have not demonstrated any major changes in the composition or size of the electorate, the use of absentee voting is spreading and there is the potential for it to increase turnout if it mobilizes casual voters upon implementation. States should examine Oregon's VBM system, using it as an example of how gradual changes supported by research and testing can lead to an effective and convenient new method of voting. Further development of absentee voting practices will be helpful to many U.S. citizens who enjoy the convenience of voting from home, but it is especially important that states continue to focus on easing the absentee voting process for active duty military members and their families who rely on absentee voting in order to cast their votes.

FURTHER READING

Alvarez, R. Michael, Hall, Thad E., and Betsy Sinclair. 2008. "Whose Absentee Votes Are Returned and Counted: The Variety and Use of Absentee Ballots in California." *Electoral Studies* 27 (4): 673–683.

Alvarez, R. Michael, Hall, Thad E., and Brian F. Roberts. 2007. "Military Voting and the Law: Procedural and Technological Solutions to the Ballot Transit Problem." *Fordham Urban Law Journal* 34: 933–996.

Alvarez, R. Michael, and Thad E. Hall. 2004. *Point, Click, and Vote: The Future of Internet Voting*. Washington, DC: Brookings Institution.

Alvarez, R. Michael, and Thad E. Hall. 2006. "Controlling Democracy: the Principal–Agent Problems in Election Administration." *Policy Studies Journal* 34 (4): 491–510.

Berinsky, Adam J. 2005. "The Perverse Consequences of Electoral Reform in the United States." *American Politics Research.* 33: 471–491.

Berinsky, Adam J., Burns, Nancy, and Michael W. Traugott. 2001. "Who Votes by Mail? A Dynamic Model of the Individual-Level Consequences of Voting-by-Mail Systems." *Public Opinion Quarterly* 65 (2): 178–197.

DMDC. May 2, 2013. "2012 Post-Election Quantitative Voting Survey." Note No. 2013-006.

DMDC. July 2015. "2014 Post-Election Voting Survey of Local Election Officials: EAC Statistical Methodology Report." DMDC Report No. 2015-014.

EAC EAVS. 2012. "Election Administration and Voting Survey, 2012." Election Assistance Commission.

EAC EAVS. 2014. "Election Administration and Voting Survey, 2014." Election Assistance Commission.

FVAP. 2012. "2012 Post-Election Report to Congress." Federal Voting Assistance Program. https://www.supportthevoter.gov/files/2013/08/2012-FVAP-Report.pdf.

Gronke, Paul, Galanes-Rosenbaum, Eva, Miller, Peter A., and Daniel Toffey. 2008. "Convenience Voting." *Annual Review of Political Science* 11: 437–455.

Gronke, Paul, Galanes-Rosenbaum, Eva, and Peter A. Miller. 2007. "Early Voting and Turnout." *PS: Political Science and Politics* 40 (4): 639–645.

Gronke, Paul, and Peter Miller. 2012. "Voting by Mail and Turnout in Oregon Revisiting Southwell and Burchett." *American Politics Research* 40 (6): 976–997.

Huefner, Steven F. 2013. "Lessons from Improvements in Military and Overseas Voting." *University of Richmond Law Review* 47: 833–880.

Karp, Jeffrey A., and Susan A. Banducci. 2001. "Absentee Voting, Mobilization, and Participation." *American Politics Research* 29: 183–195.

NCSL. 2015a. "Absentee and Early Voting." National Conference of State Legislatures. http://www.ncsl.org/research/elections-and-campaigns/absentee-and-early-voting.aspx.

NCSL. 2015b. "Electronic Transmission of Ballots." National Conference of State Legislatures.

Patterson, Samuel C., and Gregory A. Caldeira. 1985. "Mailing in the Vote: Correlates and Consequences of Absentee Voting." *American Journal of Political Science* 29 (4): 766–788.

Piven, Frances F., and Richard A. Cloward. 2000. *Why Americans Still Don't Vote: And Why Politicians Want It That Way.* Boston, MA: Beacon Press.

Rosenfield, Margaret. September 1995. *Innovations in Election Administration 11.* Washington, DC: National Clearinghouse on Election Administration.

Tokaji, Daniel P., and Ruth Colker. 2007. "Absentee Voting by People with Disabilities: Promoting Access and Integrity." *McGeorge Law Review.* 38: 1015.

U.S. Census. 2002. https://www.census.gov/prod/2002pubs/p20-542.pdf.

9

It's Not Convenient: Should Other States Follow the Northwest and Vote by Mail?

Priscilla L. Southwell

Vote-by-mail elections, also referred to as all-mail elections, have been used for many types of elections in the states of Oregon and Washington over the previous two decades, and now this method is being used for all elections conducted in these two states. Vote-by-mail eases the burden of voting by reducing the impact of unanticipated difficulties, such as illness or inclement weather, that often prevent individuals from voting on Election Day. With vote-by-mail, a potential voter also does not have to worry about long lines at the polling place, transportation to the polling place, or making special work arrangements. As such, vote-by-mail simply makes it easier to vote and is very popular in both these states. As this chapter demonstrates, the result of vote-by-mail has been a modest increase in voter turnout since its adoption in Oregon and Washington. Vote-by-mail has also been shown to facilitate the voting of certain ethnic and racial groups that may fear intimidation or other obstacles at the polling place. In addition, vote-by-mail also reduces the amount of "ballot roll-off"—that is, where a voter only votes in federal and state races that appear at the top of the ballot but does not vote in local races or ballot measures at the end of the ballot. Vote-by-mail is not a cure-all for the low voter turnout in the United States. However, in presidential and "special" elections, it can increase voter turnout by about three to five percentage points.

BACKGROUND OF VOTE-BY-MAIL IN OREGON

The first time a vote-by-mail election was used to decide a federal election was in December 1995, in a special election to replace Senator Bob Packwood (X-OR). Prior to the December 1995 primary and January 1996 general elections that determined Packwood's replacement, vote-by-mail had been used only for local contests or statewide ballot measures (Hamilton 1998), primarily as a measure to lower administrative costs. From 1981 to 1983, the Oregon State Legislature tested vote-by-mail in local elections. In 1987, the legislature made vote-by-mail an option for local and special elections. A majority of counties then adopted vote-by-mail for local elections. In 1993, vote-by-mail was used, for the first time, in a statewide ballot measure election.

In 1995, the Republican-controlled state legislature passed a bill that would have used vote-by-mail for all types of elections. The impetus for this bill was the high level of absentee voting (22 percent of all votes cast) in the 1994 general election, which delayed the certification of certain electoral outcomes for many weeks. However, John Kitzhaber, Oregon's Democratic governor, vetoed this bill. He argued that it was too early for Oregon to adopt such a drastic electoral reform without further study or experimentation (Esteve 1995b).

Senator Packwood's resignation in the fall of 1995 and the "special" nature of both the December 1995 primary and the general election in January 1996 allowed then Secretary of State Phil Keisling to adopt the vote-by-mail format for these two elections. Keisling chose the vote-by-mail format because he was a strong supporter of vote-by-mail, and given the governor's explanation for his veto of the vote-by-mail bill, this election provided an opportunity for the experimentation the governor felt was needed. As secretary of state, Keisling had the right to determine the format of any "special" election—that is, an election not held on one of the four designated election dates in the year. Nearly 58 percent of eligible voters participated in the December 1995 primary election, and approximately 66 percent of Oregon's registered voters cast a ballot in the January 1996 general election. Controversy then brewed between both major parties as to whether vote-by-mail conferred a particular advantage to one party over another. As a result, the push for making it a permanent feature lost support among most party leaders (Cain 1995). However, the Oregon League of Women Voters led a successful petition drive to put a vote-by-mail measure on the 1998 general election ballot, and this ballot measure passed by a 67 percent margin. Since that time, all elections in Oregon have been conducted by mail.

BACKGROUND OF VOTE-BY-MAIL ELECTIONS IN WASHINGTON

The adoption of vote-by-mail in Washington was more gradual, as the state liberalized its absentee voting laws over the years and also allowed an all-mail election option at the county and precinct level. In 1965, the Washington State Legislature authorized county election officials to conduct vote-by-mail elections in precincts of less than 200 voters (Pirch 2012). The state legislature also authorized "no-excuse" absentee voting, in contrast to states that required voters to certify their absence was due to one of a list of predetermined acceptable reasons in order to be able to vote by absentee ballot. In early iterations of this concept, Washington voters still had to request an absentee ballot for every election. In 1993, the legislature authorized anyone to request permanent status as an absentee voter (State of Washington, Secretary of State 2015). By 1996, Washington led the nation in the percentage of requested absentee ballots.

In 2002, five rural eastern Washington counties constructed precinct populations at less than 200 registered voters each in order to conduct all their elections by mail. This move prompted the 2005 legislature to authorize any county to conduct all their elections by mail if authorized by the respective county commissions. Almost immediately, 23 other counties joined these original 5 in conducting elections entirely by mail. The remaining 11 counties, mostly nonrural, used a hybrid mail and poll site electoral process (State of Washington, Secretary of State 2015).

When given the choice to vote either at polling sites or by mail, Washington voters made their preference known. From 1993 to 2008, an increasing number of registered voters chose a permanent absentee status, rising to 90 percent by 2006 (Gronke, Galanes-Rosenbaum, and Miller 2007). In 2004, Washington's hybrid system was a major cause of concern in the aftermath of the closest governor's race in U.S. history and the judicial challenges that followed (Southwell 2011). This election signaled a critical juncture for Washington's electoral process. The popularity of vote-by-mail and difficulties at polling places led state and local leaders to favor vote-by-mail (McDonald 2014, unpublished data). By 2011, only one county (Pierce, Tacoma area) still used a hybrid electoral process; in 2011, legislation passed that required only voting by mail in all counties. The 2011 primary election was the first held entirely by mail.

THE PHYSICAL AND PSYCHOLOGICAL DIMENSIONS OF VOTE-BY-MAIL

Under vote-by-mail in both states, all registered voters are sent a ballot prior to Election Day. In Oregon, the period is 14–21 days prior, and in Washington, the period is at least 18 days prior. Ballots are not forwarded if the voter no longer lives at the address on record. Voters then put their ballots first into a secrecy envelope that contains no identifying information and then into a second mailing envelope. It is then necessary to sign the outside of this mailing envelope and mail it or drop it off postage-free at any one of the numerous drop-off sites in one's neighborhood. This outside signature is then compared to the original registration signature on file at the local election office.

This advance voting period is a crucial element that contributes to the increased participation under vote-by-mail. In essence, the potential voter has this time to consult the official voter's guide, consult with others, or simply deliberate about the electoral choices. A previous analysis (Southwell 2009a) suggests vote-by-mail decreases the amount of roll-off voting for ballot measures that occur near the end of the ballot.

The physical process of receiving a ballot in the mail also reminds the potential voter of the upcoming election. Upon receipt, the voter makes a decision about whether or not to vote. Non-voters are required to actively decide not to vote by discarding the ballot. In contrast, in polling place elections, the potential voter must be aware of the date of Election Day and the location and hours of the polling place. Non-voters can easily ignore or forget an election conducted at the polling place; however, it is more difficult to do so under a vote-by-mail system.

RACIAL AND ETHNIC CONSIDERATIONS

Previous research has suggested that certain ethnic and racial groups will respond even more positively to the vote-by-mail method of conducting elections because the ease of voting is even more crucial to such groups (Cassel 2002; Mollenkopf, Olson, and Ross 2001). Specifically, some might prefer voting by mail because this method allows them to avoid the problems associated with getting time off work or transportation—all factors that can have a disproportional impact on Latino/as and blacks because of their economic status (La Garza and DeSipio 1992; Kam, Zechmeister, and Wilking 2008). Others might appreciate the increased amount of time and deliberation that is permitted in a vote-by-mail system because of language barriers or lower levels of educational achievement.

In addition, there are instances of efforts to intimidate racially and ethnically diverse voters through aggressive challenges or outright harassment at polling places. There are numerous examples of how poll workers—through sabotage or discrimination—can make voting more difficult on Election Day (Friedman 2005). Party activists are not immune to such tactics, either. In 2007, for example, California Republican Party leaders urged the Republican candidate Tan Nguyen to withdraw from his congressional race after his campaign sent out letters intended to prevent Latino/as from showing up at the polls (Richman 2011).

Such obstacles have become more salient as an increasing number of states are also imposing stricter voter identification laws at the polls. Vercellotti and Anderson (2006, unpublished data) have suggested that voter turnout decreases between 3 percent and 4 percent in states with stronger voter identification laws, in comparison to laws that require voters simply state their name. They also suggest that the effect increases for minority voters—as much as 5.7 percent for blacks, 10 percent for Hispanics, and 8.5 percent for Asians.

If voters receive a ballot in the mail, they may be less likely to be affected by such tactics. Vote-by-mail will not prevent such discrimination, but it allows the voter to attempt to resolve any ineligibility issues over a two- to three-week period, rather at the polls on Election Day. For example, during the Denver citywide elections from 2005 to 2007, both Latino and black voters participated more often in vote-by-mail elections, although the black turnout increase was also affected by the recent change in Colorado's registration policies (Southwell 2010).

EFFECT OF VOTE-BY-MAIL ON VOTER TURNOUT

Research on vote-by-mail has generally supported the argument that the vote-by-mail format increases turnout, although not for every type of election. An analysis of Oregon's elections from 1980 to 2007 suggests that such turnout increases occur primarily in presidential elections and special elections (Sled 2008, unpublished data; Southwell 2009b). Similarly, Richey (2008) analyzed aggregate data from 1980 to 2006 and suggested that the vote-by-mail format increased turnout by approximately 10 percentage points, although the analysis did not include special elections in Oregon. Several studies also found that turnout increased in Oregon as a result of vote-by-mail elections, but these also suggest that vote-by-mail elections ease the participation of *likely* voters, rather than mobilizing previous non-voters (Berinsky, Burns, and Traugott 2001; Hanmer and Traugott 2004; Karp and Banducci 2000). Berinsky Burns, and Traugott (2001) conclude that a vote-by-mail election may draw a non-voter into the electorate initially, but if this format does not entice such persons past their initial exposure, it is unlikely to do in subsequent elections.

An examination of the Oregon case suggests that vote-by-mail has boosted turnout modestly, particularly in presidential and special elections. Table 9.1 presents the overall turnout in 59 Oregon elections from 1980 to 2014 by type of election.

The results are not surprising given the nature of these types of elections. Presidential elections are high-stimulus and typically motivate first time voters, including those who may have had difficulty locating their polling place in previous years but had no such problems under vote-by-mail. Special elections are usually low-stimulus elections, often centering

Table 9.1

A Comparison of Turnout of Registered Voters across Electoral Format and Election Type State of Oregon, 1980–2014

Election Type	Number	Turnout	
		Polling Place (percent)	Vote-by-Mail (percent)
Presidential elections	9	78.1	83.7
Off-year general elections	9	69.4	70.7
Primary elections	18	46.5	44.7
Special elections	23	46.8	50.5
N	59	28	31

N = the total number of elections.
Source: State of Oregon, Office of the Secretary of State 2015.

on one or a few ballot measures. In such a situation, even politically aware voters might find it less important to go to the polls for a single issue. Vote-by-mail makes it easier for them to vote on even this one item.

Discerning the effect of vote-by-mail on turnout in the state of Washington is a more complicated matter, given the gradual precinct-by-precinct, county-by-county adoption of vote-by-mail over time across the state. Simple comparison of turnout between vote-by-mail and polling place counties over the years is not sufficient, as these different political units have different demographic characteristics that also affect turnout. However, the previous two elections in Washington, for both categories of presidential and off-year general elections, have been the highest in the decade (State of Washington, Secretary of State 2015). An analysis of turnout in Washington from 2004 to 2008 suggests that vote-by-mail resulted in a modest boost in voter turnout during presidential election years and for special elections, but had little or no effect in primary or off-year elections (Southwell 2009a). This is consistent with other research in Oregon and the table presented above. An update of general elections in Washington from 1992 to 2012 (McDonald 2014, unpublished data) shows that vote-by-mail increased voter turnout and ballot completion.

Residents of Washington and Oregon, in general, have always voted at higher rates than do residents of other states, so the effect of an electoral reform such as vote-by-mail is likely to be marginal in primary and off-year general elections, but significant in presidential and special elections. For those who are likely voters, vote-by-mail may prevent them from missing an election when they have an unforeseen personal crisis on Election Day, and this is a desirable goal. Other states with typically lower rates of participation might experience a more dramatic boost in turnout under vote-by-mail because of the added convenience of voting.

Most recently, in 2013, Colorado joined Oregon and Washington by passing a bill that allows for all elections to be conducted by mail. Although 22 states have provisions to allow certain elections to be conducted completely by mail (e.g., for special districts, municipal elections, when candidates are unopposed, or at the discretion of the county clerk), most states have been slow to follow these three in the adoption of elections exclusively by mail. In 2011, Montana's House of Representatives killed a bill that would have provided for elections exclusively by mail after receiving calls from constituents about the security of elections.

According to the National Conference of State Legislatures, security concerns coupled with the tradition of voting on Election Day, and the additional printing costs that states incur when switching to vote-by-mail, are just some of the disadvantages that may dissuade a state from adopting vote-by-mail provisions. Although concerns about unintended and unforeseen consequences of any proposed electoral reform are inevitable and understandable, Oregon and Washington's experiences should dispel most of these doubts.

FURTHER READING

Berinsky, Adam J., Burns, Nancy, and Michael W. Traugott. 2001. "Who Votes by Mail: A Dynamic Model of the Individual-Level Consequences of Voting-by-Mail Systems." *Public Opinion Quarterly* 65: 178–197.

Cain, Brad. 1995. "Senate Election Prompts Vote by Mail Worries." *The Register Guard* (Eugene, Or.), October 8, 4B.

Cassel, Carol A. 2002. "Hispanic Turnout: Estimates from Validated Voting Data." *Political Research Quarterly* 55: 391–408.

Esteve, Harry. 1995a. "Voters Will Still Be Going to the Poll." *The Register Guard* (Eugene, Or.), July 15, 1A.

Esteve, Harry. 1995b. "Mail Vote Experiment to be Watched Closely." *The Register Guard* (Eugene, Or.), October 17, 1A.

Friedman, Anne K. 2005. "Voter Disenfranchisement and Policy toward Election Reforms." *Review of Policy Research* 22: 787–810.

Gronke, Paul, Galanes-Rosenbaum, Eva, and Peter A. Miller. 2007. "Early Voting and Turnout." *PS: Political Science and Politics* 40: 639–645.

Hamilton, Randy H. 1998. "American All-Mail Balloting: A Decade's Experience." *Public Administration Review* 48: 860–866.

Hanmer, Michael J., and Michael W. Traugott. 2004. "The Impact of Voting by Mail on Voter Behavior." *American Politics Research* 32: 375–406.

Kam, Cindy D., Zechmeister, Elizabeth J., and Jennifer R. Wilking. 2008. "Americans from the Gap to the Chasm: Gender and Participation among Non-Hispanic Whites and Mexican Americans." *Political Research Quarterly* 61: 205–218.

Karp, Jeffrey A., and Susan A. Banducci. 2000. "Going Postal: How All-Mail Elections Influence Turnout. *Political Behavior* 22: 223–239.

La Garza, Rodolfo O. de, and Louis DeSipio. 1992. "Making Them Us: The Political Incorporation of Culturally Distinct Immigrants and Non-Immigrant

10

Logistical Barriers to Voting

Elizabeth Bergman and Dari Sylvester-Tran

This chapter addresses physical, tangible challenges to voting. Beyond attitudinal factors like voter apathy or convenience considerations such as the need to commute to far-off polling places, voters face issues that make the physical act of casting a ballot particularly difficult. Logistical barriers, specifically voting equipment technology, can affect the voting experience of citizens with physical or cognitive impairments and aging populations. In the United States, estimates suggest this includes at least 35 million voting-age people with disabilities, and approximately 41 million people aged 65 or older (Annual Disability Statistics Compendium; U.S. Census Bureau 2011).

VOTING AND DISABILITY

Although the body of turnout research focusing on physically and cognitively challenged populations remains scant, findings consistently suggest that populations with disabilities vote significantly less than those without disabilities, and this "disability gap" persists (Matsubayashi and Ueda 2014; Schur and Adya 2012; Schur, Adya, and Ameri 2015) despite federal laws intended to improve access. In brief summary, federal law requires accessible polling places for elderly individuals and people with disabilities (Voting Accessibility for the Elderly and Handicapped Act

Minorities in the United States." In *Nations of Immigrants: Australia, the United States and International Migration*, edited by G. P. Freeman and James Jupp, 202–216. Melbourne: Oxford University Press.

McDonald, Patrick. 2014. *The Affects of Vote by Mail on Voter Turnout, Cost of Elections, and Ballot Completion in the State of Washington from 1992 to 2012.* Unpublished doctoral dissertation. Minneapolis, MN: Walden University. https://www.sos.wa.gov/_assets/elections/McDonald-Patrick-Completed-and-Approved-Dissertation-7-23-2014.pdf.

Mollenkopf, John, Olson, David, and Timothy Ross. 2001. "Immigrant Political Incorporation in New York and Los Angeles." In *Governing American Cities: Interethnic Coalitions, Competition, and Conflict*, edited by Michael Jones-Correa, 17–70. New York, NY: Sage.

Pirch, Kevin A. 2012. "When Did the Campaign End? An Examination of the Timing of Vote Returns in the 2008 General Election in Washington State." *Political Science and Politics* 45: 711–715.

Richey, Sean. 2008. "Voting by Mail: Turnout and Institutional Reform in Oregon." *Social Science Quarterly* 89: 902–915.

Richman, Josh. 2011. "Former CA House Candidate Sentenced to Prison." *Contra Costa Times*, February 14. Retrieved May 22, 2015 from http://www.ibabuzz.com/politics/2011/02/14/former-ca-house-candidate-sentenced-to-prison/?doing_wp_cron=1432326421.1307010650634765625000.

Sled, Sarah M. 2008. *It's in the Mail: The Effect of Vote by Mail Balloting on Voter Turnout and Policy Outcomes in U.S. Elections.* Unpublished doctoral dissertation. Cambridge, MA: MIT. http://hdl.handle.net/1721.1/46634.

Southwell, Priscilla L. 2009a. "Analysis of the Turnout Effects of Vote by Mail Elections, 1980–2007." *The Social Science Journal* 46: 211–217.

Southwell, Priscilla L. 2009b. "A Panacea for Voter Fatigue? Vote by Mail in the State of Oregon." *Journal of Political and Military Sociology* 37: 195–203.

Southwell, Priscilla L. 2010. "A Panacea for Latino and Black Voters? Elevated Turnout in Vote by Mail Elections." *The Social Science Journal* 47: 819–828.

Southwell, Priscilla L. 2011. "Letting the Counties Decide: Voter Turnout and the All-Mail Option in the State of Washington." *Politics and Policy* 39: 979–996.

State of Oregon, Secretary of State. 2015. "Elections." Retrieved May 18, 2015 from http://sos.oregon.gov/elections/Pages/electionsstatistics.aspx.

State of Washington, Secretary of State. 2015. "Elections and Voting." Retrieved May 18, 2015 from https://www.sos.wa.gov/elections/.

Vercellotti, Timothy, and David Anderson. 2006. "Protecting the Franchise, or Restricting It? The Effects of Voter Identification Reqirements on Turnout." Unpublished manuscript. New Brunswick, NJ: Rutgers University. http://moritzlaw.osu.edu/blogs/tokaji/voter%20id%20and%20turnout%20study.pdf.

1984), stipulates that people with disabilities have a full and equal opportunity to vote (Americans with Disabilities Act 1990), and requires jurisdictions responsible for conducting federal elections to provide at least
one accessible voting system for persons with disabilities at each polling
place (Help America Vote Act [HAVA] 2002).

We explore the attitudes and experiences of people with disabilities
using statewide surveys conducted in California by the secretary of state's
(SoS) Voting Accessibility Advisory Committee (VAAC); data were obtained
from the SoS staff. The VAAC fielded online "Voter Accessibility Surveys" to
nonrandom samples of targeted disabled communities in 2012 and 2014 to
get information about the preferences and experiences of disabled citizens
regarding voting and elections. SoS staff created the web-based survey with
the help of the VAAC; individual VAAC members then distributed the web
link to their communities and asked that everyone complete the survey.
In 2012, respondents numbered 336; in 2014, 193 people completed the online survey. The largest group of respondents was mobility impaired (31 percent), followed by those with mental health or developmental impairment
(28.5 percent) and the vision impaired (19 percent). Respondents self-
selected their classification of impairment from the following list: mobility
—use a wheelchair or other mobility aid, dexterity, mental health, developmental or intellectual, vision, hearing, and other (see Appendix A.4).

In the 2012 survey, 90 percent of respondents reported being registered
and 64.5 percent said they "always vote." The percent of registered may
seem high; however, these are self-reported data. Issues surrounding the
(un)reliability of self-reported survey data have been well documented
in the political science literature (see, e.g., Ansolabehere and Hersh
2012). For those who said they seldom or never vote, 41.3 percent said
they do not vote "because the issues are complicated and I find it over-
whelming" (what the "issues" are is not specified or defined in the survey
instrument), 11 percent said they "can't vote because registering to vote is
not accessible to me because I have a disability," and 6.5 percent said they
"don't vote because information about voting, candidates, and issues is
not accessible to me because I have a disability." More than 50 percent of
respondents prefer to vote by mail because "it is more convenient
than voting at the polls" and affords "more time with the ballot"—these
responses are across all ages of disabled voters. Among those who prefer
voting by mail, the largest number (34 percent) is mobility impaired, followed by 19 percent of voters with vision impairment, as shown in the
chart in Figure 10.1 (2014 data).

In terms of election knowledge and experience, across both surveys in
2012 and 2014, the majority of respondents reported knowing how to find
their polling place and were aware of federal accessibility and equipment
requirements; nevertheless, a substantial number of registrants did not.
To illustrate the magnitude of this lack of information, we estimate that

Figure 10.1
Percent of Voters with Disability (by type) Preferring to Vote-by-Mail

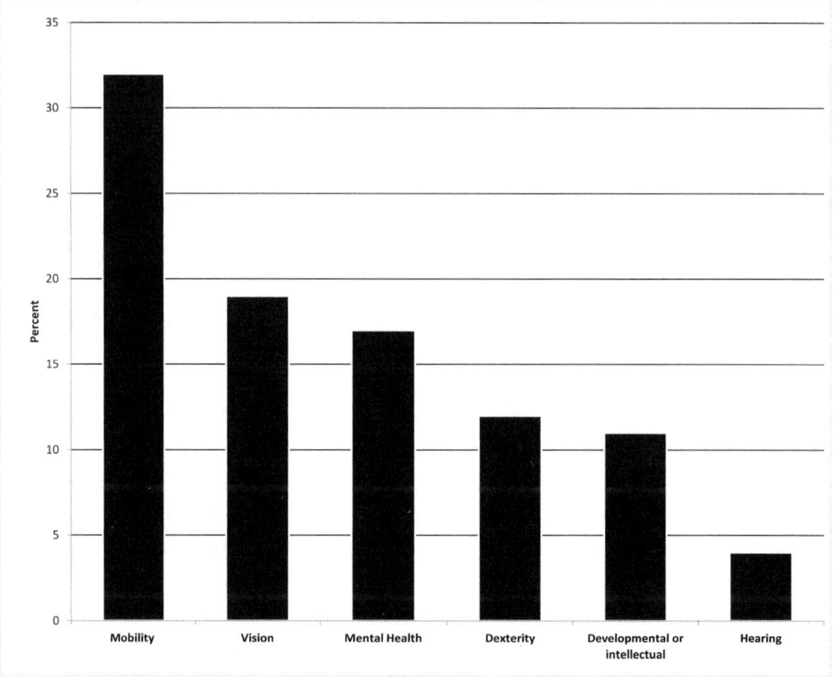

Source: California Secretary of State's Office.

approximately 1 million disabled voters in California do not know how to find out if their polling place is accessible to voters with disabilities, more than 200,000 do not know that federal law requires polling places to be accessible to voters with disabilities, and about 300,000 do not know that the law requires an accessible voting machine in polling places. These estimates were calculated using the percentage of respondents answering the applicable VAAC survey question and the voting-age disabled population in California taken from census data (from U.S. Census Bureau, 2009–2013, 5-Year American Community Survey: Disability Status of the Civilian Noninstitutionalized Population), which is approximately 1.8 million 18–64-year-olds and 1.5 million aged 65 years and older.

Among the 24.7 percent of respondents who used an accessible voting machine, 47.3 percent said it was convenient and useful and 69.4 percent said it allowed them to vote privately and independently. However, on the flip side, 75.3 percent of respondents have not used such an accessible voting machine in the past (see Appendix A.5). Why are such a large percentage of disabled voters not using accessible machines? We do not have data to answer this question, but we can surmise that there are numerous potential reasons, including voter ignorance, voter choice, poll worker failure, machine failure, and administrator failure (see Benedetti 2012). Whatever the reason is for accessible voting machine nonuse, higher percentages of target population utilization across the entire nation may be unattainable without considerable additional financial investment. Since 2002, federal law requires the deployment of accessible machines in every precinct in America—a mandate staggering in both cost and implementation considering that according to the most recent U.S. Election Assistance Commission Election Day Survey Report (2004), there were 185,994 precincts nationwide—and that number remains substantially the same 10 years later. Yet, the record speaks for itself; according to the General Accounting Office 2013 report of an eight-year (2000–2008) review of HAVA compliance across the 50 states: "All but one polling place GAO visited had an accessible voting system—typically, an electronic machine in a voting station—to facilitate private and independent voting for people with disabilities."

Our findings are corroborated by recent research (Matsubayashi and Ueda 2014; Schur and Adya 2012; Schur, Adya, and Ameri 2015) that has found that the participation gap between people with and without disabilities did not disappear over the past three decades despite the presence of federal laws aimed at removing barriers to voting. However, it is worth noting that researchers have relied on national surveys and, as far as we are aware, scholars have not published state-level studies on this population.

VOTING AND AGE

The relationship between aging and turnout has been typically characterized as curvilinear with a decline occurring in late age though others have likened it more to a "roller coaster" (Bhatti and Hansen 2012); in addition, certain policy areas (e.g., Social Security, Medicare) can effectively mobilize senior populations (Binstock 2012). To analyze the impact of the growth of voting by mail on aging voter populations and propose new policies aimed at increasing turnout in this demographic, we use our unique and large dataset containing the officially validated voter records of more than 2.4 million voters across five of the most ethno-racially diverse counties in California (Alameda, Fresno, Marin, San Mateo, and Santa Clara). We narrowed our analysis to those aged 65 and over, as these individuals are most likely to experience obstacles to in-person voting and therefore more likely to benefit from alternatives to polling place voting such as vote-by-mail.

Our sample includes the percentage of voters aged 65 and over who voted either absentee (called Permanent Absentee Voters, or "PAV") or at a polling place in primary and general elections in 2006 and 2008. The five-county data are shown in Table 10.1. The results reveal a number of significant and key findings.

Table 10.1
Percent Age 65+ Voting 2006 and 2008: Absentee (PAV)* and Polling Place

5-County Sample n = 2,439, 711 Voters	How voted	2006 Midterm Election		2008 Presidential Election	
		Percent Voted June Primary	Percent Voted November General	Percent Voted June Primary	Percent Voted November General
Alameda	Polls	42.2	56.7	33.4	66.8
	PAV	69.7	81.9	63.2	88.9
Fresno	Polls	38.8	58.6	37.5	70.2
	PAV	65.1	80.8	69.6	87.8
Marin	Polls	63.9	83.8	54.4	93.3
	PAV	72.4	86.9	72.3	94.8
San Mateo	Polls	49.3	71.4	38.7	81.6
	PAV	68.8	82.9	65.2	93.5
Santa Clara	Polls	57.3	52.1	30.9	68.9
	PAV	77.4	78.5	63.2	90.8

*PAV are mail-only voters.
Source: Alameda, Fresno, Marin, San Mateo, Santa Clara Counties—Registrar of Voters.

First is the consistently higher turnout among PAV versus polling place voters across both midterm and presidential elections among millions of older voters. Second, in no election does the turnout of polling place voters ever exceed that of PAVs. Third, controlling for election type (e.g., midterm versus presidential), there is significant growth in PAV voting from November 2006 to November 2008 across all five counties. Some of this increase may be due to the greater emphasis parties and campaigns place on "get out the vote" (GOTV) efforts targeted at absentee voters in presidential years (Hagle 2014), but we argue that some of the increase is due to the shift of voters from polling place to the PAV method of voting as well. Of note with respect to this last finding is that the increase in our election-to-election turnout data is among PAVs with previous experience in voting by mail. Prior experience or exposure to voting by mail is important because when individuals are required to switch from polling place to voting by mail scholars have found that turnout goes down (Bergman and Yates 2011). However, research has shown that after having experience with mail voting, individuals' support for all-mail balloting paralleled that of voters who voluntarily chose to vote by mail (Bergman 2012).

VOTING EQUIPMENT TECHNOLOGY

The presidential election of 2000 demonstrated how voting equipment (including ballots) can have a significant impact on the accuracy and viability of votes cast. At the time of the 2000 presidential election, the majority of counties in the United States were utilizing Votomatic punch-card devices to record votes. This equipment, considered a high-tech innovation in the early 1960s when it was introduced, ultimately became discredited for causing voting errors, including undervoting and unintentional voting (Gritzalis 2012). Some of these issues occurred due to the machine itself and how it marked votes, some were due to voter mistakes, and others occurred during the counting process. Although voting equipment technology in the post–Votomatic era alleviated some of these issues, newer voting technology still presents challenges. For example, optical scan machines improved upon the punch-card marking problems such as "hanging chads" by requiring a paper ballot fed into a machine that would tabulate votes electronically. However, other marking errors can occur. Touch screen technology allows for better control of over-voting and undervoting, but the interface can be confusing to some voters, causing them to vote for an unintended candidate or proposition. The possibility of coding errors also exists, which can result in spoiled ballots or completely voided ballots. Scholars (Roseman and Stephenson 2005; Tomz and Van Houweling 2003) have found that older voters express trepidation over how to properly use touch screen machines, and the rate of voided ballots can be exacerbated by the type of technology employed.

Based on people's experience with technology in other domains—banking and shopping are two popular and prevalent examples—it might seem that high-tech election approaches are an obvious solution. A common refrain is: "Are we not able to vote on the Internet?" Unfortunately, it is not that simple. Voting is a unique transaction that requires casting an anonymous, yet verifiable and trackable, vote—the key part of this transaction, unlike banking and shopping, is that it be anonymous because elections also require a secret ballot. Furthermore, once cast, there is no acceptable margin for error in processing, recording, or counting that vote (Hasen 2012). Vote tabulation systems must be reliable, accurate, and free from tampering (aka "hacking"). Such requirements preclude Internet voting for the foreseeable future.

In the relatively short term, we are likely to witness marginal technology advances in election administration. In the long(er) term, our anecdotal evidence from conversations with election officials indicates an interest in open source voting systems. Open source systems are designed such that the computer programming code that controls the system would be publicly available for review as opposed to the current undisclosed and proprietary code used by vendors. At the time of this writing, Los Angeles County (CA) and Travis County (TX) are exploring options for open source voting systems.

POLICY—INCREASING TURNOUT AMONG DISABLED AND OLDER VOTERS

The California data show that both voters with disabilities and those over the age of 65 prefer to vote by mail, and voting by mail increases turnout significantly among older voters. We suggest that expanding the availability of mail voting will increase turnout among disabled and older voters. There are other policy changes that could also enhance voter participation for voters that face obstacles in casting a ballot. For example, California election law specifies who may return a ballot on behalf of another individual; at the time of this writing, only a voter's spouse, child, parent, grandparent, grandchild, brother, sister or a person residing in the same household as the voter may return another voter's ballot. This restriction effectively limits the franchise for absentee voters who live alone, without access to any of the individuals named in the law, and who are unable to return their ballots either by mail or in person.

WHAT IS NEXT?

Although logistical barriers to voting are widely acknowledged by citizens and election administrators, measures are being proposed to help ameliorate these barriers in a number of ways. In the midst of record lows in voter turnout, during the 2015 session, the California State Assembly considered more than a dozen bills aimed at improving turnout, including an update of the Motor Voter legislation that would automatically register voters at driver's license locations. The results and recommendations we have presented are specific to one state, and we cannot speculate beyond California. We believe, however, that the size and diversity of California provide important and illuminating information about the continuing challenges faced by disabled and aging voter populations.

FURTHER READING

Ansolabehere, Stephen, and Eitan Hersh. 2012. "Validation: What Big Data Reveal about Survey Misreporting and the Real Electorate, 2012." *Political Analysis* 20 (4): 437–459.

Benedetti, Robert R. 2012. *More Votes That Count: A Case Study in Voter Mobilization.* Edited by Robert Benedetti. Berkeley, CA: Berkeley Public Policy Press.

Bergman, Elizabeth. 2012. "Administering Democracy: Public Opinion on Election Reform in California." *California Journal of Politics and Policy* 4 (1): 1–23.

Bergman, Elizabeth, and Philip A. Yates. 2011. "Changing Election Methods: How Does Mandated Vote-by-Mail Affect Individual Registrants?" *Election Law Journal* 10 (2): 115–127.

Bhatti, Yosef, and Kasper M. Hansen. 2012. "The Effect of Generation and Age on Turnout to the European Parliament—How Turnout Will Continue to Decline in the Future." *Electoral Studies* 31 (2): 262–272.

Binstock, Robert H. 2012. "Older Voters and the 2010 U.S. Election: Implications for 2012 and Beyond?" *The Gerontologist* 52 (3): 408–417.

Gritzalis, Dimitris A. 2012. *Secure Electronic Voting*. Vol. 7. New York, NY: Springer Science and Business Media.

Hagle, Timothy. 2014. "Iowa Voting Series, Paper 6: An Examination of Iowa Absentee Voting Since 2000." Department of Political Science, University of Iowa.

Hasen, Richard L. 2012. *The Voting Wars*. New Haven, CT: Yale University Press.

Matsubayashi, Tetsuya, and Michiko Ueda. 2014. "Disability and Voting." *Disability and Health Journal* 7 (3): 285–291.

Reilly, Shauna, and Sean Richey. 2011. "Ballot Question Readability and Roll-Off: The Impact of Language Complexity." *Political Research Quarterly* 64: 59–67.

Roseman Jr., Gary H., and E. Frank Stephenson. 2005. "The Effect of Voting Technology on Voter Turnout: Do Computers Scare the Elderly?" *Public Choice* 1 (2): 39–47.

Schur, Lisa. 2003. "Contending with the 'Double Handicap': Political Activism among Women with Disabilities." *Women and Politics* 25 (1–2): 31–62.

Schur, Lisa, Adya, Meera, and Mason Ameri. 2015. "Accessible Democracy: Reducing Voting Obstacles for People with Disabilities." *Election Law Journal* 14 (1): 60–65.

Schur, Lisa, and Meera Adya. 2012. "Sidelined or Mainstreamed? Political Participation and Attitudes of People with Disabilities in the United States." *Social Science Quarterly* 94 (3): 811–839. doi: 10.1111/j.1540-6237.2012.00885.x.

Schur, Lisa, Shields, Todd, Kruse, Douglas, and Kay Schriner. 2002. "Enabling Democracy: Disability and Voter Turnout." *Political Research Quarterly* 55 (1): 167–190.

Schur, Lisa, Shields, Todd, and Kay Schriner. 2005. "Generational Cohorts, Group Membership, and Political Participation by People with Disabilities." *Political Research Quarterly* 58 (3): 487–496.

Tomz, Michael, and Robert P. Van Houweling. 2003. "How Does Voting Equipment Affect the Racial Gap in Voided Ballots?" *American Journal of Political Science* 47 (1): 46–60.

11

Voter Identification Requirements and Participation: A Cause for Alarm?

Ryan Voris

In 2008, the U.S. Supreme Court ruled on the constitutionality of requiring voters to present government-issued photo identification (photo ID) at the polls on Election Day. The case stemmed from an Indiana law that at the time was the strictest in the country. Many feared the law, and others like it, would prevent thousands of citizens from voting in elections, with minorities and other disadvantaged groups bearing the brunt of the impact. Supporters argued identification requirements were necessary to prevent election fraud and protect voter confidence in the electoral process. *Crawford v. Marion County* (2008) upheld government-issued photo ID requirements but did not end the controversy surrounding voter identification laws. Voter identification (voter ID) laws first emerged on the political scene in the aftermath of the 2000 U.S. presidential election, and scholars continue to be divided as to their impact on the American political system. This chapter examines requirements across the states with particular focus on changes since the Help America Vote Act (HAVA) of 2002 and the effects of voter ID practices on voter turnout.

VOTER IDENTIFICATION LAWS IN AMERICA

During most elections, focus centers on the competition between the two major parties and the mechanics of the electoral process are left to the background. Both major parties devote a large portion of their resources toward getting supporters to the polls, including passing legislation designed to ease the voting process. Many states passed reforms that allowed voters access to absentee ballots without requiring an excuse or instituted periods where they could vote in-person before Election Day, with Oregon switching all elections to vote-by-mail in 1998 (Gronke et al. 2008).

The 2000 presidential election between George W. Bush and Al Gore shifted this focus to the mechanics of electing the president. The election was one of the closest on record, with Bush being declared the winner based on 537 votes in the state of Florida. Over the next several weeks, media coverage centered on the manual recount that was underway in several Florida counties. Viewers saw volunteers attempt to determine the will of individual voters on thousands of punch-card ballots. Nearly a month after the election, the Supreme Court effectively ended the recount through its 5-4 decision in *Bush v. Gore* (2000). This decision galvanized public opinion on the need to modernize the electoral process across the country. Congress was among the first to act with the passage of the HAVA. Many of the provisions of the bill were designed to remedy issues that plagued the 2000 election by providing states with funds to update election machinery. The Election Assistance Commission was created to disburse and monitor funds for new electronic voting systems and to serve as an information clearinghouse, among other functions. Both Congress and President Bush hoped the broad guidelines would spur the states to undertake further reform.

Although HAVA passed with widespread support, the bill's identification requirements proved to be an area of significant disagreement between the major parties. Republican politicians desired a requirement that would force all voters to show identification in all federal elections, a measure they stated would prevent voter fraud. Democrats believed such requirements would prevent many citizens from participating in elections. Then-Senator Hillary Clinton (D-NY), one of two to vote against HAVA in the Senate, believed the voter ID requirement would prevent many recently naturalized citizens and millions of other New Yorkers who did not possess a driver's license from voting (Pear 2002). In the end, political compromise limited the ID requirement to first time voters and allowed for multiple forms of documentary identification so long as the documentation contained the voter's name and address.

Between 2002 and 2006, 10 states created identification requirements for all voters in state elections. Most states adopted HAVA provisions for all elections, which allowed a wide variety of documents and did not require photo ID. Also, these laws contained provisions that enabled individuals without proper identification to cast either a provisional ballot, similar to HAVA, or allowed voters to cast a regular ballot through other means (such as signing an affidavit of identity or allowing the poll workers to waive the requirement). Indiana and Georgia were the only states to go beyond the HAVA minimum requirements and require government-issued photo ID of all voters in order for ballots to be counted. All states reviewed their voter ID provisions as a consequence of HAVA; states that subsequently adopted requirements more stringent than the HAVA minimum were more likely to be controlled by Republican governors and legislatures (Hale and McNeal 2010).

The Indiana photo ID law came to centralize the debate over identification requirements for all voters. Unlike HAVA, Indiana's photo ID requirement was passed in a straight party line vote after Republicans took control of the state government in 2004. The law required all voters to present photo ID at the polls. Voters without proper identification would be required to cast a provisional ballot. The provisional ballots would only be counted if they returned to the Board of Elections with acceptable proof of identification by noon the Monday after the election. Challenges to the law followed quickly, as some estimated that nearly 13 percent of all Indiana voters lacked acceptable identification under the law (Urbina 2008). After the 2006 midterm elections, numerous reports surfaced of voters being temporarily denied a ballot; among these were several nuns in northern Indiana, incumbent U.S. House member Julia Carson (D-IN, and 32 residents of Marion County).

Court challenges began immediately after the election, with various cases being consolidated into *Crawford v. Marion County Board of Elections* (2008). The case attracted attention as one of the most important election law cases in decades to come before the Court, with the constitutionality of identification requirements hanging in the balance (Urbina 2008). In the end, the Supreme Court upheld Indiana's ID requirement, calling these laws an appropriate means for states to protect the "integrity and reliability of the electoral process" (*Crawford* 2008, 7). While the court did not deny that ID requirements placed a barrier on some voters, it relied on lower court findings that these did not qualify "as a substantial burden" or even "significant[ly] increase the usual burdens" of voting (*Crawford* 2008, 15).

While the *Crawford* decision upheld the legality of government-issued photo voter ID requirements, it did not end the controversy surrounding these laws. Since 2008, 22 states have enacted voter ID requirements, with 14 of those enacting photo ID requirements. As of March 2016, 33 states have voter ID in place for the 2016 presidential election (NCSL 2016). Numerous advocacy groups and scholars note that millions of otherwise legally eligible citizens may lack acceptable forms of photo ID that meet the stricter voter ID requirements. Further, those that lack photo ID tend to be disproportionately minority voters (American Civil Liberties Union [ACLU] 2011; Barretto, Nuno, and Sanchez 2007; Brennan Center for Justice 2012). District Court Judge Richard Posner, who authored the opinion largely upheld in *Crawford*, has also recently dissented from opinions upholding voter ID requirements in part citing the partisan motivation behind these laws. As the 2016 election draws closer, ID requirements are likely to again take center stage.

VOTER IDENTIFICATION AND VOTER PARTICIPATION

Voter ID laws vary widely from state to state, but each law specifies the forms of identification that are acceptable in the state and the procedures available for those without acceptable ID. Many researchers and media outlets refer to these laws using the classification developed by the National Conference of State Legislators (NCSL). The NCSL classifies laws according to the type of identification requested and whether individuals are required or requested to show that identification. These identification requirements specify that voters bring the required/requested documentation with them to the polls on Election Day. These voter ID requirements contrast with those of other states, which simply require that voters state or sign their name and that poll workers match the voters' signatures against the signatures on the registration record.

Currently, 33 states request voters to bring identification with them to the polls on Election Day. The NCSL divides these laws into two major dimensions. The first deals with which type of identification voters are to present, either with or without a photograph. Of the states with voter ID laws, 17 specify that the ID have a picture of the voter. The other 16 *non-photo ID* states generally apply HAVA recommendations to all voters in elections. The second dimension of these laws is referred to as "strictness," generally referring to whether the law *requests* or *requires* voters to present identification. Each of these dimensions will be discussed in turn.

The first dimension refers to the nature of the identification itself. Generally speaking, non-photo ID laws permit any form of identification with the voter's name and address. Most common are current utility bills or bank statements, though statutes may expand the number of acceptable documents. Some examples include the acceptance of Social Security cards in Connecticut, hunting licenses in Alaska, or credit cards in Kentucky (NCSL 2016). Photo ID laws generally require the ID to be issued by a government entity, such as a driver's license or military ID card. Other states expand this to include student identification cards, neighborhood association ID, or tribal ID, provided each has a picture of the voter on it.

The second dimension of these laws covers the procedures used for voters without proper identification. The NCSL refers to these laws as either "strict" or "non-strict" based on whether the laws require acceptable ID of all voters or contain provisions for those without acceptable ID. Under "strict" ID statutes, voters without acceptable identification are required to cast a provisional ballot that is only counted if voters return with acceptable ID within a specified period of time after the election. Generally, these laws require voters to return to the Board of Elections within one week after the election with appropriate identification, though some states limit the period to three days. If the individual does not return, the ballot is not counted. In "non-strict" states, officials typically *request* the specified form of identification and voters without acceptable ID are still allowed to cast a regular ballot through other measures. Typically, these other measures include signing an affidavit of identity; in some states, if poll workers know the voter they are permitted by law to waive the requirement for that reason. In these cases, the ballots are counted without additional effort by the voter.

States can thus be classified as one of four categories: strict photo, non-strict photo, strict non-photo, and non-strict non-photo. Figure 11.1 depicts the array of state voter ID laws in the country as of early 2016. Changes to these existing classifications are possible both through new legislation (e.g., North Carolina relaxed its photo ID law prior to the law going into effect) and as a result of legal challenges (e.g., a Texas photo ID law was upheld in 2015 but faces continuing challenges).

Of these laws, the strict photo ID laws have attracted the most attention. These laws require photo ID of all voters and face criticism for the difficulty of some individuals to obtain identification. States that require photo ID of all voters offer free voter ID cards to those who otherwise lack acceptable photo ID. Although the voter ID card itself may be free, obtaining the other documents and traveling to the location imposes costs of both time and money on those seeking the ID. Individuals must first travel to the location where the IDs are available, most often the Division or Bureau of Motor Vehicles, during normal business hours. In addition, citizens must bring proof of residency and identity. For most individuals this requires obtaining their original or a certified copy of their birth certificate, in addition to other documents. In addition to fears that these costs will reduce voter turnout, many groups fear that some segments of the population are more likely to be impacted by these laws. Using exit polls from the 2006 elections, Barreto, Nuno, and Sanchez (2007) found that racial minorities and immigrants are less likely to have access to the photo ID required by many of the stricter voter ID requirements. These findings have been

Figure 11.1
Voter Identification Laws in 2016

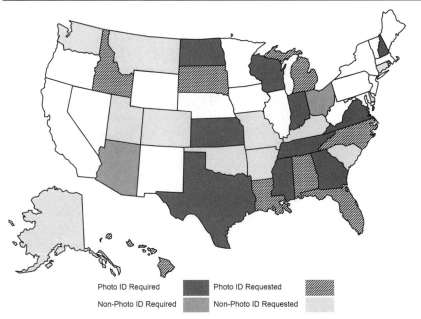

Source: National Conference of State Legislatures, http://www.ncsl.org/research/elections-and -campaigns/voter-id.aspx.

supported by numerous other studies that show racial minorities and lower income individuals are less likely to have a driver's license, although this documentation is nearly universal among other groups of the population (Pastor et al. 2010).

The literature is considerably mixed on whether these requirements depress voter turnout in elections. Studies of their impact began shortly after HAVA requirements went into effect after the 2004 presidential election. One of the earliest studies noted that although there appeared to be no impact on voter participation, it was likely still too early to tell as the laws were not in widespread use across the county (Lott 2006). Later studies examined turnout at the national level and in individual states after photo ID laws were enacted and found no evidence of a decline in turnout associated with these laws (Muhlhausen and Sikieh 2007; Mycoff, Wagner, and Wilson 2007).

In contrast, other research finds support for claims that stricter requirements depress voter turnout. Alvarez, Bailey, and Katz (2008) find that stricter identification requirements lead to a decline in voter turnout, with photo ID requirements having the most negative impact. Hood and Bullock (2012) similarly find evidence of a negative impact on voter turnout, but note that disproportionate impact falls only on those without photo ID and not on racial minorities per se. Still other researchers have found evidence that stricter requirements have a negative impact on voter participation and that this impact disproportionately harms minority turnout (Barreto, Nuno, and Sanchez 2007). Extrapolating their findings to other races across the country, Barretto and colleagues find that the impact may be strong enough to flip election outcomes in close races for both the U.S. House and the Senate. They predict that, had photo ID been required of all voters in 2006, 12 U.S. House seats and 3 Senate seats would not have switched from Republican controlled to Democratic controlled.

These findings present an interesting puzzle for research on political participation. Many researchers approach the study of voting behavior with the assumption that increasing the costs of participation will decrease overall levels of participation. In fact, reforms such as early voting and no-excuse absentee are designed to reduce costs for voters in hopes of increasing turnout. In fact, some administrative procedures deter people from voting and some reforms boost voter participation. The mixed findings about the effect of voter ID requirements on turnout have prompted exploration about why the effect of stricter identification requirements is not more apparent.

One potential explanation is that even stricter identification requirements are of little concern to most voters. Pastor et al.'s (2010) survey of registered voters in three states found that over 95 percent of registered voters could provide a driver's license. Additionally, many of the groups most suspected to lack identification also happen to be groups that have historically been found to vote at lower rates than the general population. Thus for the vast majority of voters, identification requirements present no additional barrier, and those who are most likely to be deterred already vote at lower levels.

Political party strategy may be another reason for the mixed findings of previous research on the impact of these laws. One of the major goals of political parties is to win elections, and parties appear to have two major strategies: one is to write laws that provide advantage over the opposition and the other is to mobilize their supporters. Republicans may be acting strategically to pass voter ID laws to help them continue to win elections; this approach may have been made possible by the number of states over which Republicans have gained unified control in recent elections, particularly given the historic association of Republican control and stricter voter ID requirements (Hale and McNeal 2010; Hicks et al. 2015). However, Democrats suspect these laws may harm key segments of their coalition, and consequently, mobilize supporters to counter these laws. Media accounts contain some evidence of groups using voter ID to encourage citizens to vote in Indiana (Adler 2008), Wisconsin (Issenberg 2012), and North Carolina (Portnoy 2014) around the time laws were changed.

Recent research is beginning to explore this possibility that voter ID laws may increase turnout. Voris (2015) examined state turnout in elections after 2000 and found that photo ID requirements lead to an increase in average turnout levels in presidential elections. This finding is consistent with civic group strategies to take advantage of the increased attention drawn to presidential elections to motivate those who traditionally do not vote in elections. Other researchers find that messages about identification requirements motivate partisans to participate in elections (Citrin, Green, and Levy 2015). This suggests that political parties and other groups are using the divisive nature of identification laws to motivate their supporters to participate in elections. These findings are challenged by analysis of the two Obama elections in 2008 and 2012, which occurred during the same period many states first enacted voter ID laws. The Obama campaign was able to mobilize many groups that did not typically vote at high rates, including many of the same groups thought to be most negatively impacted by identification requirements. It remains difficult to disentangle the mobilization efforts of the Obama campaign with independent groups organized around voter ID, or whether the mobilization effects achieved in 2008 and 2012 will continue with President Obama no longer on the ballot.

FURTHER READING

Adler, Ben. 2008. "Young Activists Mobilize against ID Law." *Politico*, January 21. Retrieved March 13, 2015 from http://www.politico.com/news/stories/0108/8001.html.

Alvarez, Michael, Bailey, Delia, and Jonathan Katz. 2008. "The Effect of Voter Identification Laws on Turnout." In *The Effect of Voter Identification Laws on Turnout*. California Institute of Technology, Social Science Working Paper 1267R.

American Civil Liberties Union (ACLU). 2011. "Oppose Voter ID – Fact Sheet." American Civil Liberties Union. Retrieved November 15, 2012 from http://www.aclu.org/voting-rights/oppose-voter-id-legislation-fact-sheet.

Barreto, Matt, Nuno, Stephen, and Gabriel Sanchez. 2007. "Voter ID Requirements and the Disenfranchisements of Latino, Black and Asian Voters." Vol. 30. *Annual Meeting of the American Political Science Association*, Chicago, IL.

Brennan Center for Justice. 2012. "Voter ID." Brennan Center for Justice, New York University School of Law. Retrieved November 19, 2012 from http://www.brennancenter.org/analysis/voter-id.

Citrin, Jack, Green, Donald P., and Morris Levy. 2015. "The Effects of Voter ID Notification on Voter Turnout: Results from a Large-Scale Field Experiment." *Election Law Journal* 13 (2): 228–242.

Crawford v. Marion County Election Board (2008) 553 U.S. 181.

Gronke, Paul, Galanes-Rosenbaum, Eva, Miller, Peter, and Daniel Toffey. 2008. "Convenience Voting." *Annual Review of Political Science* 11: 437–455.

Hale, Kathleen, A., and Ramona McNeal. 2010. "Election Administration Reform and State Choice: Voter Identification Requirements and HAVA." *Policy Studies Journal* 38 (2): 281–302.

Hicks, William, McKee, Seth, Sellers, Mitchell, and Daniel Smith. 2015. "A Principle or a Strategy? Voter Identification Laws and Partisan Competition in the American States." *Political Research Quarterly* 68 (1): 3–17.

Hood III, M. V., and Charles Bullock III. 2012. "Much Ado about Nothing? An Empirical Assessment of the Georgia Voter Identification Statute." *State Politics and Policy Quarterly* 12 (4): 394–414.

Issenberg, Sasha. 2012. "Don't Let Them Disenfranchise You: Can Democratic Organizers Use Voter ID Laws to Mobilize Outraged Supporters?" Retrieved March 30, 2016 from http://www.slate.com/articles/news_and _politics/victory_lab/2012/09/voter_id_laws_will_they_mobilize_angry _democrats_.html.

Lott, John. 2006. "Evidence of Voter Fraud and the Impact That Regulations to Reduce Fraud Have on Voter Participation Rates." Available at SSRN 925611.

Muhlhausen, David, and Keri Sikich. 2007. "New Analysis Shows Voter Identification Laws Do Not Reduce Turnout." A Report of The Heritage Center for Data Analysis. CDA07-04. September 10.

Mycoff, Jason, Wagner, Michael, and David Wilson. 2007. "The Empirical Effects of Voter-ID Laws: Present or Absent?" *PS: Political Science and Politics* 42 (1): 121–126.

National Conference of State Legislatures. 2016. "History of Voter ID." National Conference of State Legislators, January 4, 2016. Retrieved from http:// www.ncsl.org/research/elections-and-campaigns/voter-id-history.aspx.

National Conference of State Legislatures. 2016. "Voter Identification Requirements: Voter ID Laws." National Conference of State Legislatures. Updated January 4, 2016. Retrieved from http://www.ncsl.org/research/elections- and-campaigns/voter-id.aspx#.

Pastor, Robert A., Santos, Robert, Prevost, Alison, and Vassia Stoilov. 2010. "Voting and ID Requirements: A Survey of Registered Voters in Three States." *American Review of Public Administration* 40 (4): 461–481.

Pear, Robert. 2002. "Congress Passes Bill to Clean Up Election System." *The New York Times*, October 17. Retrieved May 26, 2015 from http://www.nytimes .com/2002/10/17/politics/17VOTE.html.

Portnoy, Jenna. 2014. "Virginia Voting Rights Groups Mobilize for Election Day and New Photo ID Law." *The Washington Post*, October 29. Retrieved March 15, 2015 from http://www.washingtonpost.com/local/virginia -politics/virginia-voting-rights-groups-mobilize-for-election-day-and-new -photo-id-law/2014/10/29/156b071e-5fa1-11e4-9f3a-7e28799e0549_story .html.

Urbina, Ian. 2008. "Voter ID Laws Are Set to Face Crucial Test." *The New York Times*, January 7. Retrieved May 27, 2015 from http://www.nytimes.com /2008/01/07/us/07identity.html?pagewanted=all.

Voris, Ryan. 2015. "Voter Identification and Minority Turnout: Reexamining the Evidence." Paper presented at the 2015 Annual Meeting of the Midwestern Political Science Association. Chicago, IL.

12

Barred from the Booth: Felony Disenfranchisement

Bridgett A. King

Felony disenfranchisement is the loss of the right to vote after conviction for a felony level offense. Although some American citizens may refrain from voting because of administrative and logistical barriers, political preferences, or lack of interest, in many states individuals with felony convictions are legally barred from voting. In the United States, an estimated 5.85 million voting-age citizens were ineligible to vote during the November 2014 midterm election due to felony conviction. This includes 2.6 million citizens who have completed their sentences (Sentencing Project 2014). Of those who are currently disenfranchised, 75 percent live in their communities, either under judicial supervision (probation or parole) or having completed their sentences.

HISTORY OF FELONY DISENFRANCHISEMENT

The presence of felony disenfranchisement as a part of the American legal system is a result of English colonization. During the colonization of what would eventually become the United States, the English brought with them much of their legal tradition. This included the removal of legal rights and privileges as a result of criminal conviction (Pettus 2005;

Reiman 1995). From 1776 to 1821, 11 states retained provisions in their constitutions denying voting rights to convicted felons or giving power to their state legislature to do so. Prior to the Civil War, 24 of the 34 states had legal provisions that allowed for the exclusion of felons from voting (Keyssar 2000).

Following the Civil War, states, particularly those in the South, expanded voting restrictions. States expanded the criminal codes to punish offenses that they believed freedmen (former slaves) were most likely to commit. These crimes included vagrancy, petty larceny, miscegenation, bigamy, and receiving stolen goods (Ewald 2002, 1088–1089). During the Jim Crow Era, the expansion of voting restrictions continued as states enacted voting bans for felons alongside grandfather clauses, constitution interpretation tests, literacy tests, and poll taxes. Although the 1965 Voting Rights Act invalidated laws, institutional arrangements, and administrative practices that denied American citizens the right to vote because of race, states continue to deny millions of Americans the right to vote. In the 21st century, disenfranchised citizens with felony convictions constitute the largest population of American citizens legally denied the right to vote (Keyssar 2000, 308).

JUSTIFICATION FOR DISENFRANCHISEMENT

There are two normative justifications used to support the disenfranchisement of felons: preserving the purity of the ballot box and maintaining the social order. Preserving the purity of the ballot box suggests that offenders must not be allowed to vote because they are untrustworthy. There is an expectation that because offenders have been convicted of crimes, they are untrustworthy and would potentially vote to weaken criminal law and form an antilaw enforcement voting bloc if given the opportunity (Clegg 2001). Essentially, this line of reasoning argues that felons would use their voting power to corrupt existing law enforcement institutions by voting for policies and politicians that would help criminals.

The second argument used by supporters of felony disenfranchisement is a need to preserve the social order. This argument suggests that convicted felons should be barred from voting because "the right to political participation should be conditioned on some kind of behavior or contribution" (Ewald 2004, 119). By allowing people who lack the appropriate qualities to participate, the social order is threatened. Because felons have broken the law and consequently rejected the social order, they have lost the right to participate in the governance of the whole (Silber 2000).

In hearing cases that have challenged the legitimacy of felony disenfranchisement statutes, courts in the United States have repeatedly upheld the right of states to disfranchise felons. In *Green v. Board of Elections*, Justice Friendly asserted:

> It can scarcely be deemed unreasonable for a state to decide that per-petrators of serious crimes shall not take part in electing the legislators who make the laws, the executives who enforce these, the prosecutors who must try them for future violations, or the judges who are to con-sider their cases. This is especially so when account is taken for the heavy incidence of recidivism and the prevalence of organized crime. (*Green v. Board of Elections*, 380 F.2d 445 (2nd Cir. 1976))

Although courts have consistently sided with states when presented with legal challenges to felony disenfranchisement statutes, civil rights chal-lenges regarding felony disenfranchisement laws have resulted in several states changing their laws to include the return of voting rights to certain segments of the disenfranchised felony population.

FELONY DISENFRANCHISEMENT TODAY

Current felony disenfranchisement restrictions in the United States fall into one of five categories: no restriction; restriction while in prison; restriction while in prison and on parole (probationers may vote); restriction while in prison, on probation, and on parole; and permanent restriction for some or all felony offenses. Table 12.1 presents the array of disenfranchisement approaches across the states. Only two states—Maine and Vermont—currently allow all felons to vote, including those who are incarcerated. Those individuals who are permanently restricted from vot-ing make up approximately 45 percent of the disenfranchised population in the United States (Chung 2015).

Between 1997 and 2010, 23 states reformed their laws to expand the franchise to ease voting rights restoration procedures (Porter 2010). Eight states repealed or amended lifetime disenfranchisement laws, 2 states expanded voting rights to persons under community supervision, 10 states eased the restoration process for persons seeking to have their voting rights restored after the completion of a sentence, and 3 states improved data and information sharing to facilitate restoration of the abil-ity to vote. From these policy changes, it is estimated that 800,000 persons have regained the right to vote (Chung 2015).

In addition to the legally disenfranchised population, a number of ex-felons may not be voting because they are under the mistaken belief that they have permanently lost the right to vote due to their felony conviction. Consequently, some ex-felons who are eligible to vote are not participating due to a misunderstanding of the laws in their state. This misunderstanding

Table 12.1
Categories of State Felony Disenfranchisement Restrictions, 2014

		Type of Restriction		
None	While in Prison	While in Prison or on Parole	While in Prison or on Parole or Probation	Permanent for Some or All Offenses
Maine	Hawaii	California	Alaska	Alabama
Vermont	Illinois	Colorado	Arkansas	Arizona
	Indiana	Connecticut	Georgia	Delaware
	Massachusetts	New York	Idaho	Florida
	Michigan		Kansas	Iowa
	Montana		Louisiana	Kentucky
	New Hampshire		Maryland	Mississippi
	North Dakota		Minnesota	Nebraska
	Ohio		Missouri	Nevada
	Oregon		New Jersey	Tennessee
	Pennsylvania		New Mexico	Virginia
	Rhode Island		North Carolina	Wyoming
	Utah		Oklahoma	
			South Carolina	
			South Dakota	
			Texas	
			Washington	
			West Virginia	
			Wisconsin	

Source: Chung 2015.

is attributable not only to the variation in disenfranchisement laws across the states, but also to dramatic changes that have occurred within states.

Florida, for example, has gone through a series of changes to its disenfranchisement policy in the past decade. In 2004, under Governor Jeb Bush, the state adopted civil rights restoration procedures that made the restoration process easier. Felons who had been arrest-free for five years were able to have their rights restored without a hearing, unless they owed restitution or were convicted of violent crimes. Felons who remained arrest-free for 15 years or more could have their rights restored without a hearing, regardless of crime unless they owed restitution. In 2007, under Governor Charlie Crist, automatic civil rights restoration became a reality for nonviolent ex-offenders upon release from prison. Felons no longer had to file a petition for restoration, nor were they required to have a hearing with the Clemency Board. Ex-offenders were automatically reviewed by the Parole Commission to determine their eligibility for restoration of civil rights without a hearing (Florida Commission on Offender Review, n.d.). From 2009 to 2010, 30, 672 ex-offenders had their rights resorted (Florida Parole Commission 2001). Most recently, under Governor Rick Scott, the automatic restoration procedures that were in effect under Governor Crist were rescinded. The new mandates not only required that each clemency application be reviewed by the Clemency Board, but also that an ex-offender wait five to seven years before applying for rights restoration. Under this new policy, 2,462 ex-offenders had their rights restored from 2011 to 2014 (Florida Parole Commission 2015). Beyond the required waiting period, offenders may also face an additional delay in rights restoration due to administrative backlog. In July 2011, the state of Florida reported 89,959 people waiting to have their rights restored. As of July 2014 this number has decreased to 20,258 (Florida Commission on Offender Review 2015).

Similarly, Iowa has undergone dramatic changes to felony disenfranchisement policy. Prior to July 2005, ex-felons were required to submit an application for rights restoration. A recommendation was then received by the governor from the Iowa Board of Parole; the governor then made the final decision regarding voting rights restoration. Through Executive Order 42, issued by former Governor Thomas Vilsack in 2005, the requirement of a voting rights application was eliminated. Executive Order 42 also provided for the retroactive restoration of voting rights for all individuals who had completed their sentences on or before the issuance of Executive Order 42. In 2011, Governor Terry Branstad signed Executive Order 70, which reinstated the application process that existed prior to Executive Order 42.

The way these policy changes are communicated and understood can have a dramatic effect on the likelihood that an eligible ex-offender will register and vote. In a 2014 study of ex-felon voting in Iowa, Maine, and Rhode Island, Meredith and Morse (2014) address the role of misinformation in voter turnout among ex-offenders. They suggest that an ex-felon who is uncertain about his or her right to vote may choose to err on the side of caution. This is especially true given that the punishment for voting when one is not eligible is itself a felony. Much of this uncertainty they attribute not only to the variation and complexity of state laws, but also a lack of accurate information among election administrators and justice officials (Allen 2011; Ewald 2002) and limited effort on the part of candidates, parties, and interest groups to mobilize and inform ex-offenders. Utilizing corrections' records, they find that notifying ex-felons that their voting rights have been restored increases both the likelihood of registration and voting. This is especially true in Rhode Island, where inmates are provided upon release with a voting rights information session during which the opportunity to register to vote is provided.

In addition to a misunderstanding of the laws, ex-felons may also be subject to documentary discrimination. Allen (2011) found that election officials often require documents from those who are attempting to re-register after being identified as ineligible due to a felony conviction that are impossible to obtain. In a 2002–2003 investigation of the administration of felony disenfranchisement laws in New York, Allen (2011) found that election officials in almost half of New York's counties were demanding that individuals with felony convictions provide documentation that they had completed their sentences. Both the "Certificate of Relief" and "Certificate of Good Conduct" can be presented to demonstrate relief from civil disability; however, these are rarely provided to ex-offenders and not readily accessible. In addition, some election boards required a "Certificate of Release," which is a document that does not exist in New York. In response to these findings, the New York State Board of Elections issued a memo to all counties requiring them to change their practices and asserted that "everyone who presents themselves to register, completes the [registration] form and signs the affidavit, is presumed to be eligible and should be registered" (New York State Board of Elections 2003, 1). In a follow-up study, researchers at the Brennan Center for Justice at New York University School of Law found that in spite of the 2003 directive from the New York State Board of Elections, three years later more than one-third of the election boards continued to require documentation. The documentation requested included the nonexistent "Certificate of Release," "a pardon from the court," and a letter from the judge or parole officer. Allen (2011) finds that the requests for documentation are not isolated incidents. During the 2008 presidential election, people in St. Louis, Missouri, who had completed their sentences, were being prevented from registering by election boards that were requiring them to produce "unspecified documents." Similar studies have identified administrative practices and procedures of election officials in New Jersey, Washington, Idaho, and Colorado that diverge from state law and which may be inappropriately disenfranchising ex-offenders. Given this, estimates of the disenfranchised population may not assess the full impact of felony disenfranchisement laws (Hoffman 2003; Manza and Uggen 2004) and the administration of those laws on registration and turnout.

Beyond those who are legally disenfranchised, a study of voter turnout shows that, in states that have the most restrictive disenfranchisement policies, turnout is lower, even among individuals who are legally able to vote (Mauer 2004a). Bowers and Preuhs (2009) find this to be especially true for racial and ethnic minority groups and those with lower socioeconomic status. Mauer (2004a) suggests that reduced turnout among citizens who are eligible to vote may be a consequence of the communal nature of voting. Voting is a task that we engage in together with our families and communities. However, when a substantial number of people in a community are unable to participate, that may reduce the enthusiasm shared by those who are able to vote as well (Mauer 2004a, 616; Burch 2014). Communities with high rates of people with felony convictions have fewer votes to cast. All residents of these neighborhoods, not just those with a felony conviction, become less influential. Disenfranchisement laws are also affecting a large segment of the younger population. The increasing tendency to charge juveniles with adult crimes is causing a greater number of 16- and 17-year-olds to lose the right to vote, in some cases permanently before they are even able to cast their first ballot (Mauer 2004b).

Although all states have a process available for felons to regain their voting rights (civil rights restoration), this process can be misunderstood, complicated, and expensive. The state of Alabama, for example, requires individuals who committed disenfranchising felonies (those of moral turpitude) to seek a pardon from the Board of Pardons and Paroles. In Mississippi, an individual who commits a disenfranchising felony must either secure an executive order from the governor or convince a state legislator to introduce a bill on his/her behalf, obtain a two-thirds majority in the legislature, and have the bill signed by the governor.

FELONY DISENFRANCHISEMENT AND ELECTORAL OUTCOMES

Assessment of the effect of felony disenfranchisement on election outcomes has produced mixed results. When estimating the turnout and the voting preferences of convicted felons, some studies find that felon voters have a strong preference for Democratic candidates in presidential and senatorial elections (Uggen and Manza 2002). Other studies find that the party preferences of offenders closely mirrored those of the general population during the 2000 and 2008 presidential elections (Burch 2011, 2012).

Uggen and Manza (2002) conclude that if felons were allowed to vote, Democrats would have received 7 of every 10 votes cast by felons and ex-felons in 14 of the 15 U.S. Senate elections from 1972 to 2000. The Democratic Party would have gained control of the Senate from 1986 to 2000, which would have resulted in at least two important policy consequences: key Senate committees would have shifted from Republican to Democratic control, and with a shift in the balance of power, the Clinton administration may have been able to gain approval for a greater portion of its federal justice nominees (Uggen and Manza 2002, 794). Further, when considering the outcome of the 2000 presidential election, they find that if disenfranchised felons had been allowed to vote, Gore's margin of victory in the national popular vote would have surpassed 1 million. If disenfranchised felons had been allowed to vote in Florida, Gore would have not only carried the state, but the election (Uggen and Manza 2002, 792). However, not all research regarding felony disenfranchisement and electoral outcomes arrive at this conclusion.

Burch (2011) suggests that expecting ex-offenders to vote at the same rate as everyone else is overly optimistic. When estimating the turnout of ex-felons, we should not consider them to be core voters who vote regularly in every national election. She suggests that ex-felons are peripheral voters, meaning that they are voters who vote occasionally and participate when stimulated or mobilized (Burch 2012). It may be the case that enfranchising offenders will have little effect on turnout because offenders come from a population that generally does not regularly vote. Because of party preferences that vary by demographic characteristics, Burch concludes that disenfranchisement in Florida did not alter the outcome of the 2000 presidential election, but that disenfranchisement may affect future elections especially if the disenfranchised population continues to grow.

Given recent changes that have occurred regarding felony disenfranchisement statutes in the states, it is important to consider public opinion about the inclusion or exclusion of offenders and ex-offenders in the franchise. Two national studies have examined this issue. One (Pinaire, Huemann, and Bilotta 2003) hypothesized that among citizens the "right to vote" would be considered one of the most important rights in a democracy, but expected public support for the "right to vote" to decrease when extending this right to convicted felons was considered. Using a national telephone survey, they found no consensus as to when the right to vote should be restored or removed. 81.7 percent of the individuals surveyed felt that felons should regain their right to vote at some point. 9.9 percent felt felons should never lose the right to vote, 31.6 percent felt felons should lose the right to vote only while incarcerated, 5 percent felt felons should lose the right to vote only while on parole or probation, and, 35.2 percent felt felons should lose the right to vote while incarcerated, on parole, or on probation.

The method of the second study was similar. Using a national telephone survey with 1,000 adult participants, researchers tried to determine the effect of offender status (prison, probation, parole, or ex-felons) and the type of crime committed on public attitudes toward disenfranchisement. Manza, Brooks, and Uggen (2004) found that 80 percent of those who participated in the survey supported restoring voting rights to ex-felons who no longer had any official contact with the criminal justice system, 68 percent supported restoration for probationers, 60 percent supported restoration for parolees, and 31 percent supported the restoration of voting rights for individuals presently incarcerated. When looking at the category of crime committed, there was public support for restoration across a variety of offense types. 63 percent of survey participants support restoration for white-collar offenses, 66 percent support restoration for violent offenses, and 52 percent support restoration for sex crimes. Across crime categories and categories of judicial control, a majority of the public endorsed the restoration of rights for felons and ex-felons, with the exception of those offenders currently incarcerated.

Enfranchisement is a mark of citizenship and participation (Shapiro 1993). Although it is true that disenfranchisement polices have existed in the United States since its founding, changes in punishment philosophy have resulted in an increasing number of American citizens who are temporarily or permanently unable to register and vote. It is also true that, despite the recent changes to state disenfranchisement policies which have created greater opportunity for ex-offenders to register and vote, the United States remains the only democracy in the world that prohibits millions of its voting-age citizens from voting.

FURTHER READING

Allen, Jessie. 2011. "Documentary Disenfranchisement." *Tulane Law Review* 86: 389–464. University of Pittsburgh Legal Studies Research Paper No. 2012-02.

Bowers, Melanie, and Robert Preuhs. 2009. "Collateral Consequences of a Collateral Penalty: The Negative Effect of Felon Disenfranchisement Laws on the Political Participation of Nonfelons." *Social Science Quarterly* 90: 722–743.

Burch, Traci. 2011. "Turnout and the Party Registration among Criminal Offenders in the 2008 General Election." *Law and Society Review* 45: 699–730.

Burch, Traci. 2012. "Did Felony Disenfranchisement Laws Help Elect President Bush? New Evidence on the Turnout Rates and Candidate Preferences of Florida's Ex-Felons." *Political Behavior* 34: 1–26.

Burch, Traci. 2014. "Effect of Imprisonment and Community Supervision on Neighborhood Political Participation in North Carolina."*Annals of the American Academy of Political and Social Science* 651: 184–201.

Chung, Jean. 2015. "Felony Disenfranchisement: A Primer." Washington, DC: The Sentencing Project.

Clegg, Roger. 2001. "Who Should Vote?" *Texas Review of Law and Politics* 6: 157–177.

Ewald, Alec C. 2002. " 'Civil Death': The Ideological Paradox of Criminal Disenfranchisement Law in the United States." *Wisconsin Law Review* 5: 1045–1138.

Florida Commission on Offender Review. n.d. "Executive Clemency Timeline 1991–2015." Retrieved March 30, 2016 from https://www.fcor.state.fl.us/docs/clemency/ClemencyTimeline.pdf.

Florida Commission on Offender Review. 2015. "2015 Annual Report." Retrieved March 31, 2016 from https://www.fcor.state.fl.us/docs/reports/FCORannualreport201415.pdf.

Florida Parole Commission. 2011. "Status Update: Restoration of Civil Rights' (RCR) Cases Granted 2009 and 2010." Retrieved December 15, 2015 from https://www.fcor.state.fl.us/docs/reports/2009-2010ClemencyReport.pdf.

Florida Parole Commission. 2015. "Restoration of Civil Rights' Recidivism Report for 2013 and 2014." Retrieved March 30, 2016 from https://www.fcor.state.fl.us/docs/reports/RecidivismReport2013-2014.pdf.

Green v. Board of Elections of City of New York, 380 F.2d 445 (2d Cir. 1967).

Hoffman, Wayne. 2003. "Some Counties May Not Let Felons Vote." *Idaho States-man*, August 25, 3a.

Keyssar, Alexander. 2000. *The Right to Vote: The Contested History of Democracy in the United States*. New York, NY: Basic Book.

Manza, Jeff, Brooks, Clem, and Christopher Uggen. 2004. "Public Attitudes toward Felony Disenfranchisement in the United States." *Public Opinion Quarterly* 68: 275–286.

Manza, Jeff, and Christopher Uggen. 2004. "Punishment and Democracy: Disen-franchisement of Nonincarcerated Felons in the United States." *Perspectives on Politics* 2 (3): 491–505.

Manza, Jeff, and Christopher Uggen. 2008. *Locked Out: Felon Disenfranchisement and American Democracy*. New York, NY: Oxford University Press.

Mauer, Marc. 2004a. "Thinking about Prison and Its Impact in the Twenty-First Century." *Ohio State Journal of Criminal Law* 2: 607–617.

Mauer, Marc. 2004b. "Political Report: Disenfranchising Felons Hurts Entire Com-munities." Trend Letter: Joint Center for Political and Economic Studies.

Mauer, Marc, and Meda Chesney-Lind. 2002. *Invisible Punishment: The Collateral Consequences of Mass Imprisonment*. New York, NY: New Press.

Meredith, Mark, and Michael Morse. 2014. The Politics of the Restoration of Ex-Felon Voting Rights: The Case of Iowa. Working paper. Retrieved March 30, 2016 from http://www.sas.upenn.edu/~marcmere/working papers/IowaFelons.pdf.

New York State Board of Elections. 2003. Registration of Former Felons [Memorandum], October 29. Albany, NY: New York State Board of Elec-tions. Retrieved March 30, 2016 from https://www.brennancenter.org/ sites/default/files/analysis/NY%208%20Memo%20Registration%20of %20Former%20Felons.pdf.

Pettus, Katherine. 2005. *Felony Disenfranchisement in America: Historical Origins, Institutional Racism, and Modern Consequences*. New York, NY: LFB Scholarly Publications, Inc.

Pinaire, Brian, Huemann, Milton, and Laura Bilotta. 2003. "Barred from the Vote: Public Attitudes toward the Disenfranchisement of Felons." *Fordham Urban Law Journal* 30: 1519–1550.

Porter, Nicole. 2010. "Expanding the Vote: State Felony Disenfranchisement Reform, 1997–2010." Washington, DC: The Sentencing Project.

Reiman, Jeffrey. 1995. *The Rich Get Richer and the Poor Get Prison* (4th ed.). Boston, MA: Allyn & Bacon.

Shapiro, Andrew. 1993. "Challenging Criminal Disenfranchisement under the Voting Rights Act: A New Strategy." *Yale Law Journal*, 103: 537–566.

Silber, John. 2000. "Inmates Shouldn't Vote." *Boston Herald*, October 24, 33.

Uggen, Christopher, and Jeff Manza. 2002. "Democratic Contraction? Political Consequences of Felon Disenfranchisement in the United States." *American Sociological Review* 67: 777–803.

13

Politics of Representation: The Two-Party System

Linda M. Trautman

In contemporary American politics, political parties play a pivotal role in promoting interest in, awareness of, and participation in elections. Political parties are also the architects of the mechanisms that structure American elections. They register voters and nominate candidates to compete for political office. The two-party system is essential in representing the interests of their core base of supporters. However, in recent times, attachments to political parties have waned and a greater number of voters identify as Independent. Recent estimates indicate that about 40 percent of the American electorate identifies as Independent rather than maintaining strong allegiance to either of the two major political parties (Pew Research Center 2015). Trends in American partisanship over time are shown is Figure 13.1, which shows the growth in voters who self-identify as Independent compared to Democrat and Republican across the period 1939–2014.

Over the past several years, the steady decline in party identification among voters is a significant trend that affects voter turnout. Political scientists have long argued that voters with strong partisan and organizational ties are more likely to vote than Independent voters (Campbell et al. 1960; Leighley and Nagler 2013). Party identification is a key

Figure 13.1
Trends in Party Identification, 1939–2014

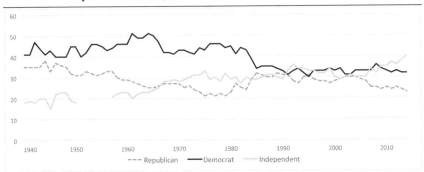

Source: Pew Research Center. 1939–1989 yearly averages from the Gallup Organization interactive website. 1990–2014 yearly totals from Pew Research Center aggregate files. Based on the general public. Data unavailable for 1941. Independent data unavailable for 1951–1956.

psychological factor in fostering political involvement, interest, and participation (Campbell et al. 1960).

Some scholars and pollsters caution, however, that surveys of voter behavior also need to take into account "leaners"—people who describe themselves as Independents for whatever reason but reliably pull the lever for one party or the other when the time comes. "Although independents claim no outright allegiance to either major party, it is well-known that they are not necessarily neutral when it comes to politics," stated one 2015 report by the Gallup polling organization.

> When pressed, most independents will say they lean to one of the two major parties. For example, last year an average of 17% of Americans who initially identified as independents subsequently said they 'leaned' Republican, 15% were independents who leaned Democratic, with the remaining 11% not expressing a leaning to either party. Since partisan leaners often share similar attitudes to those who identify with a party outright, the relative proportions of identifiers plus leaners gives a sense of the relative electoral strength of the two political parties, since voting decisions almost always come down to a choice of the two major-party candidates. In 2014, an average 45% of Americans identified as Democrats or said they were Democratic-leaning independents, while 42% identified as Republicans or were Republican-leaning independents. (Jones 2015, 3)

Several theories and perspectives exist about the apparent detachment from identification with contemporary major U.S. political parties. Some scholars maintain that parties have failed to uphold their collective responsibility of mobilizing the American electorate (Wattenberg 1999). Political scientists have argued that political parties have lost their intensity and strength in terms of activating and maximizing voter participation. Partisan responsiveness, therefore, to voters' preferences and issues have declined in American elections. Scholars such as Alan Abramowitz and Steven Webster have also cited the rise of "negative partisanship" as an important factor. "Measured by self-identification, partisanship is actually declining—growing numbers of Americans describe themselves as 'independent' rather than loyal to one of the parties," explained political pundit Jon Chait.

> But measured by actual voting behavior, the opposite is happening: Straight ticket voting continues to grow. . . . One common explanation is that it has become increasingly vogue, especially among college-educated voters, to describe yourself as independent, which implies that you form educated judgments about politics rather than blindly following the dictates of a party. Abramowitz and Webster add to this by introducing a phenomenon they call *negative partisanship.* That is to say, voters form strong loyalties based more on loathing for the opposing party than on the old kind of tribal loyalty. (Chait 2015, 2)

Based upon American National Election Studies (ANES) data, which is a nationally representative survey conducted by the University of Michigan Research Center since 1948, evidence suggests that major political parties have fallen short in engaging and mobilizing American voters in recent presidential elections. An analysis of the 2012 presidential election indicates a lack of political mobilization of American voters by the major political parties.

The ANES includes a question that asks voters whether or not a political party contacted them during the 2012 presidential election as a measure of party mobilization. The results show that about 52 percent of the electorate reported low party mobilization of voters (no contact), compared to approximately 41 percent who reported mobilization efforts by the major political parties (contact). The lack of partisan mobilization effort is a potential source of voter dissatisfaction with the two-party system. Low levels of mobilization coupled with a continuous decline in partisanship can be contributing to why more people do not vote in American elections. According to Wattenberg (1999), the inability of parties to mobilize voters and lower levels of partisanship have negatively impacted voter turnout.

CLASSIC LITERATURE: DUVERGER'S LAW ON PARTY SYSTEMS

Dominance of the two-party system in American politics has long been recognized by scholars (Schattschneider 1942, 69). The classic understanding of this dominance is reflected in Duverger's Law (Duverger 1959). Adopting a comparative approach to understand the nature of partisan politics, Duverger's Law suggests that the plurality electoral structure (i.e., winner-take-all electoral contests, "first past post") is conducive to the maintenance of a two-party system. Voter dependency upon the two major political parties and the lack of alternative party options play a part in dissuading electoral participation and interest in American elections.

Historically and in contemporary politics, the influence of the major political parties undermines the viability of minor parties also known as "third parties." Minor parties do not succeed under the current two-party electoral system because of the "monopoly of power" by the major political parties and the winner-take-all system (Duverger 1959; Schattschneider 1942). Unlike proportional representational party systems, which more clearly reflect voters' preferences by awarding seats based upon percentage of votes won in an election, minor party candidates are not viewed as serious contenders in American elections.

MINOR PARTIES: BALLOT ACCESS RESTRICTIONS, CAMPAIGN FUNDING, AND THE MEDIA

Partisan representation is significantly limited within the American political system due to the small number of party choices and inherent systematic biases against third parties. Even though many minor parties have emerged over time, they have been less than successful in penetrating the party power structure in the United States. Evidence of this reality is observed by the difficulties third parties experience in gaining ballot access in the 50 states. Such ballot regulations have deep consequences for the extent of voters' choices regarding party candidates.

Ballot access laws are determined by each state and vary widely across states. State-level ballot access rules generally include filing fees and/or nomination petitions accompanied by specific signature requirements and numerical thresholds. In many states, both conditions must be met in order for a candidate's name to appear on the ballot (Streb 2015). A further deterrent for potential minor party candidates is the costs incurred as a result of seeking the required number of signatures by state (if applicable).

Some states have flexible ballot access laws while other states have restrictive ballot access laws. For example, in Colorado, the only ballot access requirement is a $1,000 filing fee and in Louisiana, a $500 filing fee with no signature requirements (Streb 2015). In Arkansas, access to the ballot requires only 1,000 signatures. Conversely, states such as Massachusetts and Missouri require 10,000 signatures for ballot access. Ballot access laws are more stringent in other states: California requires 178,039 signatures for Independent candidates seeking to compete in the 2016 presidential election (Streb 2015). Ohio has also maintained very rigid ballot access laws that date back to the 1968 presidential election and are designed to protect the political standing of the two major parties. During the 1968 election, political tactics were used to prohibit George Wallace's name, a former segregationist governor of Alabama and an Independent minor party candidate, from appearing on the ballot in Ohio.

The Ohio situation generated legal action in the landmark case of *Williams v. Rhodes* (1968). The U.S. Supreme Court resolved the issue and Wallace's name was placed on the ballot. The Court ruled that blocking access to the ballot for third party candidates was a violation of the Equal Protection Clause of the U.S. Constitution and violated the constitutional rights of potential third party voters.

As Streb (2015) notes, recent court rulings on ballot access laws have advantaged the Republican and Democratic parties while suppressing minor party competition. In 2015, a federal District Court decision upheld Ohio ballot access laws that required third parties to collect a total of 28,000 signatures, including 500 each from at least half of Ohio's 16 congressional districts. The Court ruling in this case, *Libertarian Party of Ohio v. Husted*, effectively prevented minor parties such as the Libertarian Party and the Constitution Party from challenging major party candidates in the 2014 election cycle in Ohio. Both minor parties maintained that Ohio ballot access laws were a violation of equal protection rights and were designed to protect incumbents, which are problems commonly associated with ballot access rules. As Streb (2015) notes, recent court rulings on ballot access laws have advantaged the Republican and Democratic parties while suppressing minor party competition. State regulation of ballot access results in less competitive elections and fewer voter choices due to the constraints these laws impose upon minor parties.

Along with stringent state ballot access laws, third party candidates are severely disadvantaged by a lack of financial support and resources. In comparison to the major party candidates, campaign contributors are less likely to donate to the campaigns of minor party candidates because their prospects of winning an election are very low. To overcome this barrier, a few third party candidates have self-financed their political campaigns. In 1992, Ross Perot competed as an Independent candidate and single-handedly funded his campaign. His personal financial investment paid off as he managed to get his name on the ballot in all 50 states, which is a rarity for minor party candidates. A clear departure from the norm for minor party candidates, Perot garnered 19 percent of the popular vote share in the 1992 presidential election. Notwithstanding, third party candidates for president have rarely succeeded in winning more than one-fourth of the popular vote in presidential elections. Perot's candidacy represented the potential impact minor party candidates can have upon American elections when they have access to or acquire the necessary campaign funding and support. Further, it symbolized voter discontent with the major political parties (Rosenstone, Behr, and Lazarus 1996) and the potential threat minor parties can pose for the two-party system (Lee 2012). The public financing system of presidential campaigns also disadvantages minor party candidates. Established as a result of the Federal Election Campaign Act of 1971 and supplemented by additional state requirements, the public financing system established general eligibility requirements for public funding that require candidates to raise campaign funds of $5,000 in contributions of $250 or less in 20 states. Once this condition is met, public funds match individual contributions up to $250 (Hershey and Aldrich 2016). These stipulations contribute to the difficulties that minor parties experience in acquiring public funding. Also, if minor party candidates qualify for public funding, they receive campaign funds later in the presidential campaign season than major party candidates. Major party candidates are eligible for a preelection subsidy. For third party candidates, public funds are dispersed only after the November election and are contingent upon whether the candidate appeared on the ballot in at least 10 states and attracted at least 5 percent of the popular vote.

Minor parties also suffer from a lack of media access and coverage. Given that minor party candidates typically are viewed as less competitive than those representing the two major political parties, minor party candidates experience a difficult time gaining the attention of the media even when campaigning in national elections. Related to media coverage, the rules established by the Presidential Debate Commission present a major challenge for third party candidates. The Presidential Debate Commission is responsible for scheduling and coordinating most of the presidential debates that occur after the Republican and Democratic Party have formally named their candidates for president. Because of the power of the two major parties, rules established by the Presidential Debate Commission usually exclude minor party candidates from participating in televised presidential debates.

Strict ballot rules and lack of campaign funding present a formidable system that has stifled the efforts of minor parties to become viable party alternatives with electable candidates in U.S. elections. Media coverage is lower as a result. Rosenstone, Behr, and Lazarus (1996) state that obstacles have been created to preserve the power and status of major political parties at the expense of third parties. However, lowering such barriers may facilitate the growth of minor party politics in the United States.

MINOR "THIRD" PARTIES AND "WASTED VOTE SYNDROME"

Although minor parties have existed in the United States since the 1800s, they receive very limited support from American voters. On average, minor party candidates win less than 2 percent of the vote in presidential elections. A common explanation as to why third parties acquire less voter support is "wasted vote syndrome" (Allen 2012; Duverger 1959; Hershey and Aldrich 2016). Voters view a vote for minor or third party candidate as "wasteful" because the candidates from these parties have a very small chance of winning an election. Thus, even if a minor party or minor party candidate is a voter's preferred option, the voter will abstain from casting a vote that truly reflects their political preferences. Those votes that are cast for minor party candidates are perceived as taking away pivotal votes from major party candidates. These votes are important because they can sway the outcome of an election. This phenomenon is known as the "spoiler effect." Third parties tend to share at least some of the same ideas and principles of one of the major political parties. As a result, the electoral chances of the major political party candidate(s) whose views more closely reflect the ideals of the minor party candidate are negatively affected. For example, the "spoiler effect" played out during the highly contested 2000 presidential election campaign between Al Gore, the Democratic candidate, and George W. Bush, the Republican candidate. Although the third party candidate Ralph Nader, of the Green Party, received a very small proportion of the vote share (roughly 2 percent), it was perceived that since his Green Party has some ideological tenets similar to the Democratic Party, he hurt Gore far more than Bush. Similarly, during the 1992 presidential campaign, Ross Perot was criticized as potentially taking away votes from the Republican Party because his campaign platform reflected priorities of special resonance to Republican voters, such as fiscal responsibility and accountability, balanced budgets, and deficit reduction. Perot could also be perceived as a centrist candidate because he appealed to voters on both sides of the political aisle. Overall, Perot's candidacy was a direct challenge to the entrenched two-party system. Perot largely drew his electoral support from first-time Independent voters who otherwise would have retreated from voting without a third party option (Gillespie 2012).

ELECTORAL COLLEGE AND MINOR PARTIES
IN PRESIDENTIAL ELECTIONS

Minor parties encounter further hurdles as a result of the Electoral College. The Electoral College allocates electors to each state based on the number of members the state has in the House of Representatives and the Senate. Across the states, state legislators in nearly every state have established rules to allocate electoral votes based upon a winner-take-all system. Maine and Nebraska are exceptions; these states allocate votes using the Congressional District Method. Thus, in 48 of the 50 states, the candidate who wins the largest share of the popular vote secures all of the state's electoral votes, based on this winner-take-all approach. Consequently, it is very difficult for minor parties to win electoral votes. Constraints on minor parties related to the Electoral College are associated with wasted vote syndrome. Since voters generally perceive casting a vote for a minor party candidate as a "wasted vote," minor party candidates have been unsuccessful in capturing electoral votes. Throughout the history of presidential elections, minor parties have won only a small fraction of electoral votes. Since the 1890s, no minor party candidate has received more than 10 percent of the electoral votes in any given presidential election. Perot's candidacy depicts the significant challenge that minor parties experience when competing for electoral votes. Although Ross Perot won almost 20 percent of the popular vote (approximately 19 million votes), he was unable to secure any electors due to the winner-take-all system.

TWO-PARTY SYSTEM VERSUS MULTIPARTY SYSTEM
AND VOTER TURNOUT

In contrast to the winner-take-all system in the United States, minor parties fare better in multiparty parliamentary systems based upon proportional representation. In a proportional representation system, minor parties have a greater chance of electoral success due to allocation of seats based upon the proportion of votes received by parties or candidates in an election. Minor parties tend to achieve some form of representation and influence in multiparty systems. As a result, voters' preferences are more likely to be satisfied in a multiparty parliamentary system. A broader spectrum of views and perspectives within the electorate is accommodated by a variety of viable party choices. Thus, multiparty parliamentary systems are less likely to encounter the problem of the "wasted vote syndrome" (Karp, Banducci, and Bowler 2007, 95) and as a result, levels of political efficacy among voters are usually higher in multiparty electoral systems (Karp and Banducci 2008). Adoption of a multiparty system, however, would challenge the hegemony of the Republican and Democratic parties in the United States.

Although an issue of debate within the literature on comparative electoral systems, research suggests that multiparty parliamentary systems produce higher voter turnout and political participation rates compared to the plurality electoral method (Allen 2012; Grofman and Lipjhart 1986; Hill 2006; Karp, Banducci, and Bowler 2007, 109). Drawing upon survey data, Karp, Banducci, and Bowler (2007, 109) show that voter turnout rates are between 7 and 9 percent higher for multiparty systems. Elections are typically more competitive in multiparty systems compared to a two-party system due to the large number of party options. A multiparty system may also remedy the condition of safe seats and, related in some cases, minority underrepresentation (Allen 2012).

In contrast, the lack of party options under a two-party system limits voter turnout and participation (Schraufnagel 2011; Zipp 1985). A variety of party choices may lead to higher levels of voter engagement and participation. Voters are likely to opt out and make the decision not to vote when party or candidate options do not reflect their interests and preferences. According to Zipp (1985), the decreases in voter turnout in presidential elections since the 1960s are a reflection of poor representation of voters' preferences and issues by the major party candidates. Empirically analyzing the importance of third parties in American politics, Schraufnagel (2011) contends that minor party candidates who offer a viable and serious alternative to the major political parties can promote higher levels of voter turnout and citizen participation in presidential elections. Viable minor party competition and choices beyond the two-party system can lead to greater voter participation.

More recently, an exception to the downward trend in American voter turnout was the 2008 presidential election. The presence of party candidates from traditionally underrepresented groups, such as women and African Americans, facilitated the mobilization of new voters and younger demographic groups. The 2008 presidential election symbolized hope for encouraging party participation and engagement among disaffected groups. Despite these efforts, voter turnout declined from 62 percent in 2008 to 57 percent in the 2012 presidential election. One pattern affecting the 2012 presidential election was the weakening of partisan attachments among the American electorate. Although ANES data indicate that approximately 25 percent of voters strongly identified with the Democratic Party and 12 percent self-identify as Republican, noticeably, roughly about the same percent of respondents identify as weak Democrats (14.7 percent) and weak Republicans (10.5 percent). This suggests that the two major political parties are not as appealing to American voters as they were prior to the 1960s. Evidence suggests that partisan attachments were mildly declining during the late 1960s. The 1970s marked a critical period of an increase in the number of Independent voters. The number of voters identifying as Pure Independents suggests that a

Table 13.1
Party Identification, 1960 and 2012 Presidential Elections

Party Identification	1960 (percent)	2012 (percent)
Strong Democrat	22.6	25.1
Weak Democrat	23.8	14.7
Independent-leaning Democrat	6.0	12.6
Independent	8.9	13.4
Independent-leaning Republican	6.2	10.3
Weak Republican	13.7	10.5
Strong Republican	14.7	12.9

Source: 2012 National Election Study (Center for Political Studies), University of Michigan; National Election Study Cumulative File, 1948–2012.

proportion of the electorate does not feel a strong connection with the two major parties (see Table 13.1). The results show that a greater number of voters identified as Pure Independents in the 2012 presidential election compared to the 1960 presidential election. About 13 percent of respondents identified as Pure Independents in 2012, compared to about 8.9 percent in 1960. Such reality has important implications for American democracy particularly because, historically, political scientists have observed partisanship to be the most stable predictor of political participation and engagement. Voter involvement and participation will likely continue to suffer unless viable and diverse party and voter choices are offered within the American electoral system.

FURTHER READING

Abramowitz, Alan, and Steven Webster. 2015. "All Politics Is National: The Rise of Negative Partisanship and the Nationalization of U.S. House and Senate Elections in the 21st Century." Stevenwebster.com. Retrieved January 14, 2016 from http://stevenwwebster.com/research/all_politics _is_national.pdf.

Allen, Christopher. 2012. "The Case for a Multi-Party U.S. Parliament?" In *Annual Editions: Comparative Politics 12/13*, edited by Fiona Yap, 167–175. New York, NY: McGraw-Hill Higher Education.

Campbell, Angus, Converse, Philip, Miller, Warren, and Donald Stokes. 1960. *The American Voter*. Chicago, IL: University of Chicago Press.

Chait, Jonathan. 2015. "How 'Negative Partisanship' Has Transformed American Politics." *New York Intelligencer* [online], April 17. Retrieved January 14, 2015 from http://nymag.com/daily/intelligencer/2015/04/negative -partisanship-has-transformed-politics.html.

Duverger, Maurice. 1959. *Political Parties, Their Organization and Activity in the Modern State*. London: Methuen & Co.

Gillespie, David. 2012. *Challengers to Duopoly: Why Third Parties Matter in American Two-Party Politics.* Columbia: University of South Carolina Press.

Grofman, Bernard, and Arend Lipjhart. 1986. *Electoral Laws and Their Consequences.* New York, NY: Agathon Press.

Gryskiewicz, Jon. 2013. "Williams v. Rhodes: How One Candidate, One State, One Week, and One Justice Shaped Ballot Access Law." *The Journal of Law and Politics* 28: 185–229.

Hershey, Majorie, and John Aldrich. 2016. *Party Politics in America.* New York, NY: Routledge.

Hill, David. 2006. *American Voter Turnout: An Institutional Perspective.* Boulder, CO: Westview Press.

Jones, Jeffrey M. 2015. "In U.S., New Record 43% Are Political Independents." Gallup.com, January 7. Retrieved January 14, 2016 from http://www.gallup.com/poll/180440/new-record-political-independents.aspx.

Karp, Jeffery, Banducci, Susan, and Shaun Bowler. 2007. "Getting Out the Vote: Party Mobilization in a Comparative Perspective." *British Journal of Political Science* 38: 91–112.

Karp, Jeffery, and Susan Banducci. 2008. "Political Efficacy and Participation in Twenty-Seven Democracies: How Electoral Systems Shape Political Behaviour." *British Journal of Political Science* 38: 311–334.

Lee, Daniel. 2012. "Major Party Positioning and Third Party Threat." *Political Research Quarterly* 65: 138–150.

Leighley, Jan, and Jonathan Nagler. 2013. *Who Votes Now? Demographics, Issues, Inequality and Turnout in the United States.* Princeton, NJ: Princeton University Press.

Pew Research Center. 2015. "A Deep Dive into Party Affiliation: Sharp Differences by Race, Gender, Generation, Education." Pewresearch.org, April 7. Retrieved September 25, 2015 from http://www.people-press.org/2015/04/07/a-deep-dive-into-party-affiliation.

Rosenstone, Steven, Behr, Roy, and Edward Lazarus. 1996. *Third Parties in America: Citizen Response to Major Party Failure.* Princeton, NJ: Princeton University Press.

Schattschneider, E. E. 1942. *American Government in Action: Party Government.* New York, NY: Farrar and Rhinehart.

Schraufnagel, Scot. 2011. *Third Party Blues: The Truth and Consequences of Two-Party Dominance.* New York, NY: Routledge.

Streb, Matthew. 2015. *Rethinking American Electoral Democracy* (3rd ed.). New York, NY: Routledge.

Sundquist, James. 1983. *Dynamics of the Party System: Alignment and Realignment of Political Parties in the United States.* New York, NY: The Brookings Institution.

Wattenberg, Martin. 1999. *The Decline of American Political Parties: 1952–1996.* Cambridge, MA: Harvard University Press.

Williams v. Rhodes. (1968) 393 U.S. 23.

Zipp, John. 1985. "Perceived Representativeness and Voting: An Assessment of the Impact of Choices vs. Echoes." *American Political Science Review* 79: 50–61.

14

Geography of Representation: Gerrymandering, Representation, and Turnout

Christopher N. Lawrence

Gerrymandering, the manipulation of geographic political boundaries for political advantage, is almost as old as representative government itself. By changing the boundaries of districts to favor the representation of some interests over others, gerrymandering may influence not only who is elected but also what policies are put in place. Usually, gerrymandering is considered in the context of creating districts for state legislatures or the U.S. House of Representatives, but gerrymandering can also take place in drawing districts for other multimember bodies such as city councils, school boards, county commissions or boards of supervisors, and even judicial bodies such as state supreme courts. Because redistricting must take place every 10 years in response to changing population trends, there are perennial opportunities for state legislatures to engage in gerrymandering.

The term "gerrymandering" was first used in 1812, in reference to a plan for redrawing district boundaries for the Massachusetts State Senate during the administration of Governor Elbridge Gerry. The plan included a district with a number of towns that, together, were said to appear like a salamander partially encircling several others, in a shape vaguely similar to that of a salamander. Hence, the rather lengthy "Gerry's salamander" was abbreviated as "gerrymander," and a new word was born.

Just because a legislative district has unusual boundaries, however, does not necessarily mean it is the result of gerrymandering. Many natural features, such as rivers and ridgelines, have quite convoluted shapes, as do boundaries of cities, counties, and states that follow these and other natural features. The settlement patterns of citizens, as affected by the natural environment, can also appear to be the product of a deliberate, convoluted design rather than random happenstance. Further, it is important to distinguish between gerrymandering and partisan determination of the geographic boundaries of political participation. The latter is the norm in American states and localities; the most common methods used to determine political boundaries require either that state legislatures or local elected bodies draw boundary lines, or that these bodies approve plans drawn by other groups (Hale, Montjoy, and Brown 2015). The essence of gerrymandering is the manipulation of boundaries between districts to achieve a political end, and although the shapes of districts can suggest that manipulation has taken place, the shapes do not tell the full story.

TYPES OF GERRYMANDERS

Three major forms of gerrymandering can be identified. Historically, the most obvious and common form would be *partisan* gerrymandering: creating districts to favor the election of one party's candidates over those of other parties. The original gerrymander itself was part of a partisan redistricting plan for the State Senate of Massachusetts: Gerry and his fellow Democratic-Republicans sought to preserve as many seats for their party as possible, despite their party's declining popularity at the time due to the impending War of 1812, which was supported by the Democratic-Republicans, but unpopular in New England and opposed by the Federalist Party. Although the political landscape of American politics has evolved over the past two centuries, the partisan gerrymander remains alive and well today.

The second form is *incumbent-protection* gerrymandering. The goal of protecting incumbents is a bit different than a partisan gerrymander, as the purpose is to ensure as many incumbents as possible are reelected, regardless of their party affiliations. There are two major reasons why an incumbent-protection approach might be taken. First, it might be the only way to ensure the redistricting plan will pass, particularly if one chamber of the state legislature is controlled by one party while the other is controlled by their opponents or to avoid a possible veto if the governor is from the opposing major party. Incumbent protection would presumably satisfy the greatest number of representatives. A second reason for this approach is to preserve the power and influence of incumbent politicians. Long-time incumbents generally have both greater formal and informal power in the lawmaking process than newly-elected representatives; for example, in the U.S. House of Representatives, key positions like committee chairs and party leadership jobs are awarded in part based on the seniority of lawmakers. In most states, the state legislatures design the districts for members of the U.S. House; thus, state lawmakers can help their state receive benefits and attention from the federal government by ensuring that representatives remain in office and gain seniority regardless of party affiliation.

The third form is *racial* or *ethnic* gerrymandering, which refers to the practice of designing districts to favor or harm the prospects of particular racial or ethnic group interests. Historically, gerrymandering was one of the techniques used to effectively disenfranchise minority groups, even in states and localities where minorities were able to exercise the right to vote. By designing districts that *diluted* the voting strength of minorities— dividing their population in such a way that they would be outnumbered in most or all of the districts available—white politicians were able to maintain political power even in circumstances where there was a substantial minority voting population. Alternatively, most minority voters could be *packed* into a small number of districts, ensuring that although some minority representatives would be elected, they would be greatly outnumbered by those elected from districts with few minority voters. More recently, gerrymandering for racial and ethnic purposes has been used to *increase* minority representation, as discussed below.

THE EVOLUTION OF THE GERRYMANDER

Three major developments in American history have combined to increase the use of gerrymandering in recent decades. The first development was a change in the Supreme Court's willingness to involve itself in disputes over legislative redistricting. Until the 1960s, the federal courts generally avoided getting involved in disputes over the drawing of legislative districts, suggesting that these disputes were political questions that were to be decided by the states under their authority to create districting plans. For much of this period, state redistricting plans resulted in *malapportionment*, or legislative districts with wildly unequal populations, which typically enhanced the voting power of rural areas and reduced the voting power of cities and their suburbs. Often these districts had been frozen in place for decades, so they failed to account for population growth and the greater urbanization of the electorate. State legislatures also often had upper legislative chambers or voting rules that gave counties an equal voice regardless of their population, such as Georgia's "county unit system" rules that tended to allow the interests of a minority of voters to regularly prevail over those of the majority of the population.

A series of Supreme Court cases (most famously, *Baker v. Carr* in 1962) ruled that districts for representative bodies and other voting rules had to provide each voter with an equal opportunity for influence. This "one person, one vote" standard required that district populations had to be nearly equal, and districts needed to be redrawn regularly to ensure that this standard was maintained. The new standard also meant that legislative chambers that had been based on "one county, one vote" had to be redesigned to have approximately the same number of voters per representative, creating new opportunities for gerrymandering where they had not existed before. At the time, some states also had legislative chambers (typically their upper house) that gave each county an equal number of representatives; these court decisions also rejected those plans.

A second major development was the passage of the Voting Rights Act (VRA) in 1965, its subsequent amendments, and judicial interpretations of these. The VRA required that states take steps to ensure that African Americans (and, later, other minority racial and ethnic groups) had the ability to register to vote and cast their ballot free from discrimination in the election process. Judicial interpretations struck down voting rules that reduced minority voting strength including vote dilution. The Supreme Court ruling in *Thornburg v. Gingles* (1986) allowed minority voters to challenge redistricting plans when states or local governments failed to create opportunities for minority citizens to elect their preferred candidates to public office.

The third major development was the increased availability of computer-based systems to assist in the redistricting process. Before the 1980s, computers were generally used for large-scale scientific, military, and commercial applications, but the invention of the microprocessor and the introduction of (relatively) inexpensive desktop and workstation computers that could be operated without specialized training made new applications of computers possible. The development in particular of geographic information systems (GIS) software, that connected computer databases with mapping capabilities, made it possible for politicians, judges, interest groups, and even private citizens to consider a much greater variety of potential redistricting plans than would have been possible even a decade earlier. With redistricting no longer a process that required arduous manual computations for each permutation of a plan, it became much easier to consider a large number of plans in intricate detail and thus substantially easier to find an "optimal" plan that met particular criteria.

The confluence of these three factors led to increased opportunity and impetus for gerrymandering beginning in the 1980s. The one person, one vote standard—applied particularly strictly to districting for the U.S. House of Representatives—meant that plans that had bizarre or unusual boundaries could more easily be justified with the reasoning that a "simpler" plan that followed traditional geographic boundaries such as city and county lines would lead to unequal districts. The availability of GIS software allowed the consideration of many more potential districting plans than historically might have been the case. In addition, the VRA's requirements for the creation of districts that would afford members of minority groups an opportunity to elect the representative of their choice meant that Republicans and African American Democrats had an incentive to work together to maximize the number of "majority-minority" districts in which minority voters would form the majority of voters. These majority-minority districts would increase the number of black and Hispanic representatives in many states, but they would also (by reducing the number of black and Hispanic voters, who tend to support Democrats, in surrounding districts) weaken Democratic incumbents from surrounding districts.

The redistricting cycle following the 1990 census saw the culmination of these three factors. The 1990s also saw legal challenges to particularly bizarre redistricting plans, particularly in southern states. The 12th District of North Carolina was one notoriously gerrymandered district, stretching from Charlotte to Durham in an effort to fuse black neighborhoods in several midsized cities into one district. This district was the subject of the U.S. Supreme Court's ruling in *Shaw v. Reno* (1993). Figure 14.1 illustrates the 12th District of North Carolina as it appeared in 1992.

In this case, the Court decided that race-based redistricting plans would have to be justified under the "strict scrutiny" standard, which is the most stringent judicial standard used in discrimination cases and which is applied by the courts more generally in cases where the government makes classifications based on race or ethnicity. Since this decision, the courts have almost always rejected redistricting plans that appear to use race as the sole criterion for deciding boundaries; however, they have continued to give states wide discretion to implement partisan and incumbent-protection gerrymanders. In practice, this also means that at least some racially-motivated gerrymanders can be implemented as well, given the strong support for Democrats among minority voters, particularly among African Americans. In much of the country, a plan that effectively packs black citizens into a small number of districts would have the same effect and appearance as a plan that packs Democrats in a similar way. Although the partisan loyalties of members of other minority groups are somewhat more divided, a districting plan in the southwestern United States that favors Democrats would often also favor candidates preferred by Hispanics as well. Figure 14.2 presents one illustration of the configurations that can result; the current 4th District of Illinois is

Figure 14.1
North Carolina 12th Congressional District

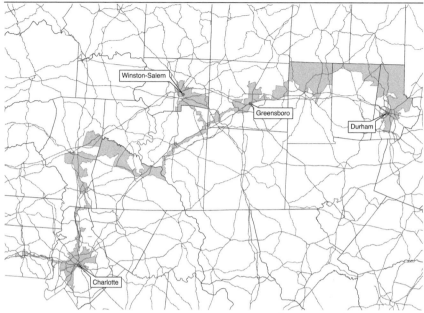

Source: Author's creation based on data from 2015 TIGER/Line® Shapefiles, U.S. Census Bureau, https://www.census.gov/geo/maps-data/data/tiger-line.html.

designed to comply with the VRA by affording Hispanics in the Chicago area an opportunity to elect representatives of their choice, linking disparate Latino/a neighborhoods on the north and south sides of the city and separated by major highways and waterways.

In the 2000s a new round of redistricting took place after the 2000 census; inevitably, some of these plans were the result of gerrymandering. Texas found itself at the center of controversy after engaging in mid-decade redistricting after Republicans gained control of both chambers of the state legislature for the first time since Reconstruction. The U.S. Constitution does not forbid states from redistricting more frequently than once a decade, and states have previously had to return to the proverbial drawing board and engage in mid-decade redistricting after court orders have required the revision of redistricting plans. However, the decision by state Republicans to adopt a new plan without any legal obligation to do so raised eyebrows. Texas Republicans argued that the existing plan (implemented by court order after the legislature was unable to pass a redistricting plan in time for the 2002 midterm elections) unfairly overrepresented Democrats; only 15 of Texas's 32 seats (47 percent) in the U.S. House of Representatives in that election had

Figure 14.2
Illinois 4th Congressional District

Source: Author's creation based on data from 2015 TIGER/Line® Shapefiles, U.S. Census Bureau,
https://www.census.gov/geo/maps-data/data/tiger-line.html.

been won by the GOP, despite Republicans winning 55 percent of the
two-party vote in those elections (Trandahl 2003). The Republican
proposal and the plan adopted—which was challenged in court and
with partial success—was clearly designed to favor the fortunes of
the GOP; after the 2004 election, 21 of the 32 seats (67 percent) were
held by Republicans despite a vote share similar to that in 2002 (Trandahl 2005). Figure 14.3 illustrates the final plan as it applied to the
areas surrounding Houston; the 2nd District is an example of partisan
efforts to unify Republican-leaning Houston suburbs. No other states
decided to follow Texas's lead and attempt a mid-decade redistricting
plan.

The Texas episode and the 2010 redistricting cycle led to renewed public attention to the issue of gerrymandering. A 2010 documentary film,
aptly entitled *Gerrymandering*, also helped to increase public interest in
the topic. Clearly there is a public perception that the manipulation of district boundaries for political gain is unseemly. However, political scientists
and legal scholars are more concerned with finding solid evidence of gerrymandering's effects.

Figure 14.3
Texas 2nd Congressional District

Source: Author's creation based on data from 2015 TIGER/Line® Shapefiles, U.S. Census Bureau, https://www.census.gov/geo/maps-data/data/tiger-line.html.

THE POLITICAL IMPACT OF GERRYMANDERING

Determining the political impact of gerrymandering has not always been straightforward. Although the use of gerrymandering since the 1980s to weaken the position of moderate southern Democrats has been well documented, and gerrymandering appears to have increased the average margin of victory for incumbent politicians in general, other effects have proved more difficult to document. For example, although many scholars and pundits believe that gerrymandering has contributed to greater political *polarization*—greater ideological differences between elected officials affiliated with the two major parties—the evidence for this connection has been weak to nonexistent.

However, that is not to say that gerrymandering lacks any political effects. Successful gerrymanders affect political representation by altering who gets elected and who does not; depending on the intent of the gerrymander, this effect can lead to greater reelection rates for incumbent politicians, disproportionate representation for a party compared to its share of the vote, or an alteration of the racial and ethnic composition of the representative body. These effects, in turn, may alter the balance of power in the legislature or affect the fortunes of future legislative proposals quite markedly.

Gerrymandering may also affect the future political fortunes of politicians from gerrymandered legislative districts. A state legislator or member of the U.S. House of Representatives who has served a district in which there was little meaningful competition may not be well prepared if he or she seeks statewide office like a governorship or U.S. Senate seat or (particularly) the presidency, where a more vigorous campaign is virtually certain to take place. The failure of representatives from gerrymandered districts to be "battle tested" by serious competition from the other party may help account for the relatively poor showing of minority candidates, particularly Democrats, with legislative experience who have attempted to win statewide and national contests in recent decades.

Gerrymandering may also have substantial effects on voter turnout. Voter participation is encouraged by vigorous election campaigns, particularly in the general election (Hillygus 2005; Iyengar and Simon 2000). In gerrymandered legislative districts, particularly those designed to favor the reelection of incumbents, the prospect of a serious general election challenge can be limited when the electorate has been tailored to favor the incumbent party or candidate's reelection. Thus, gerrymandering may have a serious impact on voter participation, particularly in midterm, special, and off-year elections when the hoopla of a national presidential campaign is not available to help mobilize voters. For example, in the 2014 midterm elections for the House of Representatives, on average a substantially higher voter turnout rate was observed in districts that had a more competitive general election campaign. On average, for each percentage point less competitive the general election campaign was, the expected voter turnout rate was 0.16 percent lower. These estimates suggest, all things being equal, that in an election where the margin of victory was only one vote (the most highly competitive election), the expected turnout rate would be 41 percent. In addition, in an election where the leading candidate wins overwhelmingly (the least competitive election), the expected turnout rate would be approximately 33 percent. In other words, nearly 1 of every 10 (8 percent) voters would stay home in the less competitive election.

Gerrymandered districts may also be harder for candidates to effectively campaign in. For example, the 12th District of North Carolina as originally established in 1992 (and litigated in *Shaw v. Reno*) included voters in three major urban areas (Charlotte, Winston-Salem/Greensboro, and Durham) and in three separate television media markets. Television advertising is one of the greatest expenses for political campaigns, and thus, advertising in three media markets (each of which contained thousands of viewers who were not in the 12th District) would be much more

Figure 14.4
Florida 5th Congressional District

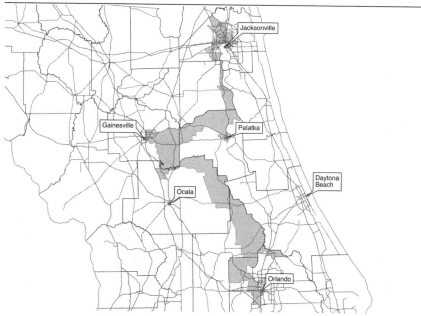

Source: Author's creation based on data from 2015 TIGER/Line® Shapefiles, U.S. Census Bureau, https://www.census.gov/geo/maps-data/data/tiger-line.html.

expensive for a candidate in that district than for a candidate whose district was included in just one market. Radio and print advertising is also similarly market-based rather than following district boundaries. This effect may be particularly pronounced for challengers, who lack the name recognition of incumbents and often are at a financial disadvantage compared to incumbent candidates. A less compact district is likely to also require more travel for candidates to successfully engage in the "retail politics" of meeting voters and holding campaign rallies. Figure 14.4 presents an example. The 5th District of Florida is a current district with an African American majority that requires candidates to campaign in three television markets—Gainesville, Jacksonville, and Orlando—along with sparsely populated areas of North Central Florida.

In recent years, a number of states have attempted to reduce the political influence on redistricting and thus decrease the use of gerrymandering, by either establishing independent commissions for redistricting or placing greater legal constraints on the redistricting plans that state legislatures can adopt. However, these changes have not been universal, and in the absence of strong political pressure from citizens on politicians in state legislatures to cede the power to draw both congressional and state districts, it seems unlikely that they would give up such a potent political tool voluntarily.

Even where they have been incorporated into law, efforts to reform the redistricting process have not been without controversy. The status of Arizona's independent redistricting commission was thrown into turmoil in 2011 when the Republican-controlled legislature, at the urging of state governor Jan Brewer, impeached and removed the chair of the commission after it released a preliminary redistricting plan that appeared to favor the election of Democrats. Although the state Supreme Court restored the chair to office, legal challenges to the authority of the commission were only settled by a U.S. Supreme Court decision in 2015 that ruled the initiative creating the commission was constitutionally permissible (*Arizona State Legislature v. Arizona Independent Redistricting Commission*, 576 US ___). In California, allegations arose in late 2011 that allegedly "Independent" witnesses who had testified before that state's redistricting commission concealed their ties to interest groups associated with both major parties in an effort to manipulate the commission's decision-making process. Florida's Congressional redistricting plans were thrown out by state courts in 2014 after it was alleged that the state legislature had not complied with requirements introduced in a 2010 state initiative for fair and equitable redistricting. These events suggest that controversies over redistricting and gerrymandering will not go away, even if reformers succeed in more states or at the national level.

FURTHER READING

Canon, David T. 1999. *Race, Redistricting, and Representation: The Unintended Consequences of Black Majority Districts*. Chicago, IL: University of Chicago Press.

Galderesi, Peter F., ed. 2005. *Redistricting in the New Millenium*. Lanham, MD: Lexington Books.

Hale, Kathleen, Robert Montjoy, and Mitchell Brown. 2015. *Administering Elections: How American Elections Work*. New York, NY: Palgrave MacMillan.

Hillygus, D. Sunshine. 2005. "Campaign Effects and the Dynamics of Turnout Intention in Election 2000." *Journal of Politics* 67 (1): 50–68.

Iyengar, Shanto, and Adam F. Simon. 2000. "New Perspectives and Evidence on Political Communication and Campaign Effects." *Annual Review of Psychology* 51 (1): 149–169.

Lublin, David. 1999. *The Paradox of Representation: Racial Gerrymandering and Minority Interests in Congress*. Princeton, NJ: Princeton University Press.

Miller, William J., and Jeremy D. Walling. 2013. *The Political Battle over Congressional Redistricting*. Lanham, MD: Lexington Books.

Trandahl, Jeff. 2003. "Statistics of the Presidential and Congressional Election of November 5, 2002." Retrieved July 14, 2015 from http://clerk.house.gov/member_info/electionInfo/2002election.pdf.

Trandahl, Jeff. 2005. "Statistics of the Presidential and Congressional Election of November 2, 2004." Retrieved July 14, 2015 from http://clerk.house.gov/member_info/electionInfo/2004election.pdf.

Winburn, Jonathan. 2008. *The Realities of Redistricting: Following the Rules and Limiting Gerrymandering in State Legislative Redistricting*. Lanham, MD: Lexington Books.

15

Dynamics of Direct Democracy and Voter Turnout

Dominic D. Wells

The initiative, referendum, and recall are major political reforms that date from the Progressive Era (1890–1920), meant to provide citizens with direct involvement in policymaking as an alternative to relying on the choices made by state legislatures as representative decision-making bodies. Direct democracy methods such as these were intended to empower average citizens and allow them to make policy decisions by bypassing the political establishment and powerful interest groups.

It was initially believed that direct democracy would increase American engagement in politics and weaken the power of elected officials and interest groups. A century later, however, many states still do not allow citizens to use the initiative, referendum, and recall to address political grievances or advance political goals. Table 15.1 lists the states that have each form of direct democracy. Studies of direct democracy show that in states with the initiative, referendum, and/or recall, there is a modest positive effect on voter turnout at best. Direct democracy campaigns have become very expensive and professionalized, allowing special interests to capture the process and undermine the initial intent of the reforms. The dynamics of the process may help explain why direct democracy reforms have not greatly mobilized American voters.

Table 15.1
States with Direct Democracy Provisions

State	Initiative	Referendum	Recall
Alaska	X	X	X
Arizona	X	X	X
Arkansas	X	X	–
California	X	X	X
Colorado	X	X	X
Florida	X	–	–
Georgia	–	–	X
Idaho	X	X	X
Illinois	X	–	X
Kansas	–	–	X
Louisiana	–	–	X
Maine	X	X	–
Maryland	–	X	–
Massachusetts	X	X	–
Michigan	X	X	X
Minnesota	–	–	X
Mississippi	X	–	–
Missouri	X	X	–
Montana	X	X	X
Nebraska	X	X	–
Nevada	X	X	X
New Jersey	–	–	X
New Mexico	–	X	–
North Dakota	X	X	X
Ohio	X	X	–
Oklahoma	X	X	–
Oregon	X	X	X
Rhode Island	–	–	X
South Dakota	X	X	–
Utah	X	X	–
Washington	X	X	X
Wisconsin	–	–	X
Wyoming	X	X	–
Total Number	24	23	19

Source: National Conference of State Legislatures.

DIRECT DEMOCRACY AND THE PROGRESSIVE ERA

During the Progressive Era, many citizens asserted that electoral politics had become strongly controlled by interest groups and elected representatives who were unresponsive to the will of ordinary citizens. In response, political reformers advocated for the adoption of direct democracy mechanisms to circumvent political parties and allow the public to decide policy issues. From 1898 to 1996, 33 states adopted forms of direct democracy (National Conference of State Legislatures 2015). The practice became embedded in the culture of the United States, especially in the West. The initiative, referendum, and recall all enable citizens to circumvent the political power of parties and interest groups through the collection of a specified number of signatures on petitions, which allow them to put legislative measures directly on the ballot. The initiative allows citizens to write legislation and place it on a ballot for public vote. The referendum allows citizens to vote on the modification, elimination, or maintenance of legislation that has already been passed by the legislature. The recall allows citizens to hold a special election, forcing an elected representative to run for their office again before their term is over. These reforms were innovations of the Progressive Era (Goebel 2002).

Progressive reformers had high expectations for direct democracy to clean up corruption and fix the system of representative democracy, which they viewed as a failure. They believed that through direct democracy the people would act collectively to educate themselves about issues and would collectively vote in their own interests. Soon after states adopted direct democracy measures, it was evident that the referendum, initiative, and recall would fall short of the high expectations of reformers. Many states did not experience more civic engagement or a more politically educated public (Goebel 2002).

Direct democracy may not have lived up to the high expectations of Progressive Era reformers, but it nonetheless gave the public additional mechanisms for self-governing. The 1930s was an era characterized by the increased use of the ballot initiative. The decade saw a total of 246 ballot initiatives. The use of ballot initiatives dropped dramatically in the 1940s, 1950s, and 1960s, before experiencing a slow resurgence in the early 1970s.

A major event in the history of direct democracy in the United States occurred in 1978 with California's Proposition 13 (Prop 13). The initiative was a part of a revolt against rising property taxes. Prop 13 placed a cap on future property tax increases in California and the public voted overwhelmingly in favor of the initiative, though business interests and the political establishment were strongly against it. Notwithstanding the policy outcome, Prop 13 was a major victory for grassroots efforts against special interests and the political establishment (Goebel 2002). In many regards, the success of Prop 13 is generally accepted as the beginning of the modern direct democracy movement as the number of initiatives and referenda has expanded considerably in subsequent elections.

The direct democracy reforms of the Progressive Era continue to be used today. Though business interests have often found themselves on the defensive, when it comes to direct democracy campaigns, direct democracy has been subject to the same dynamics that affect other types of political campaigns. Money is especially important as it takes a lot to collect signatures and pay for television and radio advertisements (Goebel 2002). The massive amount of money necessary to compete in a direct democracy campaign has limited the influence of grassroots campaigns and allowed special interests to continue to play a large role.

For example, in 2012, Wisconsin governor Scott Walker was forced into a recall election after citizens and labor union interests collected signatures in response to the curbing of collective bargaining rights for public sector union workers. About $33 million was spent on the recall campaign with special interests such as the Republican Governors Association, Americans for Prosperity, Wisconsin Manufacturers and Commerce, the American Federation of State, County, and Municipal Employees (AFSCME), the American Federation of Labor, and the Congress of Industrial Organizations (AFL-CIO), each contributing over a million dollars (Hirschkorn and Cordes 2012). In a similar collective bargaining case, a referendum was held in Ohio for the public to decide whether a bill curbing the collective bargaining rights of public employees should become law. Labor union interest groups raised millions in a successful effort to defeat the collective bargaining law; the largest contributions came from teachers' unions (Siegel and Vardon 2011).

DIRECT DEMOCRACY AND VOTER TURNOUT

It is reasonable to think, as many did, that allowing citizens to vote directly on legislation would increase voter turnout. One might think that people do not vote because they feel disconnected from the policy process. Direct democracy brings the legislative process to the public and allows them to decide on individual policies, rather than working indirectly through a system of representation. The exact impact of the initiative, referendum, and recall remains unclear.

Scholars have studied the impact of direct democracy on turnout using the number of initiatives (or referendums) on a ballot in states that permit the initiative process. It is expected that a greater number of initiatives on the ballot during an election would lead to greater voter turnout. Studies do show a positive relationship between the number of initiatives and voter turnout in some elections, but not all. There is evidence of a positive relationship for specific elections throughout the 1990s (Smith and Tolbert 2004; Tolbert, McNeal, and Smith 2003). There is also some evidence of a positive relationship for elections in the 2000s (Tolbert, Bowen, and Donovan 2009). However, positive relationships are not found in all elections and there is some evidence that the impact of direct democracy on voter turnout is larger for midterm election years than presidential election years (Smith and Tolbert 2004; Tolbert and Smith 2005). Studies that find a relationship between the number of initiatives and voter turnout estimate the impact to be anywhere from half of 1 percent to 4 percent for each initiative on the ballot.

In an effort to understand the lack of consistency between the initiative and voter turnout, scholars have questioned whether all initiatives are created equal. It may not be the number of ballot initiatives that determines whether more citizens decide to vote, but instead it may be the content of the ballot initiative that is important. Salient issues may bring citizens to the polls more than other issues. An issue is salient when it is considered well known and important to the general public. For example, a ballot initiative to legalize recreational marijuana may be considered salient because the issue is featured in the news and the public is generally aware. However, an initiative to increase the retirement age of state Supreme Court justices may not be considered salient because it may not be featured in the news and the general public may not know or care about the issue. There is some evidence that the content of the ballot initiative is an important indicator of its impact on voter turnout. An increase in the number of initiatives dealing with social issues, such as same-sex marriage, drug legalization, or abortion, are associated with higher turnout in all midterm elections and some presidential elections (Biggers 2011).

In sum, there is evidence that the number of initiatives on the ballot in an election has a positive impact on voter turnout, though most studies find that the impact is modest. The relationship between the number of initiatives and turnout is generally stronger for midterm elections than it is for presidential elections. This is likely because turnout in presidential election years is higher than turnout in midterm election years. Initiatives cannot mobilize people to the polls to vote in elections in which they are already planning to vote. Additionally, not all initiatives have the same impact on voter turnout. Highly salient social issues tend to motivate people to the polls at a higher rate than other issues.

The recall is a less commonly used form of direct democracy. On only 38 occasions since 1913 have citizens gathered enough signatures to force a recall election for state legislators. On only three occasions have citizens gathered enough signatures to force a recall election for governor. Two of the three governors recalled, Lynn Frazier in North Dakota (1921) and Gray Davis in California (2003), lost their recall elections. Wisconsin Governor Scott Walker (2012) became the first recalled governor to survive a recall election. Currently, 19 states along with the District of Columbia permit the recall of state officials (National Conference of State Legislatures 2013).

The limited number of recall elections makes drawing any conclusions on the impact of the recall on voter turnout difficult. However, the two most recent recall elections of governors did have high voter turnout. Turnout in the recall of California Governor Gray Davis was about

60 percent. This was 9 percent higher than the previous election won by Governor Davis in 1999 (Finnegan 2003). The recall election of Wisconsin Governor Scott Walker saw the highest turnout in the state for a nonpresidential election in more than 60 years (Gilbert 2012). Citizens may have been more inclined to go to the polls for these high profile recall elections because they received media coverage nationwide.

Even if direct democracy lived fully up to the initial expectations of mobilizing citizens, it is important to note that many states do not allow initiatives, referendums, and/or recall elections. Only 24 states allow the initiative process, 23 states allow referendums, and 19 states allow the recall of state level officials (National Conference of State Legislatures 2015). Citizens in many areas of the country simply cannot be persuaded to vote through direct democracy mechanisms because the opportunity to participate in direct democracy is not afforded to them. In the states that do allow direct democracy, contemporary social issues have been the focus of national media attention.

MARIJUANA LEGALIZATION INITIATIVES

Social issues important to the public may motivate citizens to the polls. One issue that has recently appeared as a direct democracy initiative in several states is the legalization or decriminalization of marijuana.

Support for the legalization of marijuana for recreational use has skyrocketed over the past decade. In 2003, only 34 percent of Americans supported legalization, but by the end of 2014 a slight majority, 51 percent, supported legalization. The most supportive are those Americans ranging from ages 18 to 34, with 64 percent saying they support legalization (Saad 2014). The increase in support has led some to speculate that marijuana ballot initiatives would help drive up voter turnout, especially among young voters who generally turn out in lower numbers than older voters.

As of 2015, four states and the District of Columbia have legalized marijuana for recreational use. Colorado and Oregon voted in favor of legalization in 2012 and Alaska, Oregon, and the District of Columbia voted in favor of legalization in 2014. These were not the first attempts to legalize the use of the drug. California was the first state to vote on marijuana legalization in 1972. The initiative was soundly defeated. California rejected marijuana legalization again in 2010 (Lacey 2010).

Most ballot initiatives to decriminalize or legalize marijuana have been voted on since 2000. Decriminalization is not the same as legalization. Decriminalization initiatives make owning a small amount of marijuana similar to a traffic violation. A person may be punished by a ticket or a fine, but would not have to appear in criminal court. Table 15.2 lists voter turnout rates in states that had decriminalization or legalization initiatives on the ballot during presidential and midterm election years from 2000 to

Table 15.2
Marijuana Ballot Initiatives and Voter Turnout, 2000–2014

Presidential Election Year	State	Approved	Turnout (percent)	Previous Presidential Election Turnout (percent)	Difference (percent)
2000	Alaska	No	65.5	59.9	+5.6
2004	Alaska	No	65.0	65.5	−0.5
2008	Massachusetts	Yes	61.3	63.7	−2.4
2012	Colorado	Yes	65.4	62.5	+2.9
2012	Oregon	Yes	63.3	62.6	+0.7
2012	Washington	Yes	60.7	62.6	−1.9

Midterm Election Year	State	Approved	Turnout (percent)	Previous Midterm Election Turnout (percent)	Difference (percent)
2002	Arizona	No	36.8	33.8	+3.0
2002	Nevada	No	37.0	33.1	+3.9
2006	Colorado	No	49.9	45.7	+4.2
2006	Nevada	No	37.3	37.0	+0.3
2010	California	No	39.2	38.4	+0.8
2014	Alaska	Yes	53.8	48.6	+5.2

Sources: United States Census Bureau; United States Elections Project.
Note: All turnout numbers are from the United States Census Bureau with the exception of Alaska in 2014. The United States Census Bureau did not have the turnout reports for 2014 at the time of this writing. The source for turnout in Alaska in 2014 is the United States Elections Project.

2014. The table also includes turnout comparisons from the year of the ballot initiative to the previous presidential or midterm election (presidential election years are compared with previous presidential election years and midterm election years are compared with previous midterm election years). Given that turnout is systematically higher in presidential election years, this makes for a fairer comparison.

At first glance, voter turnout when marijuana legalization or decriminalization is on the ballot is higher than in the previous similar election year. Higher turnout is consistent across 9 of the 12 marijuana issue elections since 2000. This may indicate that direct democracy involving social issues, and marijuana issues more specifically, has a positive impact on voter turnout. However, on average, the difference between elections with marijuana legalization or decriminalization issues on the ballot and the previous similar election is a very modest +1.8 percent, or about 446,000 out of a total of 24,772,000 votes cast. It is important to note that some of the differences in turnout are within the margin of error for the measure of turnout for the election. Polls are not perfectly accurate and every poll has some margin of error. If two reported values are within the margin of error, then the real difference between them could be zero. For example, turnout in Nevada in 2006 was 37.3 percent, but the poll had a margin of error of 1.9 percent. This means that the real turnout for the election in Nevada was anywhere from 35.4 percent to 39.2 percent. When compared to the reported turnout for 2002 (37.0 percent), it is unclear whether turnout actually decreased, increased, or stayed the same from one election to the next. It can only be certain that turnout increased or decreased when values fall outside of the margin of error.

These comparisons are also strictly comparisons of turnout that do not take into account other factors such as elections for statewide office, the excitement around national candidates for office, or even other issues on the state ballot that may be driving turnout. If there is a discernable impact of marijuana initiatives on turnout, it appears to be a very modest one that has not engaged voters to the extent imagined by Progressive Era reformers. Given the support for legalization/decriminalization among citizens aged 18–34, some Democratic Party strategists believe that marijuana legalization is a ballot issue that can motivate young Americans to the polls. Marijuana legalization is more popular with younger demographics than it is with older demographics, and younger Americans vote in smaller numbers than older Americans. Younger voters also identify with the Democratic Party more than their older counterparts. However, there is some evidence that marijuana ballot initiatives have not motivated younger Americans to vote. Eighteen to 29-year-olds actually represented a smaller portion of the electorate, a decrease of 0.2 percent, when compared to the previous similar election (Enten 2014).

Marijuana ballot initiatives are similar to others in that interest groups play an important role in the process. Direct democracy campaigns are expensive and a lot of resources are needed to circulate petitions and collect signatures. In 2015, the interest group Responsible Ohio collected signatures to place an initiative for the legalization of medical and recreational marijuana on the ballot in Ohio. The firm was paid $6 million to run the campaign. Investors contributed $20 million to the campaign, while also committing to another 20 million to purchase land and 300 million to build facilities. The large amount of money spent and the highly professionalized process involving Responsible Ohio are prime illustrations of the ways in which direct democracy has been captured by special interests. Money and special interests are not unique to the marijuana issue or Ohio; signature gathering companies are paid millions each year to get issues on the ballot in states that allow the initiative process (Whyte 2015).

Marijuana ballot initiatives exhibit some of the traditional problems with direct democracy. Ballot access obstacles favor organized interests over the interests of individuals because organized interests have the means to overcome the obstacles of ballot access, such as time limitations, costs, and the collection of hundreds of thousands of signatures. This is not to argue that citizens would be better off if states abolished direct democracy altogether. Groundbreaking public policies have been adopted first through the initiative process. Several western states voted in favor of women's suffrage using the initiative process and some states abolished poll taxes by initiative (Cronin 1989). Nonetheless, direct democracy has not lived up to the expectations of Progressive Era reformers. The increase in turnout as a result of ballot initiatives is either very modest or nonexistent. The lack of access, role of interest groups, the massive amount of money involved, and the professionalization of the initiative process may help explain why direct democracy has not mobilized voters to the extent initially expected.

FURTHER READING

Biggers, Daniel R. 2011. "When Ballot Issues Matter: Social Issue Ballot Measures and Their Impact on Turnout." *Political Behavior* 33: 3–25.

Cronin, Thomas E. 1989. *Direct Democracy: The Politics of Initiative, Referendum, and Recall*. Cambridge, MA: Harvard University Press.

Enten, Harry. 2014. "Sorry Democrats, Marijuana Doesn't Bring Young Voters to the Polls." Retrieved May 23, 2015 from http://fivethirtyeight.com/features/sorry-democrats-marijuana-doesnt-bring-young-voters-to-the-polls/.

Finnegan, Michael. 2003. "Gov. Davis Is Recalled; Schwarzenegger Wins." *Los Angeles Times*, October 8. Retrieved June 2, 2015 from http://articles.latimes.com/2003/oct/08/local/me-recall8.

Gilbert, Craig. 2012. "Impressive Voter Turnout for Recall Election." *Milwaukee Journal Sentinel*, June 27. Retrieved June 4, 2015 from http://www.jsonline.com/news/statepolitics/impressive-voter-turnout-for-recall-election-t15uajf-160606775.html.

Goebel, Thomas. 2002. *A Government by the People: Direct Democracy in America, 1890–1940*. Chapel Hill: University of North Carolina Press.

Hirschkorn, Phil, and Nancy Cordes. 2012. "A Record Amount of Money Spent on Wisconsin Recall." *CBS News*, June 7. Retrieved June 21, 2015 from http://www.cbsnews.com/news/a-record-amount-of-money-spent-on-wisconsin-recall/.

Lacey, Marc. 2010. "California Rejects Marijuana Legalization." *New York Times*, November 3. Retrieved June 6, 2015 from http://www.nytimes.com/2010/11/03/us/politics/03ballot.html?_r=0.

National Conference of State Legislatures. 2013. "Recall of State Officials." Retrieved June 2, 2015 from http://www.ncsl.org/research/elections-and-campaigns/recall-of-stateofficials.aspx.

National Conference of State Legislatures. 2015. "Initiative, Referendum, and Recall." Retrieved July 20, 2015 from http://www.ncsl.org/research/elections-and-campaigns/initiative-referendum-and-recall-overview.aspx.

Saad, Lydia. 2014. "Majority Continues to Support Pot Legalization in U.S." *Gallup*, November 6. Retrieved June 6, 2015 from http://www.gallup.com/poll/179195/majority-continuessupport-pot-legalization.aspx.

Siegel, Jim, and Joe Vardon. 2011. "Unions Spend Big on Issue 2: SB5 Supporters Keep Contribution Amounts a Secret." *The Columbus Dispatch* (News section), October 28. Retrieved June 21, 2015.

Smith, Daniel A., and Caroline J. Tolbert. 2004. *Educated by Initiative: The Effects of Direct Democracy on Citizens and Political Organizations in the American States.* Ann Arbor: University of Michigan Press.

Tolbert, Caroline J., Bowen, Daniel, and Todd Donovan. 2009. "Initiative Campaigns: Direct Democracy and Voter Mobilization." *American Politics Research* 37 (1): 155–192.

Tolbert, Caroline J., and Daniel A. Smith. 2005. "The Educative Effects of Ballot Initiatives on Voter Turnout." *American Politics Research* 33 (2): 283–309.

Tolbert, Caroline J., McNeal, Ramona S., and Daniel A. Smith. 2003. "Enhancing Civic Engagement: The Effect of Direct Democracy on Political Participation and Knowledge." *State Politics and Policy Quarterly* 3: 23–41.

United States Census Bureau. 2013. "Population Characteristic (P20) Reports and Detailed Tables." Retrieved May 23, 2015 from http://www.census.gov/hhes/www/socdemo/voting/publications/p20/index.html.

United States Elections Project. 2014. "2014 November General Election Turnout Rates." Retrieved June 25, 2015 from http://www.electproject.org/2014g.

Whyte, Lyz E. 2015. "How an Ohio Ballot Measure Could Create a Marijuana Monopoly." *Time Magazine*, June 18. Retrieved June 25, 2015 from http://time.com/3921751/ohio-marijuana-ballot-measure/.

16

Midterm Election Blues

Robert Postic

Midterm elections—those elections for national office held in between presidential elections—are notorious for having low voter turnout. Indeed, as the historical data demonstrate, over the past 50 years, midterm voter turnout has never exceeded 50 percent of eligible voters. Additionally, the 2014 midterm election saw the lowest voter turnout in over 70 years, with just less than 36 percent of the voting eligible population taking the time to vote. This point is illustrated by Figure 16.1, which displays turnout in midterm elections from 1962 to 2014 (McDonald 2015).

Low midterm election turnout has caused a number of concerns that range from the theoretical to the practical. Theoretically, one concern is whether a society can claim to be democratic when less than a majority of its population votes. Practically, another concern is the real possibility that elections and ultimately public policy are determined by a minority of voters who may not reflect the views or demographics of the populace. After the historically low voter turnout in the 2014 midterm election, the reaction from the media was as predictable as it was apocalyptic. A *New York Times* editorial indicated that while the turnout was bad for the Democrats, "it was even worse for democracy."

As somewhat of an historical oddity, midterm elections have not always had low voter turnout. Additionally, there was a time when voter turnout during midterms exceeded that of presidential elections. From the late

Figure 16.1
Midterm Voter Turnout, 1962–2014

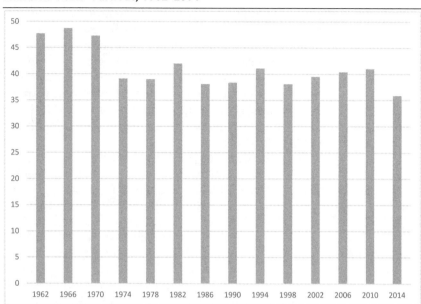

Source: McDonald, Michael P. 2015. "Voter Turnout." *United States Elections Project.* Retrieved June 25, 2015, from http://www.electproject.org/national-1789-present.

1700s into the early 1800s, midterm election turnout exceeded that of presidential elections. Even so, for those early elections, the turnout of eligible voters was below 50 percent for both midterm and presidential elections. In fact, in one election, turnout was as low as 10 percent. Of course, the election that saw such an abysmal turnout was the election of 1820 in which President Monroe effectively ran unopposed. In the mid to late 1800s, however, voter turnout was easily above 60 percent for both presidential and midterm elections.

WHO VOTES AND WHY

One of the more interesting questions revolving around the question of participation in midterm elections is the issue of who takes the time to vote and who does not. In some respects, voters at midterm elections are fairly similar to voters in any other elections. Voters tend to be older, better educated, and have higher income. Nevertheless, a central question is whether or not midterm election voters vary ideologically with those of the presidential elections. This is important because lower voter turnout provides those who vote with a vote that has more relative power. As turnout rates increase, the impact of a person's vote decreases. And if particular groups are more mobilized at one election over another, then that group's impact may be greater. In other words, if those at the ideological extreme (i.e., extremely liberal or extremely conservative) are more likely to vote during midterm elections, then they might well have an effect on the ideological composition of a state legislature or of the governor's mansion.

In comparing two recent elections, the results go against conventional wisdom. Conventional wisdom suggests that because voter turnout is lower during midterms and the demographics of midterm voters are quite different from presidential elections, Republicans benefit. And if that is true, then public policy ultimately could be affected because Republicans differ from Democrats in terms of their policy preferences. This type of conventional wisdom caused considerable angst among some just before the 2014 midterm election, with some liberal pundits suggesting that the Democrats were doomed in the November elections. *FiveThirtyEight Politics* provides an excellent comparison between the 2010 election and the 2012 election (Enten 2014). Minority and young voter turnout in 2010 was notably low in comparison to 2012, although whites over 30 (the most Republican group) composed a greater share of the voting public in 2010 than 2012 (plus six percentage points). If 2012 turnout demographics (increased levels of minority and young voter participation) were applied to the 2010 election, Republicans would have won regardless. This analysis reflects other research that suggests voter turnout has less of an effect on the political outcome than conventional wisdom suggests (Citrin, Schickler, and Sides 2003). That is not to say that we should embrace low voter turnout, but it does suggest that automatically questioning the legitimacy of election outcomes (winners and losers) simply because of low voter turnout is unwarranted.

Although relatively low rates of midterm voter turnout may not be enough to affect the outcomes of elections, the question of what motivates midterm voters still remains. As with all elections, voters are motivated by a number of things, including a sense of civic duty, interest in politics, interest in a candidate, or a feeling of political efficacy (the feeling that one's vote matters and makes a difference). Even so, during midterms, extra motivation on the part of voters may exist. At the state level, many states provide voters with the ability to recall public officials, place initiatives directly on the ballot, or hold referendums on legislation that has been enacted. These activities, when present, may motivate voters. Gubernatorial recall is one example. In 2003, California held a memorable recall election that ousted Governor Gray Davis and led to the election of Governor Arnold Schwarzenegger. At the national level, however, there is no mechanism in place that would allow voters to recall the president if the voters are unhappy with his performance. Short of impeachment and conviction, there is no way to remove a president from office. This leaves voters with few other avenues to express their displeasure with White House policies from the two previous years. Midterm elections may serve as a proxy for the referendum that voters lack at the national level. The 2006 and 2010 midterms provide illustrations of this concept.

MIDTERMS AS REFERENDUM ELECTIONS

In 2006, the War in Iraq had been ongoing for over three years, with Americans showing considerable weariness with the war and its costs in both lives and money. By the time of the 2006 midterm election, according to Gallup, over a majority of Americans consistently indicated they thought the war to be a mistake (Gallup 2015). In CNN exit polls, almost 60 percent of voters indicated they disapproved of how President George W. Bush was doing his job, and two-thirds of voters stated the Iraq War was an important issue (CNN 2006). Although the issue did not appear to have an impact on voter turnout, it is clear that it had an effect on the election results. Republicans lost control of the both the U.S. House and Senate and, at the state level, the Democrats gained six gubernatorial seats and established majority control of the governors' mansions. Holding a majority of gubernatorial seats was something the Democrats had not done since the Republican revolution of 1994. During his post-election press conference, President Bush acknowledged that the midterm vote was a reaction to Iraq: "I know there's a lot of speculation on what the election means for the battle we're waging in Iraq. I recognize that many Americans voted last night to register their displeasure with the lack of progress being made there." The president went on to say the defeat "was a thumping." Even though the turnout was abysmal, with about 41 percent of eligible voters taking the time to cast a ballot, the results were far reaching in terms of changes in partisan control and possibly policies that were or were not implemented during the remaining years of Bush's presidency (Bush 2006).

In 2010, the discussion no longer focused on Iraq. Rather, the discussion revolved around the Patient Protection and Affordable Care Act (PPACA), commonly called the Affordable Care Act (ACA), as well as the economic policies of President Barack Obama's administration. According to Pew Research, 38 percent of voters indicated that they cast their midterm 2010 vote to express opposition to Obama. Additionally, 48 percent of voters felt that health care reform should be repealed. Although that is less than a majority, it nevertheless demonstrates a considerable amount of displeasure with the law among the electorate. With respect to the economy, however, the numbers were more stark. More than 60 percent of voters stated they believed the country was on the wrong track, and 89 percent of voters stated they believed the economy was "not good" or "poor" (Pew Research Center 2010).

The effects of the 2010 election were as remarkable as 2006. The Republicans picked up 63 seats and regained control of the U.S. House of Representatives, and they picked up six seats in the Senate. At the state level, Republicans once again enjoyed a majority of gubernatorial seats, occupying 29 of 50. In his post-election news conference, President Obama admitted that his administration took a "shellacking" and, similar to President Bush in 2006, stated that the two parties would need to work together. In 2014, the Republicans were able to increase their majority in the House and regain control of the Senate. Similar to President Bush in 2006, the 2010 and 2014 midterm elections certainly "narrowed" the possibilities of how an Obama administration could affect public policy going forward (Gage 2015).

REASONS FOR LOW TURNOUT

If low voter turnout is undesirable and yet we experience it, then possible explanations matter. Here, we have a few choices. Political parties may be less vigorous in their voter mobilization efforts than in years past (Rosenstone and Hansen 1993). To be sure, the political parties do conduct "get out the vote" campaigns. Nevertheless, the political parties are not really interested in increasing voter turnout as much as they are interested in ensuring that voters who support their candidate will vote on Election Day. The political parties are more likely to target individuals who they reasonably believe are already somewhat motivated to vote. This is to be expected because they have limited resources and are focused on winning a campaign, not simply increasing political participation.

State election calendars may also influence turnout during midterm elections. However, states have generally worked to make midterm elections more meaningful to voters. Today, 36 states hold their gubernatorial election during the midterm. Ostensibly, this is to help insulate the states and their political fortunes from what may be happening at the national level. By having their gubernatorial elections coincide with midterm elections, states increase the importance of the elections, which should increase voter turnout. Everything else being equal, the more important an election is, as perceived by the voters, the more likely voters are to participate. This is easily demonstrated by looking at the last few presidential elections.

For various reasons, the presidential elections of 1992, 2000, 2004, and 2008 were all considered to be important elections. In 1992, voters saw a strong challenge by Ross Perot as a third party candidate and the economy was a major campaign issue. In 2000, the election was highly competitive and ended with a margin of victory of 537 votes. In 2004, many saw the election as referendum on U.S. involvement in Iraq. In 2008, voters had the opportunity to, and did, elect the first African American president.

The average voter turnout for those elections was 58.4 percent. The election of 1996, however, was not considered to be an important election. Arguably, the differences between the Republican candidate, Bob Dole, and the Democrat incumbent, President William Clinton, were not very great. Additionally, the nation's economic health was good. Predictably, voter turnout in 1996 was seven percentage points lower than the average for those other years and a full 10 points lower than 2008, which was considered to be an historic election with the first African American candidate representing the Democratic Party.

With qualifications, the same patterns hold in the states for midterm elections. During the 2014 midterm, 36 states held gubernatorial elections. The average voter turnout for those states was approximately 40.4 percent. The average turnout for the 14 states that did *not* elect a governor was 36.6 percent. Although turnout in the states that elected governors was almost four percentage points higher than those that did not, there are two points to consider about these data. First, the difference between the two groups could be explained by other factors such as ballot initiatives, diversity of voter registration laws, state political culture, or other factors. The second point is that turnout in both cases remained well below a majority. Even though states may be helping to increase voter turnout by holding their gubernatorial elections at that time, the effect in these years is not dramatic.

The best hint of an explanation for midterm election turnout is provided by the comparison of the turnout in the presidential elections of 1992 through 2012. When a presidential election is perceived as being less important, fewer voters show up at the polls. By their very nature, midterm elections are considered less important because these elections do not choose a president. Midterm elections are less visible to voters and receive less attention and fewer resources from the political parties. Related, the media does not pay as much attention to midterm elections as they do presidential elections. Moreover, many congressional races are not competitive. Pew Research reports that in 2006 only about 14 percent of all House seats were competitive; in 2010, the number increased slightly to approximately 19 percent. In spite of this increase, over 80 percent of all House seats remain noncompetitive. In both midterm elections, there were also candidates who faced no effective competition (8 percent in 2006 and 3 percent in 2010; Desilver 2014). Finally, one of the explanations may be that voters have the blues. Voters may simply be experiencing voter fatigue. It may seem that the American public is constantly voting; between primary elections, midterm and presidential elections, local and state elections, as well as the occasional special election, Americans are asked to vote on a fairly frequent basis. Moreover, the elections (especially presidential elections) have become drawn-out affairs. More than a dozen candidates had announced their candidacy for the

2016 November presidential election by July 2015. As Thomas Patterson (2002, 101) has commented, "The long campaign dulls citizens' interest and taxes their attention."

FIXING THE PROBLEM

One option for addressing low turnout in midterm elections is to impose mandatory voting. In early 2015, President Obama made news and received considerable criticism when he floated this idea. Of course, the concept of mandatory voting as reform is not new. It is used in other democracies, such as Australia. Leading political scientists have also advocated for mandatory voting believing it will help make government more equitable; one example is Arend Lijphart, former president of the American Political Science Association, who advocated for mandatory voting in 1997.

The reaction of the American public to President Obama's suggestion, however, was not favorable and support for the proposal quickly faded. Despite the fact that the proposal was not successful, the event highlights two problems that occur with any proposed policy change. The first problem is one of political support. President Obama found out very quickly that getting any traction on mandatory voting was a losing cause. Although Americans generally support making voting easier or more accessible, two out of three Americans opposed the president's suggestion that people be required to vote (Moore 2015). The second problem is that the suggested reforms may not produce the desired effect. For example, in 1993 Congress passed the National Voter Registration Act (NVRA). One of the goals of NVRA (commonly called Motor Voter because of its requirement to provide voter registration at motor vehicle licensing offices, among other public office locations) was to get more people registered to vote. The presumption behind the push to increase registration reflected a bit of a "field of dreams" approach to voting—if they are registered, they will vote. And this idea does have data to support it. According to Current Population Surveys conducted by the Census Bureau, in presidential elections, as many as 85–88 percent of registered voters turn out and cast a ballot. And for 2010 midterm election, almost 70 percent of registered voters indicated they voted. The problem here is that, according to the Census Bureau, approximately 28–30 percent of Americans are not registered for any given election. Motor Voter did increase registration; nevertheless, the Motor Voter Act never lived up to its full promise. Indeed, in the next presidential election after the Act was signed into law, voter turnout for that election (1996) was the lowest in 70 years. And the turnout for the 1998 midterm was less than 40 percent of eligible voters. Although it is tempting to conclude that American elections face a registration problem, it may not be as simple as that. Of course, it is true that people cannot vote unless they are registered. But voters may have many reasons for not registering including that they have little to no interest in voting.

The lack of competitive races and the problem of voter fatigue deserve particular mention as systemic factors. To address either of these factors would mean that we would somehow have to rethink how we structure our government or how we structure our elections. We could make elections more competitive, for example, if we were to move away from a single-member district format. We could potentially decrease voter fatigue if we were to consolidate elections and have fewer of them. It is unlikely that these changes will occur, given the entrenched support for the current system.

Although there may be no policy fix for the midterm blues, there are several positive aspects of the discussion of lower voter turnout in midterm elections. First, lower voter turnout should not affect our perceptions about the legitimacy of the elections. Few, if any, election results would change if voter turnout were higher. Second, a fairly high percentage (as much as 70 percent) of registered voters actually do vote. Finally, the midterm blues highlight the beauty of democracy and American politics. Our midterm elections remind those in power that they have to attend to those who happen to be in the political minority at the time. The cure for the midterm blues is to remind ourselves that those who are really blue after midterm elections are those of the party that was in power. Voters can take solace in the fact that their voices have been heard.

FURTHER READING

Bush, George. 2006. "President Bush on Election Results." *The New York Times*, November 8. Retrieved March 30, 2016 from http://www.nytimes.com/2006/11/08/washington/08bush-transcript.html?pagewanted=print&_r=0.

Citrin, Jack, Schickler, Eric, and John Sides. 2003. "What If Everyone Voted? Simulating the Impact of Increased Turnout in Senate Elections." *American Journal of Political Science* 47: 75–90.

CNN. 2006. Exit Polls. Retrieved August 16, 2015 from http://www.cnn.com/ELECTION/2006/pages/results/states/US/H/00/epolls.0.html.

Desilver, Drew. 2014. "For Most Voters, Congressional Elections Offer Little Drama." Retrieved March 30, 2016 from http://www.pewresearch.org/fact-tank/2014/11/03/for-most-voters-congressional-elections-offer-little-drama/.

Editorial Board. 2015. "The Worst Voter Turnout in 72 Years." *The New York Times*. Retrieved June 25, 2015 from http://www.nytimes.com/2014/11/12/opinion/the-worst-voter-turnout-in-72-years.html?_r=0.

Enten, Harry. 2014. "Midterm Election Turnout Isn't So Different from Presidential Year Turnout." *FiveThirtyEight Politics*. Retrieved June 25, 2015 from

http://fivethirtyeight.com/features/midterm-election-turnout-isnt-so
-different-from-presidential-year-turnout/.

Gage, Beverly. 2015. "A Liberal Standard Bearer He's Not." *POLITICO Magazine.*
Retrieved June 23, 2015 from http://www.politico.com/magazine/story/
2014/02/barack-obamas-paragraph-103572_Page2.html#.VY1_9OePZLp.

Gallup. 2015. Foreign Affairs Poll: Iraq. Retrieved August 16, 2015 from http://
www.gallup.com/poll/1633/iraq.aspx.

Lijphart, Arend. 1997. "Unequal Participation: Democracy's Unresolved
Dilemma." *The American Political Science Review* 91: 1–14.

McDonald, Michael P. 2015. "Voter Turnout." *United States Elections Project.*
Retrieved June 25, 2015 from http://www.electproject.org/national-1789
-present.

Moore, Peter. 2015. "Americans: Make Voting Easier, Not Mandatory." Retrieved
March 30, 2016 from https://today.yougov.com/news/2015/03/30/make
-voting-easier-not-mandatory/.

Patterson, Thomas. 2002. *The Vanishing Voter: Public Involvement in an Age of
Uncertainty.* New York, NY: Alfred A. Knopf.

Pew Research Center. 2010. "A Clear Rejection of the Status Quo, No Consensus
about Future Policies." Retrieved March 30, 2016 from http://www
.pewresearch.org/2010/11/03/a-clear-rejection-of-the-status-quo-no
-consensus-about-future-policies/.

Rosenstone, Steven J., and John Mark Hansen. 1993. *Mobilization, Participation and
Democracy in America.* New York, NY: Macmillan.

Wattenberg, Martin P. 2008. *Is Voting for Young People?* New York, NY: Pearson/
Longman.

17

Political Polarization: The Shift from the Middle

Benjamin W. Cole

Party polarization is the phenomenon whereby political parties in a political system become 1) increasingly distinct and ideologically unified internally and 2) increasingly isolated externally in their interactions with other political parties (Fiorina 1999). Although there are a multitude of political parties that officially exist in the American political landscape, we generally see the most interaction and polarization between the Republican and Democratic political parties. Because these two political parties dominate the American political landscape, the political polarization phenomenon is driven by the interaction between them.

HISTORY OF PARTY POLARIZATION

Political parties have been a fundamental instrument in the American republic since the ratification of its Constitution. The Federalists, for example, rallied around the creation of a strong central government, while the anti-Federalists rallied around the protection of individual rights. In contemporary American politics, political parties are most often used to champion ideas, bring awareness to issues, help electoral candidates raise funds for their campaigns, unify like-minded individuals, and help organize and rally support for legislative efforts. Political parties also help voters through the decision process by providing partisan cues that give voters some insight into what policies, values, and ideologies a particular candidate or group of candidates may subscribe to and support when in office.

Prior to the dawn of the 20th century, political parties were not considered terribly divisive. Though the political parties of the 18th and 19th centuries had their fair share of political squabbles, Paul Frymer (2011) argues that the polarization phenomenon did not begin to dominate and reshape the political landscape until Woodrow Wilson's presidency (1913–1921). President Wilson believed that America's two-party system was broken and needed to be reformed, and he advocated for more "responsible" national political parties. According to Wilson, stronger party leadership and more distinct party ideologies would make it easier for voters to make decisions about which candidate is best aligned with their personal beliefs and values. Wilson's motivation was not to create a highly polarized political atmosphere; instead, he envisioned a party system where the parties had strong values and leadership that individual citizens could easily understand and, therefore, align with the party of their choice. He also believed that strong party leadership would help to unify the party platforms and make coordination and compromise between the parties easier. He felt that having strong and "responsible" national political parties would foster democratic ideals and cooperation between them.

In the 1950s, the American Political Science Association (APSA) published a report that echoed some of President Wilson's ideals. It called for stronger national political parties with clearly defined ideologies and agendas. The APSA diverged from President Wilson's views about how the two parties should interact. The APSA believed that distinct parties gave the voting public prominent options when choosing representatives or policy alternatives. Like Wilson, the Association felt that "responsible" parties were highly coherent and unified in ideology. However, the prominent political scientists of the APSA also believed that it was the job of the opposition party to critique and challenge the positions, policies, and actions of the party in power.

In his article, "A Goal for Reform: Make Elections worth Stealing," Donovan (2007) discusses how the American political landscape has become increasingly polarized since the 1970s. He uses the congressional floor votes of the members of the 109th Congress (January 2005 to January 2007) to illustrate how Democratic candidates who were deemed "safest" for reelection tended to have more liberal voting records than Democrats who were considered "marginal" for reelection and who tended to have more centrist or moderate voting records. This trend was the same for Republican candidates as well. The "safest" Republican candidates were those whose voting records during the same Congress were more conservative than that of the national "median voter." As with Democrats, the "marginal" Republican candidates were those whose voting records during the same Congress tended to be more moderate and closer to the national "median voter" (Donovan 2007). Donovan (2007) also notes that among the public, feelings toward Republican politicians by individuals who identify as Democrats have become less positive, or cool, since 1978. Similarly, feelings toward Democrats by those who identify as Republicans have become less positive since 1990.

Median Voter Theorem and Potential Causes of Polarization

The median voter theorem offers one explanation of how candidates position themselves along the political spectrum to win elections. The median voter theorem posits that most voters are truly aligned more toward the political center rather than the far left or the far right (Fiorina 1999). If candidates truly want to win elections, their platforms cannot deviate too far in either political direction lest they risk giving up votes from the majority of voters in the median. If, for example, we assume that policy preferences can be plotted across a single dimension, the median voter theorem suggests that candidate A and candidate B will move closer toward the center, the area of the dimension occupied by the median voter (M), in order to gain a greater percent of the vote share in addition to those voters that they expect they have already captured.

That said, in today's political landscape, the median voter theorem has broken down. Political scientists cite various phenomena that may contribute to the breakdown of the median voter theorem including the lack of alternatives in a two-party system, zero-sum politics, single-member electoral districts, the cost of moderate politics, and policy orientation.

The two-party system increases polarization because it limits the number of real alternatives (Fiorina 1999). Although there are no laws that necessarily restrict the number of political parties that can operate or produce candidates for an election, the political culture in the United States is dominated by the Republican and Democratic parties at the national level. There are some smaller political (third) parties that exist, but none of them currently have any representation in the current Congress (Bernie Sanders, the U.S. Senator from Vermont, served as an Independent until 2015, when he joined the Democrats). States retain the right to determine ballot access laws and which political parties they will formally recognize for elections. Ballot access laws determine the critical actions needed to place candidate names on the ballot, including the number of signatures required, filing fees, and the voter turnout thresholds necessary for party recognition. For example, in the state of Alabama, there are four ways for a potential candidate to be placed on a ballot to be elected to state or federal office: 1) official endorsement by a recognized party (the Republican and Democratic parties are the only two officially recognized parties in Alabama); 2) an official endorsement by a minor party seeking official recognition; 3) as an independent candidate after petitioning the Alabama Secretary of State; and 4) as a write-in candidate (Code of Alabama Title 17). Generally, when any candidate wants to be placed on the ballot for elections in the state, multiple petitions to the Alabama Secretary of State are required in order to announce one's candidacy and formally create committees to report campaign information to the state. It is easy to see how having the formal endorsement of one of the two recognized parties makes this process a lot easier. Although these requirements do not explicitly ban third parties, they do create such a high threshold for resources that it has the effect of making third party competition unfeasible in most cases. Although some of third party candidates have occasionally achieved national recognition (i.e., Ross Perot in 1992 and Ralph Nader in 2000) they are rarely successful.

Having only two major parties to choose from may also contribute to party polarization as it makes the political arena function like a zero-sum game where one party must always be the winner and the other must always be the loser. In this system, leaders from the winning party tend to take on "mandates" of leadership. A presidential candidate is said to have won a mandate of leadership when he or she wins the presidential election and enough senators and representatives from his or her own party to secure a majority in both chambers of Congress. This then makes it considerably easier for the new president to push an agenda through the legislature without significant minority party cooperation. Additionally, this zero-sum perspective of winners and losers possibly has the effect of making individuals more intolerant of others who hold opposing views. This does not leave a lot of room in the American political landscape for moderate politicians or moderate views. It also makes it particularly hard for individuals who do hold more moderate views to find and support a candidate whom they feel will represent their moderate views.

Single-member districts propagate the same zero-sum problem. A single-member district is an electoral jurisdiction where only one individual is sent to a legislature or council to represent the entire district. Because only one individual may win any given election in a single-member district, the competition between candidates can be extremely high requiring incredible amounts of resources to win. These resources include campaign funds, volunteers, and time dedicated to reaching voters. Because the resources needed to win elections in a single-member district are so great, candidates rely on strong parties and party support to help provide the resources necessary for a successful campaign. The distribution of resources to the candidates represented by the two major parties has the effect of marginalizing third parties, third party candidates, and the voters who support them. The overall consequence is to limit the number of candidates available for voters.

Some political scientists also note that in today's political climate, there may be a high cost associated with centrist moves by potential candidates. This idea, called abstention (Downs 1957; Fiorina 1999), runs contrary to the median voter theorem. It posits that candidates may actually lose votes if they try to reach a moderate base rather than trying to reach out to the distinct left or right partisan base. This is because median voters tend to be indifferent toward more extreme candidates regardless of whether or not those candidates reach out to them, so a candidate on either side will not necessarily gain votes by moderating their platform or moving closer to the center. However, candidates will almost certainly lose support from voters on the political fringes if they attempt to be moderate.

Policy orientation is another phenomenon that is believed to be responsible for the breakdown of the median voter theorem (Fiorina 1999). In this paradigm, candidates are thought to have good information about the preferences of voters and will, therefore, promote policies that align with the median voter. The problem, here, is the level of trust median voters have in candidates who move toward the center. The median voter will be unlikely to trust candidates that move toward the center, and will ignore them instead of shifting their vote toward them. To win, candidates must then rely on support from the party base and will promote, support, and implement policies that reflect that base after winning the election. This, then, contributes to a more polarized political landscape.

Citizen preferences may also factor into increasing polarization (Fiorina 1999). Consistent with median voter theory, sincere citizen preferences tend to be more moderate than extreme. However, it is possible that the preferences of citizens as members of the two distinct parties have become more extreme, even though the aggregate level of polarization among all citizens has not increased. An explanation for this behavior is that while the citizenry as a whole may be more moderate, citizens who vote and participate in elections are more polarized than the citizenry at large (Collie and Mason 2000). Therefore, the citizens who turn out for elections are not representative of the entire population and lend their support to more polarized, distinct candidates.

There is ample research to support the idea that caucuses and primary elections increase political polarization in our political landscape (Fiorina 1999). In considering elections as a two-stage process, analysis of candidate positions in the primary and general election stages indicates that candidates are tempted to become more extreme and distinct to win their parties' nomination for the general election, which has the effect of making candidates more extreme in general (Coleman 1971). To illustrate this point, candidates seeking Republican Party nominations have been found to tend to move toward conservative extremes on issues like abortion to secure their party's nomination prior to the general election (Brady and Schwartz 1995).

Distributive politics and incumbency may also factor into polarizing the political landscape. Incumbents are assumed to have the advantage in elections. Typically, incumbents have had the opportunity to show the public their leadership skills, policy preferences, and ability to deliver on campaign promises. Challengers have a hard time gaining the trust of the public over the reputation of the incumbent. Often, challengers must then resort to strategies that divide the public and try to undermine the incumbent's support. Incumbents, on the other hand, rely on campaign strategies that they think will benefit a larger base. Consequently, when incumbents employ strategies that play to median and moderate voters, challengers must make themselves more distinct to gain the support of a polar side with hopes that they take away enough support from the incumbent to make them unelectable.

Entry into electoral competition itself also motivates parties to stay very distinctly on one side of the median (Fiorina 1999). In our political land-scape, if the two major parties converge closer to the median, they open up enough room for third parties to come into the electoral competition and gain support on one side of the median. Essentially, in order for the two major parties to survive and stay competitive, a polarized political landscape is necessary. A phenomenon called balancing also acts as a motivation for candidates to become more polarized (Fiorina 1999). In the context of balancing, voters are aware that when they vote, they are voting for multiple candidates to hold different types of offices and responsibilities within different branches of government. Therefore, the ballots they cast are more complex than uniform. They vote for candidates whom they think will best execute the duties and responsibilities of the specific office for which the candidates are running rather than just voting along partisan lines. This complexity in ballot choices has the effect of making candidates more distinct in multiple ways. First, because voters do not judge a candidate solely on the basis of party affiliation, a candi-date's personal preferences across multiple policy areas may become more extreme. Second, as one candidate in a particular election becomes more extreme, his or her challenger may be motivated to become more extreme, leading to a cycle of distinction that moves candidates from the center and stimulates hyperpolarization.

The behaviors of political parties also contribute to polarization (Fiorina 1999). Because multiple candidates compete for various offices on behalf of only two political parties, voters are then forced to make their electoral decisions based on party platforms rather than the platforms of individual candidates. To remain distinctive in their political views, par-ties create platforms based on the median ideas of party incumbents rather than the median electorate or the public at large. Candidates must then support and promote policies that fall within the platform of their party to maintain the support of their party and the recourses they provide. This may undermine a candidate's abilities to make moves toward the median during campaigns.

POLARIZATION-TURNOUT RELATIONSHIP

Political polarization also has an important relationship with voter efficacy and, therefore, voter turnout. Political scientists have, for years, noticed correlations between the phenomena, but it is unclear which actually causes the other. Conventional thought says that political polarization would lead to a decrease in levels of political efficacy among voters and, therefore, would decrease voter turnout (Fiorina, Abrams, and Pope 2011). Voters who have low levels of political efficacy and low levels of trust in government tend to become cynical or apathetic toward the political system as a whole. They begin to feel as though their thoughts, opinions, and values may not matter in the grander political landscape and they do not trust that any candidate regardless of which side they represent will effectively and sincerely represent their views. So, they stop seeing the utility and value in their votes and we see more political disillusionment among the citizenry and less citizens at the polls or engaging in other forms of political participation.

We know that feelings of political efficacy have a significant effect on voter turnout (Craig 1993; Pollock 1983; Southwell 2012). The more cynical and apathetic an individual feels toward his or her ability to affect political change, the less likely those individuals are to show up at the polls to cast their vote. So, we can develop some expectations for a relationship between political polarization and voter turnout. If increasing political polarization leads to a decrease in voter efficacy, then we should expect that increasing political polarization would also have a negative effect on voter turnout.

The opposite has also been argued by political scientists. It is completely possible that political polarization could be a function of the indifference of median voters. When median voters do not trust moderate candidates, or when median voters remain indifferent toward moderating candidates, they create room for polarizing candidates to gain partisan support, win elections, and then push for highly partisan measures or legislation. Dodson (2010), for example, suggests that from 1980 to 2004 increases in voters' turnout are, in part, the result of political polarization. He suggests that polarization acts as a signal for voters that the parties diverge on important issues thus raising the stakes of the policy process which may propel citizens toward greater participation. Others suggest that the American public has responded favorable to party polarization. Abramowitz and Saunders (2008), for example, find that party polarization encourages political participation and excites the American public.

There is also evidence that shows voter turnout tends to have an effect on the outcome of elections in our political landscape. A comparative study of western democracies, which included the United States, conducted by professors from the University of Aberdeen and Trinity College in Dublin found that an increase in voter turnout rates leads to less electoral success for right wing candidates and parties (Bernhagen and Marsh 2005). They also found that nongoverning, or opposition parties tend to benefit from higher voter turnout. Because voter turnout rates can significantly affect the outcome of elections, we must give continue to give consideration to the way political polarization affects voter turnout.

FURTHER READING

Abramowitz, Alan I., and Kyle L. Saunders. 2008. "Is Polarization a Myth?" *The Journal of Politics* 70: 542–555. doi:10.1017/S0022381608080493.

Alvarez, R., Atkeson, Lonna Rae, and Thad Hall. 2013. *Evaluating Elections: A Handbook of Methods and Standards.* Cambridge, England: Cambridge University Press.

American Political Science Association Committee on Political Parties. 1950. "Toward a More Responsible Two-Party System: A Report of the Committee on Political Parties, American Political Science Association." *The American Political Science Review* (Supplement: Vol. 44, September 1950, Number 3, Part 2).

Bernhagen, Patrick, and Michael Marsh. 2005. "Turnout Matters: Sometimes." Paper prepared for the Comparative Study of Electoral Systems (CSES) Conference and Planning Committee Meeting. Taipei, Taiwan. Retrieved from http://www.cses.org/plancom/2005Taipei/Bernhagen&Marsh.pdf.

Brady, David W., and Edward P. Schwartz. 1995. "Ideology and Interests in Congressional Voting: The Politics of Abortion in the U.S. Senate." *Public Choice* 84: 22–48.

Coleman, James S. 1971. "Internal Processes Governing Party Positions in Elections." *Public Choice* 11 (Fall): 35–60.

Collie, Melissa P., and John Lyman Mason. 2000. "The Electoral Connection between Party and Constituency Reconsidered: Evidence from the U.S. House of Representatives, 1974–1994." In *Continuity and Change in US House Elections,* edited by David W. Brady, Joh F. Cogan, and Morris P. Fiorina, 211–234. Redwood City, CA: Stanford University Press.

Craig, Stephen C. 1993. *Malevolent Leaders: Popular Discontent in America.* Boulder, CO: Westview Press.

Dalton, Russell J. 2008. "The Quantity and the Quality of Party Systems: Party System Polarization, Its Measurement, and Its Consequences." *Comparative Political Studies* 41: 899–920.

Dettrey, Bryan J., and James E. Campbell. 2013. "Has Growing Income Inequality Polarized the American Electorate? Class, Party, and Ideological Polarization." *Social Science Quarterly* 94: 1062–1083.

Dodson, Kyle. 2010. "The Return of the American Voter? Party Polarization and Voting Behavior, 1988 to 2004." *Sociological Perspectives* 53: 443–449.

Donovan, Todd. 2007. "A Goal for Reform: Make Elections Worth Stealing." *PS: Political Science and Politics* 40: 681–686.

Downs, Anthony. 1957. *An Economic Theory of Democracy.* New York, NY: Harper and Row Publishers.

Fiorina, Morris P. 1999. "What Ever Happened to the Median Voter?" Prepared for the MIT Conference on Parties and Congress, Cambridge, MA, October 2, 1999. Retrieved March 30, 2016 from http://web.stanford.edu/~mfiorina/Fiorina%20Web%20Files/MedianVoterPaper.pdf.

Fiorina, Morris, Abrams, Samuel J., and Jeremy C. Pope. 2011. *Culture War? The Myth of a Polarized America* (3rd Ed.). London, England: Longman.

Frymer, Paul. 2011. "Debating the Causes of Party Polarization in America." *California Law Review* 99: 335–349.

Mann, Thomas E., and Norman J. Ornstein. 2012. *It's Even Worse than It Looks: How the American Constitutional System Collided with the New Politics of Extremism.* New York, NY: Basic Books.

Massicotte, Louis, Blais, Andre, and Antoine Yoshinaka. 2004. *Establishing the Rules of the Game Election Laws in Democracies.* Toronto, Ontario: University of Toronto Press.

McCarty, Nolan, Poole, Keith, and Howard Rosenthal. 2006. *Polarized America: The Dance of Ideology and Unequal Riches.* Cambridge, MA: MIT Press.

Pollock III, Phillip H. 1983. "The Participatory Consequences of Internal and External Political Efficacy: A Research Note." *The Western Political Quarterly* 36: 400–409.

Southwell, Priscilla L. 2012. "Political Alienation: Behavioral Implications of Efficacy and Cynicism in the 2008 U.S. Presidential Election." *Review of European Studies* 4: 71–77.

Steiner, Nils D., and Christian W. Martin. 2012. "Economic Integration, Party Polarization and Electoral Turnout." *West European Politics* 35: 238–265.

18

It's Over before It Began: Pre-Election Polling and the Early Release of Election Results

Robert C. Chalwell Jr.

In the modern telecommunications era, the early release of election data and its impact on voter behavior has long been a concern of geographically large countries. In the U.S. context, although early voting does occur, national elections are primarily centered on one day. Elections are conducted in 50 states and across six time zones; poll opening and closing times also vary from state to state. For instance, based on state poll opening and closing times in 2014, when voting closed in New York, there were still two hours of voting remaining in California, and three hours remaining in Hawaii. Although the question has not been studied systematically, a limited number of field experiments suggest that the effects of political information on voter turnout vary by media source and consumption patterns, including the availability of election coverage in one's native tongue or specific ethno-culturally targeted news media, and media type preference.

POLITICAL INFORMATION AND THE MEDIA

Following the 1980 media-projected landslide victory of Ronald Reagan, the early release of election results briefly enjoyed increased interest as a causal catalyst for voter behavior. From that election to the present, the release of election projections and exit poll results by the mass media has been blamed for producing adverse public reactions despite the practice of such polling since the 1960s. These reactions range from hostility toward polling to political apathy and voter demobilization. More recent studies on the early release of poll results find that these effects vary by the extent of voter knowledge about candidates and their campaigns broadly, and whether the information received by the early release of election results is new or confirmatory. Additionally, as the digital age continues to assert itself, consumers are empowered to get their information from preferred Internet news sites, blogs, social media, and cable networks that are heavily one-sided or even blatantly biased sources of information, rather than from traditional local and national broadcast media where investigative objectivity and journalistic integrity are assumed to improve the quality of the information provided to audiences and likely voters.

Contemporary voters focus increasing amounts of their political attention on sources of political information that do not challenge the existing beliefs they hold. The impact of this trend is that if the early release election results are in line with voter expectations, there is a lower incentive to vote. Pre-election polls and the early release election results have a demobilizing effect if they confirm expectations, that is, the information indicates that the election outcome is what the voter wants. New or unexpected information, however, is likely to mobilize voters if the results provide a new or unexpected outcome. Mobilization effects may vary depending on the source of the information when considered with the normal political attentiveness of the voter. Mobilization effects may increase for particular groups if information is provided in languages other than English (e.g., Spanish language news for Hispanic voters) or disseminated via ethno-culturally targeted media (e.g., black newspapers and radio stations for black voters).

Critics of the media handling of polling data, including Roskin et al. (2010, 152), assert that "published or broadcasted poll results can distort an election." In the 1980s, several states sought to prohibit exit polling by enacting laws limiting immediate access to voters as they left polling stations. Though challenged, these laws were deemed constitutional as long as the intent is not to limit the ability of the press to relay information to the public. Albeit varied across comparative national contexts, there is ample evidence to assert commonality between the effects of the spreading of pre-election polling data and the early release of exit poll/official results. However, as issues as well as voters' minds may change during the last crucial weeks and days of an election campaign, concession must be made for the time lag effects on the quality and relevance of the pre-election data collected.

PUBLIC OPINION POLLING AND ELECTIONS

In the United States, much of the knowledge utilized by citizens and voters to hold officials accountable comes from collected data on aggregate public opinion about a particular issue or set of issues, at a specific point in time. George Gallup (1901–1983), considered the founder of modern-day polling, was quoted as saying that, "polls help speed up the process of democracy" (O'Connor, Sabato, and Yanus 2013, 251).

To their defense, public opinion polls are not the dramatic tidal changes in individual and group positions they are often portrayed as. Polls are the surveyed opinions of the American public that attempt, through stratified sampling, to capture the variety in demographic characteristics of the general population. Poll results are then conservatively generalized to be representative of the whole, accounting for a margin of error plus or minus 4 percent (O'Connor, Sabato, and Yanus 2013; Roskin et al. 2010).

In what is considered a seminal text in American politics, Odegard and Helms (1938) characterize the political process as the "translation of social pressures into policy" and emphasized the role of social group pressures on candidates. A significant part of political marketing is candidates spending money and time to promote themselves during an election with the goal of getting elected. In this context, understanding why voters behave the way they do takes on the character of an electoral "numbers game," informing campaign spending, and, in turn, sending specific signals to the voting public.

Polls are increasingly utilized as a means of filling significant gaps in individual and mass voter knowledge, sometimes known as information asymmetries. Figure 18.1 depicts the accuracy of the Gallup Organizations' presidential election predictions since 1936. The accuracy of these polls and the predictions generated are why Gallup remains one of the most trusted providers of poll data in the world. If a candidate could reliably explain, predict, and even influence how a voter will act, to the degree of accuracy exhibited by the Gallup predictions, the candidate would be able to allocate election resources strategically to efficiently insure (re)election. Specific media consumption behaviors, and how voters receive and utilize political information, particularly polling and the early release election results, arguably also act as catalysts for voter action or inaction, beyond a simple accounting of existing preferences.

Although accurate and authoritative political news is still deemed important, scholars note that voters rationally seek to reduce their expenditure of energy, effort, and resources by employing information shortcuts. Arguably, the dual utility of polling data as information on existing political preferences and as information signals as to how one *should* vote is one such shortcut. Scholars in this particular camp further assert that voter competence should not summarily be questioned because

Figure 18.1
Gallup Presidential Election Predictions Since 1936

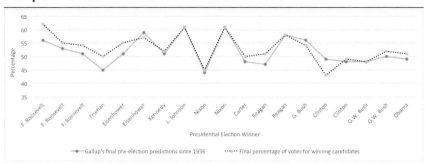

Source: Adapted from Gallup, Inc.

of imperfections in the news they consume, its source, or the limited quantity of factual political information consumed.

EARLY MEDIA PROJECTIONS, EXIT POLLS, AND VOTER TURNOUT

Beginning in the early 1960s, news organizations developed pre-election methods of statistical modeling and polling that could project likely winners. Exit polls are a post-election measurement tool used primarily to project results. Exit polls also provide data that give insight as to why voters voted the way they did and provide insight into underlying sociopolitical dynamics.

The accuracy of such projections was called into question on election night Tuesday, November 7, 2000, as candidates George W. Bush and Al Gore vied for the U.S. presidency. Gore took what appeared to be a decisive lead in the Electoral College count. Bush had 246 of the 538 electoral votes and Gore was just ahead with 260. The results of the overall popular vote also showed Gore with a slight lead.

NBC was the first to declare Al Gore the winner in Florida at 7:50 p.m. EST, followed by other networks. However, by 9:55 p.m. EST, CNN had taken back its projection for a Gore victory and other networks quickly followed. At the close of the polls on the West Coast, the still unofficial Florida count was clearly going to decide the election. At 2:16 a.m. EST Wednesday morning, Fox News declared Bush the winner, echoed minutes later by NBC, CBS, CNN, and ABC. Several early edition newspapers went to print after Florida had been called for Bush; some, such as the St. Louis Post-Dispatch, recalled these early editions and printed revised editions. Bush's victory margin of less than 0.5 percent triggered an automatic machine recount. All the major networks recalled the Bush victory projection around 4 a.m. EST. The election was not settled until after a lengthy recount process, and the decision of the U.S. Supreme Court on December 8, 2000, in *Bush v. Gore*. Bush was declared the winner, having officially won Florida's Electoral College votes.

Polls continue to be a big and growing business in elections and data collection generally. However, the impact of polls and the early release of election results on voter turnout remains unsettled, with empirical results varying across national contexts. Carpini (1984) found small but measurable impacts of the early call of the election by broadcasters on presidential and congressional turnout in 1980. The author also highlights evidence of a somewhat larger impact on depressing the vote for Democratic candidates in congressional and presidential races by 3.1 percent. In Carpini's analysis, which measures the relationship between party affiliation, voter preference, and voter turnout in pre-election call and post-election call districts, there is evidence that indicates a possible depressing effect of the early call on Republican congressional voting. The author finds that "fourteen races were decided by an amount smaller that the net Republican advantage of 4.7 percent" (Carpini 1984, 879). He additionally finds and accounts for a greater effect on voters with specific socioeconomic characteristics by assuming that better educated, higher income, white collar populations would watch the news, and perceive the projected outcome as rendering their vote noninstrumental. Busch and Lieske (1985) align with Carpini and find a demobilizing effect on West Coast voters by as much as 6–11 percent.

Those dubious of the undue effects of the early release of election results assert that only a tiny fraction of the 10–13 percent of registered voters who do not vote can possibly be affected by projections. They further contend that registered non-voters who live in states where the polls have already closed at the time the presidential call is made, those who are ill, or are turned off by the choices presented, when adequately accounted for, reduce the likely number of voters affected by the early release election results to a negligible number. The central assertion here is that "sometimes [a] non-voter is really a vote for no candidate" (Milavsky et al. 1985, 14).

MEDIA CONSUMPTION EFFECTS

Initially face-to-face interviews and exit poll data collection were primarily used to predict electoral outcomes. These methods were geographically restrictive and were prone to errors caused by unrepresentative samples. With advances in telecommunications, poll data now can be collected and disseminated with exponential reach via radio, television, the Internet, and social media. New forms of media affect turnout. Tolbert and

McNeal (2003) found that individuals with Internet access who consume on-line election information were significantly more likely to report voting in the 1996 and 2000 presidential elections. Further, simulations conducted by the authors indicate that access to the Internet and online election news increased the probability of voting by an average of 12 percent and 7.5 percent, respectively, in the 2000 election.

Communications that are targeted to reach particular groups within the overall population also matter. On the specific impact of television view-ing, Oberholzer Gee and Waldfogel (2006) found that local Spanish lan-guage public affairs programming significantly and positively increases Hispanic voter turnout in nonpresidential elections from about 30 to about 41 percent. In presidential election years, the presence of Spanish-language local television news appears to raise Hispanic turnout from about 46 to 54 percent. The findings further indicate that Spanish-language news programs boost Hispanic turnout by 5 to 10 percentage points overall. In nonpresidential election years, the effects are noticeably large and raise Hispanic turnout by 8 to 11 percentage points. Similar studies by the authors in 2005 produced similar relationships for the impact of black-targeted local papers as well as radio stations on black voter turnout.

The aggregate conclusion is that political information consumed by voters via trusted and ethno-culturally targeted media sources are likely to affect voter behavior and voter turnout specifically. However, specific questions must be considered. Under what circumstances will the early release of election results actually change voter behavior (mobilize or demobilize)? To what extent is the source of the information, separate of the media platform, likely to have a mitigating effect on voter turnout?

MEDIA TYPE PREFERENCE

According to a 2013 Nielsen Report, television (TV) remains the leader in terms of media consumption; 90 percent of Americans now consume their news via television. The spread of television between 1950 and 1970 is regularly blamed for both the decline of local newspapers and a substantial drop in voter turnout. Traditional TV viewing cumulatively accounts for up to 6 days' (or 144 hours, 54 minutes) worth of time per month, in comparison with using the Internet on a computer, which takes up 28 hours, 29 minutes. "Despite the spread of the Internet, television is still the most powerful tool that influences peoples' minds" (Lazitski 2013). This number varies across age demographics, particularly when TV viewing is separated into broadcast and cable mediums.

Although continuing to be the most trusted source of political informa-tion, TV is also criticized for restricting content along ideological lines. Many question, and indeed doubt, whether the news media provides today's voters with sufficient information to function as competent democratic citizens. Compared to 2012 presidential primary campaign coverage, the 2016 coverage to date has provided little by way of reporting which candidate led in campaign donations (a traditional indicator of likely voter support). There was, however, abundant coverage of Hillary Clinton's private e-mail server, Donald Trump's most recent offensive comments, and weekly, if not daily reports of polling data as substitute for investigative reporting on the platforms and positions of the candidates.

News consumers increasingly seek less contentious, enjoyment-based "soft news" sources via social media, infotainment, and the blogosphere. The consumption of "soft news" means that voters are not accessing investigative "hard news" to the same historically high frequency. Public affairs-oriented "hard" news is often considered unappealing or not "sexy" enough for the average media consumer/voter. Increasingly, news quality, as indicated by media consumption and voter behavior, is determined by how entertaining the news source is. As a result, for many likely voters, "soft news" is more effective than traditional "hard news" in promoting voter turnout. According to Baum and Jamison (2006), entertainment personalities such as Oprah Winfrey, Bill Maher, and John Stewart are better at mobilizing voters to turn out to the polls on Election Day. Among likely voters with limited knowledge of the candidates (the authors call this group politically inattentive), who reported consuming no hard news, as talk show (soft news) consumption increases from its minimum to maximum values, the probability of actually voting for a preferred candidate (the authors call this phenomenon voting consistently) increases by 13 percentage points.

CONCLUSION

Over the past decade, discontent with biased reporting has led to fragmentation in broadcast television news audiences. A 2004 poll found that over two-thirds of the U.S. public (69%) perceived at least a fair amount of political bias in the news, and only 7 percent perceived no bias at all (Prior 2005). The consequence of this fragmentation is a shift in preference to a wide array of cable and other news sources, thereby changing the way many Americans get their political information. Instead of demanding greater objectivity, news consumers, particularly younger news consumers, are simply choosing alternative types of consumption. Counterintuitively, studies show that the consumption of "soft news" media not only increases voter turnout but can also be a vehicle for facilitating political competence among some citizens (Bachmann et al. 2010).

Finally, pre-election opinion polls, exit polls, and the early release of election results are treated equally under the First Amendment, which does not allow for these practices to be unduly infringed upon. Although many maintain the belief that the media is obligated to keep voters sufficiently informed to make the best political choices, others observe that the media is a business, and will follow the path to profit, even if it is away from objectivity and journalistic integrity. The early release of election results and other polling data, for all of its varied and theoretical impacts on voter turnout, can be asserted to be simply another product that news media consumers can take or leave.

FURTHER READING

Anand, S. Aarthi, and Celia Joanne Jenkins. 2004. "Exit Polls: Debating Freedom or Fairness." *Economic and Political Weekly* 39 (46/47): 4971–4973.

Bachmann, Ingrid, Kaufhold, Kelly, Lewis, Seth C., and Homero Gil de Zúñiga. 2010. "News Platform Preference: Advancing the Effects of Age and Media Consumption on Political Participation." *International Journal of Internet Science* 5: 34–47.

Baum, Matthew A., and Angela S. Jamison. 2006. "The Oprah Effect: How Soft News Helps Inattentive Citizens Vote Consistently." *Journal of Politics* 68: 946–959.

Busch, Ronald J., and Joel A. Lieske. 1985. "Does Time of Voting Affect Exit Poll Results?" *Public Opinion Quarterly* 49: 94–104.

Carpini, Michael X. Delli. 1984. "Scooping the Voters? The Consequences of the Networks' Early Call of the 1980 Presidential Race." *The Journal of Politics* 46: 866–885.

Gerber, Alan, Karlan, Dean S., and Daniel Bergan. 2006. "A Field Experiment Measuring the Effect of Newspapers on Voting Behavior and Political Opinions." February 15. Yale Economic Applications and Policy Discussion Paper 12.

Lafayette, John. 2015. "28% of TV Viewing Done via Streaming." The Business of Broadcasting & Cable. Retrieved August 9, 2015 from http://www.broad castingcable.com/news/next-tv/28-tv-viewing-done-streaming/142380.

Lazitski, Olga. 2013. "Media Endarkenment: A Comparative Analysis of 2012 Election Coverage in the United States and Russia." *American Behavioral Scientist* 58: 1–30.

Milavsky, J. Ronald, Swift, Al, Roper, Burns W., Salant, Richard, and Floyd Abrams. 1985. "Early Calls of Election Results and Exit Polls: Pros, Cons, and Constitutional Considerations." *Public Opinion Quarterly* 49 (1): 1–18.

Oberholzer-Gee, Felix, and Joel Waldfogel. 2006. "Media Markets and Localism: Does Local News en Espanol Boost Hispanic Voter Turnout?" No. w12317. National Bureau of Economic Research.

O'Connor, Karen J., Sabato, Larry J., and Alixandra B. Yanus. 2013. *Essentials of American Government: Roots and Reform.* Upper Saddle River, NJ: Pearson Higher Ed.

Odegard, Peter H., and E. Allen Helms. 1938. *American Politics: A Study in Political Dynamic.* New York, NY: Harper & Brothers.

Patterson, Thomas. 2003. "The Search for a Standard: Markets and the Media." *Political Communication* 20 (April/June): 139–143.

Perez, Sarah. 2013. "Nielsen: TV Still King in Media Consumption; Only 16 Percent of Homes Have Tablets." *Techcrunch Blog*, January 13. Retrieved August 9, 2015 from http://techcrunch.com/2013/01/07/nielsen-tv-still-king-in-media-consumption-only-16-percent-of-tv-homes-have-tablets/.

Prior, Markus. 2005. "News vs. Entertainment: How Increasing Media Choice Widens Gaps in Political Knowledge and Turnout." *American Journal of Political Science* 49: 577–592.

Rietz, Thomas. 2008. "Three-Way Experimental Election Results: Strategic Voting, Coordinated Outcomes and Duverger's Law." *Handbook of Experimental Economics Results* 1: 889–897.

Roskin, Michael G., Cord, Robert L., Medeiros, James A., and Walter S. Jones. 2010. *Political Science: An Introduction* (11th ed.). New York, NY: Pearson Education, Inc.

Tolbert, Caroline J., and Ramona S. McNeal. 2003. "Unraveling the Effects of the Internet on Political Participation?" *Political Research Quarterly* 56: 175–185.

19

Tenor of Modern Political Campaigns: Alienation and Voter Turnout

Priscilla L. Southwell

"Vote, Vote, Get Out the Vote—Choose the One Who'll Cut Your Throat"

—Graffiti in Eugene, Oregon, November 2012

When potential voters are disillusioned and disenchanted with the political system, they are less likely to participate. Political alienation—as defined by feelings of powerlessness and cynicism, can influence whether an individual votes or not. Specifically, the chapter investigates the behavioral implications of these alienated attitudes on voter turnout in the 2008 and 2012 presidential elections. The analysis of recent survey data suggests that feelings of powerlessness decreased turnout in both election years, and cynicism did so in 2012.

During the late 1960s and early 1970s, Americans became less attached to the two major political parties, more cynical about elected officials and political institutions, and less confident in their own ability to influence the political system. The conduct of the Vietnam War under the Johnson and Nixon administrations, coupled with the urban unrest that erupted in the late 1960s, certainly affected the general public's assessment of the capabilities and competence of public and party officials (Tolchin 1998).

The Watergate scandal of 1972–1974 had widespread implications for other political figures outside of the Nixon White House. Its revelations led many Americans to question a political process where large campaign contributors were shown to have influenced major decisions ranging from government contracts to ambassadorial posts (Garment 1991). As additional political scandals, from the Iran-Contra affair to President Clinton's impeachment trial unfolded in subsequent decades, these feelings of alienation continued to grow among the American people. Such negative views of the political system declined at the end of the 20th century, but have risen considerably over the past decade. In 2014, the Gallup Poll reported that 65 percent of Americans are dissatisfied with the U.S. system of government and how it works—the highest percentage since 2001 (Gallup 2015).

Feelings of powerlessness, or "inefficacy," have previously been linked to lower levels of voting, as those who are not confident in their ability to influence politics are less likely to vote (Abramson and Aldrich 1982; Craig 1993; Southwell 1985, 2012; Weatherford 1991, 1992). High levels of cynicism often also invoke distrust of the political system, hence decreased participation (Hetherington 1998, 1999, 2005; Rudolph and Evans 2005; Teixeira 1987, 1992; Weakliem and Borch 2006). However, cynical individuals can also be spurred on by their desire "to throw the rascals out" (Citrin 1974, 1977, 2001).

When an individual is faced with an external situation that is perceived as undesirable, he is presented with two options: 1) take remedial action or 2) exit the scene. In an electoral context, the individual who has become disenchanted with the political system either votes or abstains. The internal or self-perceived capabilities of the individual involved may influence whether one participates or withdraws. An individual who feels powerless and cynical is less likely to become involved in politics even if one believes that the current political situation is in need of remedy. External evaluations of the political system, such as the responsiveness of political parties or the effectiveness of the electoral process, also affect one's decision to participate or abstain.

In rational choice terms, these internal and external perspectives reflect one's values about democracy, including how much individuals care which party wins the election (Downs 1957). These long-term attitudes have been shown to be deep-seated and persistent (Aldrich 1993; Fiorina 1981; Riker and Ordeshook 1968).

Contextual considerations, such as the nature of the political choices offered in any one election year, also influence the voting decision. Here the difference in perceived benefits derived if one candidate wins over another comes into play. Aldrich (1993) argues that models of voting behavior need to relate long-term attitudes toward democracy to perceived benefits of particular elections. In other words, the linkage between general orientations and election-specific forces must be better established. As an example, Aldrich (1993) suggests that high levels of powerlessness lead to lesser benefits from electing any particular candidate to office. This linkage lends support to the hypothesis that alienated individuals were more likely to abstain from voting than their more allegiant counterparts (Gilmour and Lamb 1975; Southwell 1985; Zipp 1985).

So, we might expect that the rise in political cynicism and powerlessness in recent years to decrease turnout in 2008 and 2012. Certainly, the war in Iraq and the worsening economy under the Bush administration did little to ease the concerns of Americans by 2008. However, in certain electoral contexts, many alienated individuals are provided with an outlet for their frustration at the political system. Specifically, such individuals can and do protest the current state of political affairs by voting for an "outside" or third party presidential candidate (Atkeson et al. 1996; Hetherington 1999). Many disillusioned voters, especially liberal ones, appear to have rallied behind the candidacy of Barack Obama in 2008. The assumption is that the mobilization efforts of the Democratic Party in 2007–2008, primarily directed at blacks, Latino/as, and young persons, were effective in both getting such persons to register *and* vote for the Obama/Biden ticket (Avery 2006, 2009; Nagourney 2008). In 2008, Barack Obama emerged as a candidate who could "change" the system. The historic nature of this election suggests many interesting questions. Did his candidacy alter the political landscape such that "outsiders" became more hopeful and participatory? Did he break the link between political alienation and nonvoting? Was the mobilizing effect present in 2014 as well?

THE CONCEPT OF ALIENATION

The concept of political alienation refers to a set of attitudes or opinions that reflect a negative view of the political system. Political alienation represents a less-than-positive view of the political world; it indicates displeasure with political leaders and institutions. Lane defined the concept of alienation as "an individual's disapproval of the way political decisions are made" (1962, 162). In a similar vein, Neuman describes alienation as a "conscious rejection of the whole political system which expresses itself in apathy" (1957, 290).

Political alienation, as Neuman suggests, can include a sense that one is powerless to influence the political system. Such individuals often feel incapable of having any meaningful impact on political events or developments. Although political alienation represents a general disillusionment and disenchantment with the political system, the concept includes a number of different dimensions, some of which may be present to different degrees in an alienated individual (Harder and Krosnick 2008; Herring 1989).

A major advance in approaching the definitional problems of alienation was the research on the dimensionality of this concept (see Finifter 1970 and also subsequent works by Clarke and Acock 1989; Niemi, Craig, and Mattei 1991; Weatherford 1991, 1992). This type of inquiry breaks down the larger concept of alienation in order to specify the dimensions of alienation by identifying the different ways in which political alienation may be expressed: "powerlessness," "meaninglessness" or government responsiveness, and "cynicism." *Powerlessness* reflects the individual's assessment of how much power or influence he or she can have on the course of political events and outcomes. *Meaninglessness*, or lack of government responsiveness, is closely related to powerlessness, but represents a more general evaluation of how receptive political institutions are to input from all individuals in society, not simply the individual himself or herself. This dimension refers to beliefs about whether political parties offer meaningful choices among candidates, whether elections provide an effective way for citizens to influence the political system, and whether elected bodies are representative of the general public (Gilmour and Lamb 1975). Political *cynicism* is an evaluation of whether the government is producing policies according to expectations. Politically cynical individuals are generally dissatisfied with the procedures and products of government (Erikson, Luttbeg, and Tedin 2007). The different dimensions of alienation may combine in different ways and result in a variety of behaviors. A cynical individual, who nonetheless feels that voting is an effective way to influence the political system, may be motivated to vote in order to oust the current administration or party in power. In contrast, another similarly cynical individual, who feels powerless as well, is likely to stay home on Election Day.

DATA ANALYSIS

Feelings of powerlessness and cynicism have been identified by scholars as notable factors in turnout for the 2008 and 2012 election years. The figures below show the effect of feelings of cynicism and powerlessness on the probability of voting in the presidential elections of 2008 and 2010. Figure 19.1 illustrates cynicism; Figure 19.2 illustrates powerlessness. The findings reported in these figures come from surveys conducted by the University of Michigan and are based on a multivariate analysis, which also controls for the effect of other influences on voter turnout, such as age, education, and income (see Appendix A.6 for the survey questions and Appendix A.7 results of the multivariate analysis). Both figures clearly show the impact of feelings of cynicism and powerlessness on voter turnout. In both elections, more alienated individuals are much less likely to vote.

These findings confirm the effect of negative evaluations on important political actions and behaviors. The real conundrum is how to ease these alienated feelings, when they may be based on a realistic assessment of the current state of affairs in U.S. politics. Perhaps, a comprehensive reform of

Figure 19.1
Effect of Alienated Attitudes on Probability of Voting

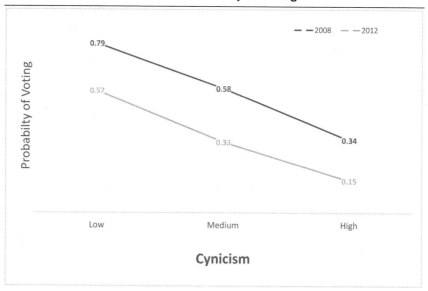

Figure 19.2

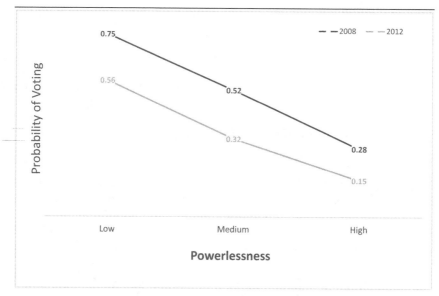

Source: American National Election Studies. 2012. "American National Election Study, 2008: Pre- and Post-Election Survey." ICPSR25383-v2. Ann Arbor, MI: Inter-University Consortium for Political and Social Research.

campaign finance or a change in the restrictiveness of electoral law for third parties would start the process.

On the latter point, there have been few times in recent U.S. politics when a viable third party presidential candidate has been present. In 1992 and 2000, the presence of a third party candidate was shown to mobilize disenchanted and disillusioned voters, such that they voted for that candidate, even as a "protest" vote (Southwell 2004; Southwell and Everest 1998). The context of the 1992 and 2000 presidential elections, with the candidacies of Ross Perot and Ralph Nader, respectively, was such that many alienated individuals were provided with alternative outlets for expressing their frustration with the political system. Specifically, alienated individuals could protest the current state of political affairs by voting for a third party presidential candidate. Because it applies to the dynamics of voter turnout and the appeal of third parties, this "protest voter" hypothesis represents an extension of the rejection voting model, where voters displeased with a certain policy or personality within their party defect to another party (Fiorina 1981; Key 1966). This phenomenon suggests that third party candidates, or even Independent candidates, have the potential to transform certain alienated individuals, from likely non-voter to voter.

The "protest voter" hypothesis differs from the strategic or "tactical" model in which individual preferences are often overridden by assessments of the competitive situation. As well-established in rational choice literature, this model assumes that an individual will vote for his or her second preference in a situation in which his or her first preference is unlikely to win, therefore avoiding a "wasted" vote (Black 1978; Cain 1978; Downs 1957; Duverger 1967).

In contrast, the alienated protest voter may behave in an opposite manner to the strategic voter. He or she may gravitate toward a third party candidate because that candidate has less chance of victory. Bowler and Lanoue describe the protest voter as one "who may vote for a third party not so much to unseat the incumbent as to reduce the majority status of that incumbent and so send a message of dissatisfaction" (1992, 489). Alienated individuals may not consider votes for unlikely winners as "wasted," but as a statement of dissatisfaction (Southwell 2003). "Alienated individuals are more likely to vote when there is a third party or independent candidate that is a symbol of their dissatisfaction. Thus, although alienation can, and often, leads to abstention, when conditions are ripe, alienation can result in electoral participation, albeit of a negative quality (Southwell 2004, 425).

THE IMPACT OF NEGATIVE POLITICAL ADVERTISING

In addition to limited political party and candidate options contributing to alienation, potential voters may increasingly feel apathetic and cynical because of the negative tone associated with political campaigns and advertisements. Although citizens may possess limited knowledge about elected officials and current events (Schenck-Hamlin, Proctor, and Rumsey 2000), campaign advertisements serve as a resource that allows citizens to learn about candidates and their positions on a variety of issues (Ansolabehere and Iyengar 1995). In today's environment much of the information that citizens learn about candidates is through negative campaign advertisements that are created by interest groups, opposing candidates, their campaigns, and supporters. The focus of these advertisements is often not to educate others on the policy positions of a candidate but to demonstrate to the public the ways that the opposing candidate is not suited, personally or professionally, to serve in the position being campaigned for.

The first presidential election that included the extensive use of television campaign advertisements was in 1952. The advertisements quickly turned negative, most notably with Lyndon B. Johnson's *Daisy Girl* advertisement from 1964, which features a little girl in a field plucking individual petals from a daisy and counting each petal. Given her age, she experiences some difficulty with the sequence of the numbers. Once she reaches nine, a male voice begins a reverse countdown in the background. Once the male voice reaches zero, an image of a nuclear explosion appears. Johnson is then heard saying, "These are the stakes. To make a world in which all of God's children can live, or to go into the dark. We must either love each other, or we must die." A final voiceover then states, "Vote for President Johnson on November 3rd. The stakes are too high for you to stay home." The intention of the advertisement was to assert Johnson as a responsible and trustworthy man while portraying Barry Goldwater as a reckless and dangerous one.

In contemporary American politics, the use of advertisements to convey a negative image of the opposing candidate persists. One of the most famous negative campaign advertisements in recent elections was the Willie Horton advertisement from the 1988 presidential election. Willie Horton, an African American man who was convicted of murder and was serving a life sentence without the possibility of parole in Massachusetts, was allowed a series of weekend furloughs. In the advertisement, the narrator informs the audience that while on furlough, Horton kidnapped a couple, repeatedly raped the woman, and stabbed her male companion. These events occurred during the time that Michael Dukakis, the then Democratic nominee for president, was the governor of Massachusetts. The advertisement, which was run by the National Security Political Action Committee (NSPAC), presented the Willie Horton story in a way that urged viewers to place the blame for the violent attacks on Dukakis. Some critics of the advertisement charged that it went far beyond painting Dukakis as soft on crime. They asserted that although the ad did not explicitly mention Horton's race, it used imagery patently designed to prey on white voters' racial fears.

Although such advertisements may be perceived as a useful tool that candidates can use to convince potential voters that their political challengers are inferior, these tactics may have a negative effect on the political attitudes, disposition, and behavior of the mass public. While scholars have asserted that there is a relationship between the tone and framing of campaign coverage by the news media, distrust, and cynicism (Ansolabehere and Iyengar 1995; Cappella and Jamieson 1996; Lipset and Schneider 1983), others have suggested that it is unclear as to whether negative advertisements cause cynicism or merely trigger underlying political cynicism (Schenck-Hamlin, Proctor, and Rumsey 2000). Further, some have found that there is in fact no relationship between campaign tone and trust in government (Jackson, Mondak, and Huckfeldt 2009; Lau and Pomper 2004).

Beyond the tone of campaign advertisements, the content of campaign advertisements may affect feelings of alienation. Utilizing campaign advertisements from the 2004 presidential election, research has found that college students feel alienated by candidates for a variety of reasons, including candidates not featuring individuals from their age demographic in advertisements and not addressing issues that are important to college students. College students also report being disappointed by the negative tone of campaign advertisements and suggest that political advertising would be better used to educate voters about the merits of a particular candidate as opposed to focusing on why the opposing candidate is not an acceptable choice. Lastly, advertisements that attacked candidates on a personal level were evaluated more negatively than those that made attacks on a candidate's policy positions (Parmelee, Perkins, and Sayre 2007).

Given that negative campaign advertisements can contribute to citizen alienation and cynicism, we might then expect that exposure to negative campaign advertisements to have an effect on voter turnout. The relationship, however, between viewing negative campaign advertisements and voter turnout is not clear. Researchers have found that negative campaigns can demobilize voters and make them less likely to turn out, generate greater interest in campaigns and mobilize voters, or have no effect on turnout (see Lau, Sigleman, and Rovner 2007 for detailed description of negative campaign studies). Beyond understanding the effect that the tone and content of political advertisements can have on citizen alienation, cynicism, and turnout, it is perhaps equally as important to try and understand why candidates for elected office continually engage in behavior that sustains a political environment characterized by limited choice, citizen mistrust, and cynicism.

FURTHER READING

Abramson, Paul, and John Aldrich. 1982. "The Decline of Electoral Participation in America." *American Political Science Review* 76: 502–521.

Aldrich, John. 1993. "Rational Choice and Turnout." *American Journal of Political Science* 37: 246–278.

American National Election Studies. 2012. "American National Election Study, 2008: Pre- and Post-Election Survey." ICPSR25383-v2. Ann Arbor, MI: Inter-University Consortium for Political and Social Research.

Ansolabhere, Stephen, and Shanto Iyengar. 1995. *Going Negative: How Political Advertisements Shrink and Polarize the Electorate.* New York, NY: Free Press.

Atkeson, Lonna R., McCann, James M., Rapoport, Ronald B., and Walter Stone. 1996. "Citizens for Perot: Assessing Patterns of Alienation and Activism." In *Broken Contract*, edited by S. C. Craig, 147–167. Boulder, CO: Westview Press.

Avery, James M. 2006. "The Sources and Consequences of Political Trust among African Americans." *American Politics Research* 34: 655–682.

Avery, James M. 2009. "Political Trust among African Americans and Support for the Political System." *Political Research Quarterly* 62: 132–145.

Black, Jerome H. 1978. "The Multicandidate Calculus of Voting: Application to Canadian Federal Elections." *American Journal of Political Science* 22: 609–638.

Bowler, Shaun, and David L. Lanoue. 1992. "Strategic and Protest Voting for Third Parties: The Case of the Canadian NDP." *Western Political Quarterly* 45: 485–500.

Cain, Bruce E. 1978. "Strategic Voting in Britain." *American Journal of Political Science* 22: 639–655.

Cappella, Joseph N., and Kathleen H. Jamieson. 1996. "News Frames, Political Cynicism, and Media Cynicism." *Annals of the American Academy of Political and Social Science* 546: 71–84.

Citrin, Jack. 1974. "Comment: The Political Relevance of Cynicism in Government." *American Political Science Review* 68: 973–988.

Citrin, Jack. 1977. "Political Alienation as a Social Indicator: Attitudes and Actions." *Social Indicators Research* 4: 381–419.

Citrin, Jack, and Samantha Luks. 2001. "Political Cynicism Revisited: Déja Vu All over Again?" In *What Is It about Government That Americans Dislike?*, edited by Elizabeth Theiss-Morse and J. R. Hibbing, 9–27. New York, NY: Cambridge University Press.

Clarke, Harold, and Alan Acock. 1989. "National Elections and Political Attitudes: The Case of Political Inefficacy." *British Journal of Political Science* 19: 551–562.

Craig, Stephen C. 1993. *Malevolent Leaders: Popular Discontent in America.* Boulder, CO: Westview Press.

Downs, Anthony. 1957. *An Economic Theory of Democracy.* New York, NY: Harper and Row.

Duverger, Maurice. 1967. *Political Parties.* London: Lowe and Brydone.

Erikson, Robert S., and Kent L. Tedin. 2007. *American Public Opinion: Its Origins, Content, and Impact.* New York, N.Y.: Pearson/Longman.

Finifter, Ada. 1970. "Dimensions of Political Alienation." *American Political Science Review* 65: 329–341.

Fiorina, Morris.1981. *Retrospective Voting in American National Elections*. New Haven, CT: Yale University Press.

Gallup. 2015. "In U.S., 65% Dissatisfied with How Gov't System Works." Retrieved May 25, 2015 from www.gallup.com/poll/166985/dissatisfoied-gov-system-works.aspx.

Garment, Suzanne. 1991. *Scandal: The Crisis of Cynicism in American Politics*. New York, NY: Random House.

Gilmour, Robert S., and Robert B. Lamb. 1975. *Political Alienation in Contemporary America*. New York, NY: St. Martin's.

Harder, Joshua, and Jon A. Krosnick. 2008. "Why Do People Vote? A Psychological Analysis of the Causes of Voter Turnout." *Journal of Social Issues* 64: 525–549. doi: 10.1111/j.1540-4560.2008.00576.x.

Herring, Cecil. 1989. *Splitting the Middle: Political Alienation, Acquiescence, and Activism among America's Middle Layers*. New York, NY: Praeger.

Hetherington, Marc J. 1998. "The Political Relevance of Political Cynicism." *American Political Science Review* 92: 791–808.

Hetherington, Marc J. 1999. "The Effect of Political Cynicism on the Presidential Vote, 1968–96." *American Political Science Review* 93: 311–322.

Hetherington, Marc J. 2005. *Why Cynicism Matters: Declining Political Cynicism and the Demise of American Liberalism*. Princeton, NJ: Princeton University Press.

Jackson, Robert A., Mondak, Jeffrey J., and Robert Huckfeldt. 2009. "Examining the Possible Corrosive Impact of Negative Advertising on Citizen's Attitudes toward Politics." *Political Research Quarterly* 62: 55–69.

Key Jr., V. O. 1966. *The Responsible Electorate*. Cambridge, MA: Harvard University.

Lane, Robert. 1962. *Political Ideology*. New York, NY: The Free Press.

Lau, Richard R., and Gerald Pomper. 2004. *Negative Campaigning: An Analysis of U.S. Senate Elections*. Lanham, MD: Rowan and Littlefield.

Lau, Richard R., Sigleman, Lee, and Ivy B. Rovner. 2007. "The Effects of Negative Political Campaigns: A Meta-Analytic Reassessment." *The Journal of Politics* 69: 1176–1209.

Lipset, Seymour M., and William Schenider. 1983. "The Decline of Confidence in American Institutions." *Political Science Quarterly* 98: 378–400.

Nagourney, Adam. 2008. "The '08 Campaign: Sea Change for Politics as We Know It." *The New York Times*, November 4, 1. http://www.nytimes.com/2008/11/04/us/politics/04memo.html?_r=0.

Neuman, Franz L. 1957. *The Democratic and the Authoritarian State*. New York, NY: The Free Press.

Niemi, Richard G., Craig, Stephen C., and Franco Mattei. 1991. "Measuring Internal Political Inefficacy in the 1988 National Election Study." *American Political Science Review* 85: 1407–1141.

Parmelee, John H., Perkins, Stephynie C., and Judith J. Sayre. 2007. " 'What about People Our Age?' Applying Qualitative and Quantitative Methods to Uncover How Political Ads Alienate College Students." *Journal of Mixed Methods Research* 1: 183–199.

Plutzer, Eric. 2002. "Becoming a Habitual Voter: Inertia, Resources, and Growth in Young Adulthood." *American Political Science Review* 96: 41–56.

Riker, William H., and Paul C. Ordeshook. 1968. "A Theory of the Calculus of Voting." *American Political Science Review*, 62: 25–43.

Rudolph, Thomas J., and Jillian Evans. 2005. "Political Trust, Ideology, and Public Support for Government Spending." *American Journal of Political Science* 49: 660–671.

Schenck-Hamlin, William J., Proctor, David E., and Deborah J. Rumsey. 2000. "The Influence of Negative Advertising Frames on Political Cynicism and Politician Accountability." *Human Communication Research* 26: 53–74.

Segura, Gary, Jackman, Simon, Hutchings, Vincent, and American National Election Studies. 2010–2012. "American National Election Studies: Evaluations of Government and Society Study 1 (EGSS 1)." ICPSR32701-v1. Ann Arbor, MI: Inter-University Consortium for Political and Social Research.

Southwell, Priscilla L. 1985. "Alienation and Nonvoting in the United States: A Refined Operationalization." *Western Political Quarterly* 38: 663–674.

Southwell, Priscilla L. 2003. "The Politics of Alienation: Nonvoting and Support for Third-Party Candidates among 18–30 Year Olds." *The Social Science Journal* 40: 99–107.

Southwell, Priscilla L. 2004. "Nader Voters in the 2000 Presidential Election: What Would They Have Done without Him?" *The Social Science Journal* 41: 423–431.

Southwell, Priscilla L. 2012. "Political Alienation: Behavioral Implications of Efficacy and Cynicism in the 2008 U.S. Presidential Election." *Review of European Studies* 4: 71–77.

Southwell, Priscilla L., and Marcy Everest. 1998. "The Electoral Consequences of Alienation: Nonvoting and Third Party Voting in the 1992 Presidential Elections." *Social Science Journal* 35: 43–51.

Teixeira, Ruy. 1987. *Why Americans Don't Vote: Turnout Decline in the United States 1960–1984*. New York, NY: Greenwood Press.

Teixeira, Ruy. 1992. *The Disappearing Voter*. Washington, DC: Brookings Institution.

The Independent, 2015, September 18. http://www.independent.co.uk/news/world/politics/pirate-party-surges-in-polls-to-become-biggest-political-party-in-iceland-10222018.html.

Tolchin, Susan J. 1998. *The Angry American*. Boulder, CO: Westview Press.

University of Michigan. 2004. "American National Election Study, 2004 Panel Study." ICPSR04293-v1. Ann Arbor, MI: Center for Political Studies.

Weakliem, David L., and Casey Borch. 2006. "Alienation in the United States: Uniform or Group-Specific Change?" *Sociological Forum* 21: 415–438.

Weatherford, M. Stephen 1991. "Mapping the Ties that Bind: Legitimacy, Representation, and Alienation." *Western Political Quarterly* 44: 251–273.

Weatherford, M. Stephen. 1992. "Measuring Political Legitimacy." *American Political Science Review* 86: 149–167.

Zipp, John. 1985. "Perceived Representativeness and Voting: An Assessment of the Impact of 'Choices vs. Echoes.'" *American Political Science Review* 79: 50–61.

20

Mobilization through Third Party Groups

Mitchell Brown

Third party groups are nongovernmental organizations whose purpose is nonetheless to affect government. With respect to elections, they operate in a number of ways, including trying to influence government by having members elected to office (called "political parties"), and by bringing attention to major issues of interest to group members through a variety of tactics, such as lobbying, litigation, research, direct service provision, training and technical assistance, public education, and encouraging people to register to vote and show up at the polls (called "interest groups"). One of the key functions of public interest groups focused on elections is to mobilize voters through so-called "get out the vote" (GOTV) efforts, though the extant literature is mixed on how and whether these efforts are effective.

There are a variety of issues that interest groups focus on to mobilize voters. In recent elections, organizations concerned about issues such as the Second Amendment and gun control, abortion, employee wages, and the environment have all been prominent. Interest groups may also use the history of a candidate to mobilize voters. During the 2004 presidential election, for example, a conservative group called Swift Boat Veterans mobilized in opposition to Democratic nominee John Kerry's presidential campaign by making controversial allegations that Kerry lied about his military record and was not fit to serve as president.

As noted above, third party groups may include political parties, but for the purpose of this chapter, the focus will only be on nonpolitical party interest groups, some of which are partisan and others of which are nonpartisan. These are also sometimes referred to as nongovernmental organizations outside of the American context. Third party groups are critical elements within the American political system writ large as they function to allow ordinary citizens to get involved in politics beyond voting and individual contact with legislators. These groups organize around particular topics or issues of interest, frequently allowing citizens to join in with other similarly minded and therefore allied people to coordinate together and advance their personal interests.

The role of the third party, or interest, group system in American politics is best characterized by the theory of pluralism. As first described by Dahl (1961), pluralism is the idea that politics in the United States is heavily influenced not just by political parties, politicians, donors, and voters, but also by groups of citizens who come together (in organized groups) to advance particular goals (or interests). Although ordinary citizens are not typically involved in politics most of the time, some will become active around issues of critical importance to them and encourage others to do so as well. Government then responds when a critical mass of citizens feel strongly about a particular issue (when this happens, the issue is sometimes referred to as salient).

The scope of interest groups in the United States is immense. The idea of working together to achieve common goals has always been ubiquitous in the American experience (see, e.g., Tocqueville 1839). In the late 1960s, America experienced an explosion of interest groups and the number and scope have expanded ever since (Loomis and Cigler 2016). These groups work at the national, regional, state, and local levels. Some operate in all or some of these levels simultaneously, while others work only in one. Some have formal organizations with large budgets and a professional staff, while others are comprised of volunteers only; most exist somewhere in between. Early interest groups formed using a federated structure, meaning that they had a national office as well as local chapters. Groups formed more recently usually have a unified structure, meaning that they have only a national, or sometimes state or local, office.

Third party groups play several key roles with respect to elections, including influencing the administration of elections, serving a watchdog function over election administration and candidates and their campaigns, working to register voters, and mobilizing voters through public information campaigns and GOTV efforts. Surveys of the major national organizations that work in elections show that they vary a great deal in terms of age, scope, and tactics (see Table 20.1). With a few recent exceptions (see discussion of Citizens United later), almost all of the third party

Table 20.1
Array of Characteristics from a Sample of Major Third Party Organization

	Range	Average
Year Organization Established	**1909–2009 (percent)**	**Median = 1990**
Focus	Disabled = 10.5 Election administrators = 10.5 General = 42 Minority = 31.6 Low income = 5.3	Mode = General population
Location*	Baltimore, MD = 5.3 Katy, TX = 10.5 Los Angeles, CA = 5.3 New York, NY = 21.1 Renton, WA = 5.3 Tacoma Park, MD = 5.3 Washington, DC = 42.1	Mode = Washington, DC
Activities	Public education = 89.5 Lobbying = 31.6 Legislative testimony = 68.4 Legalism = 68.4 Training/Technical assistance = 63.2 Research = 84.2 Registration = 26.3 GOTV = 26.3	Mode = Public education
n = 19		

*Does not equal 100 percent as one organization is defunct and no longer has a location.
Source: Hale, Montjoy, and Brown 2015.

organizations involved in GOTV efforts do so through local affiliate organizations (see Hale, Montjoy, and Brown 2015).

MAJOR THIRD PARTY GROUPS INVOLVED IN ELECTIONS

With respect to elections and voter mobilization, the oldest, largest, and arguably most important has been the League of Women Voters (LWV or the League). The League began as an offshoot of the largest women's suffrage organization, the National Woman Suffrage Association (NWSA), engaged in helping women attain the right to vote nationally. After suffrage rights were attained for women in 1920 with the passage of the Nineteenth Amendment, the NWSA became the LWV, the purpose of which then became to advance women's access to the electoral process and to enhance voter mobilization more generally. The LWV operates today using a federated structure (meaning they have a top-down organization with a national office, state organizations, and local organizations, all of which provide feedback to the national organization about leadership and organizational priorities) with a mix of paid staff and a significant number of volunteers, though their volunteer base has diminished significantly over the past 40 years. Over time, the LWV has worked to enhance elections in a number of ways, from legislative monitoring, to voter education, to advocating for better election administration practices, to voter registration drives, and to enhancing voter turnout, or GOTV. (For more information, see Brown 2005; Gidlow 2002; Hale and Brown 2015; Hale, Montjoy, and Brown 2015; Harris 1928; Harris 1929.)

The LWV is the oldest nonpartisan third party group that functions to influence elections but it is not the only one. As interest groups have proliferated in the United States generally, there has also been a groundswell of organizations focused on elections. Over time, other organizations began their own GOTV efforts to enhance turnout among group members, particularly those whose members or target audience were unlikely voters because of some form of minority status. Chief among these is the National Association for the Advancement of Colored People (NAACP). While initially working to improve conditions generally and access to voting through litigation strategies, the NAACP helped to create and then partnered with other organizations like the Southern Christian Leadership Council (SCLC) and the Student Nonviolent Coordinating Committee (SNCC) to enhance access to the polls and later encourage voter turnout. Following the passage of the Voting Rights Act (VRA) in 1965, these and other national organizations turned their attention to GOTV, and many regional and local organizations were created specifically to increase turnout among newly enfranchised minority voters. Most of the newly created organizations were not long lasting and the research on the efficacy of all of these efforts is mixed, showing that some of the organizations were initially able to increase turnout for targeted subgroup members but with lasting effects for some (Hispanic/Latino/a) voters but not for others (African American; Baker 1996; Vedlitz 1985). Further research demonstrated that the registration efforts of these groups did not translate into increased turnout; those that self-registered were more likely to cast ballots than those that were registered by third party organizations (Cain and McCue 1985).

Colleges and universities also function as third party groups when it comes to voter registration and GOTV. Student groups on college campuses are organized to increase voter registration and provide reminders for how and when to vote, either through absentee ballots for those students registered to vote in a home district away from the school or for those voting in the district(s) serving the school. These student organizations include an array of groups affiliated with various political parties and candidates, as well as nonpartisan campus wide efforts whose aim is to enhance democratic functioning by attracting youth voters more generally. The reach of these campus organizations is by definition significantly smaller than the other organizations described above; however, as a whole campus organizations represent hundreds of thousands of potential voters in every election and have been shown to have an effect on increasing student turnout as compared to citizens of the same age who are not enrolled in college (Ulbig and Waggener 2011).

Perhaps the most notorious of the third party groups working to enhance voter mobilization in the recent past is the Association of Community Organizations for Reform (ACORN). ACORN began as an advocacy organization whose purpose was to push for policy and rights change for low- and moderate-income people. Over time their agenda evolved to include registration and GOTV efforts, as well as working to elect ACORN members and ACORN-friendly politicians to office in order to affect positive policy change for members. For example, in the election following Hurricane Katrina that displaced thousands of voters, ACORN provided free bus service to refugees attempting to vote (Vanderleeu, Liu, and Williams 2008). Part of ACORN's strategy for all of its efforts, and for voter registration specifically, was to hire largely unskilled workers to advance their mission of helping low-income people gain skills and employment. In the end this strategy, coupled with canvassers who participated in illegal activity, became the downfall of the organization. Over time allegations of fraudulent practices by ACORN canvassers began to spread and were made in several states. These allegations were covered by major media outlets including the *New York Times* and *Fox News*, which aired video footage of some of the ACORN canvassers actually engaging in fraud. In some of these cases, the charges of fraud were substantiated, and over time the organization lost so much public credibility and financial support that it was forced to file for bankruptcy and shut its doors.

THIRD PARTY GROUPS AND VOTER MOBILIZATION APPROACHES

Third party mobilization efforts tend to focus either on increasing turnout generally across all groups or on increasing participation by a particular subgroup (and related, potentially decreasing participation by another). The first GOTV campaign ever run was led by the LWV in 1923 and was called the "Victory Vote Drive" (Gidlow 2002). During and following World War I, there was significant public attention paid to and discussion of the importance of democracy, but simultaneously voter turnout was less than 50 percent. Driven by the national office, local affiliate League organizations attempted to increase turnout by engaging in door-to-door canvassing, working with local boy scout troops to have members stand on street corners and *bugle* in order to announce the election, taking out advertisements in newspapers and news magazines, encouraging people to vote in community meetings, developing a national radio show whose purpose was to talk about the importance and responsibilities of citizenship, and circulating badges for people to wear, posters for buildings and poles, and billboards. These efforts were immediately popular and within just a few years were replicated by hundreds of other organizations across the United States.

GOTV efforts today are significantly more streamlined and follow a two-step process. First, organizations engaged in GOTV (whether candidate, party, or third party) work to identify those people (or groups) that they want to target. Candidates and parties tend to focus their attentions on likely supportive voters, though increasingly, allegations are made that they also target opposition voters for voter suppression by providing misinformation about candidates and elections. Third party groups either work to increase turnout generally, or focus on a specific subgroup, usually trying to attract unlikely voters. For those that focus on increasing voter turnout generally, they are largely able to skip this first step. For those that target a specific subgroup, in this stage they attempt to identify all subgroup members in their area and collect information on how best to make contact with them.

Second, the organizations target the potential voters in what is sometimes referred to as a "voter blitz" designed to ensure that the targeted audience actually turns out to vote. Contact with voters happens through various media, including door-to-door canvassing; phone contacts; *literature drops* in the form of mail, door hangers, and postcards; general advertisements (radio, television, newspapers, local magazines, or the Internet); e-mail; and text messaging. GOTV contacts always include information and sometimes offer some form of service. Nonpartisan contacts may talk about why it is important to vote generally speaking, but always provide information about when Election Day is. In addition, when possible, organizations include information about where a potential voter's polling place is and possibly provide maps or directions to that polling place. This information includes reminders about voting identification requirements where appropriate. Partisan contacts may also include persuasive messaging about why particular candidates are more or less desirable.

Sometimes, in addition to information, GOTV efforts will include the offer of services. When this occurs, it is usually in the form of transportation to and from the polls. In some rare cases, it may also include the provision of babysitting services. More recently, efforts to engage voters in active planning about how and when they will vote have been included in these services. In these cases, GOTV canvassers will work with voters to think through when they will go to the polls and how they will get there in the hopes that doing so will increase the likelihood that the potential voter will actually show up.

Over the last decade, a number of third party groups have emerged with a specific partisan focus. Among the most famous of these is a group called Citizens United, a national organization that produces documentaries about important issues related to campaigns and elections. During the 2008 primary election, they produced a 30-minute documentary about Hillary Clinton that was banned in the weeks leading up to Election Day in some areas, which the organization contested through litigation. In 2010, the U.S. Supreme Court ruled in *Citizens United v. Federal Election Commission* that the First Amendment protects the rights of corporations to spend money to engage in direct advocacy, essentially a form of GOTV. As a consequence of this ruling, many new third party groups emerged to engage in similar types of GOTV efforts; it is not yet clear what effect this form of GOTV will have on voter mobilization.

EFFICACY OF THIRD PARTY MOBILIZATION EFFORTS

Over the last 15 years, research on the efficacy of different types of GOTV efforts has proliferated through the increased use of field experiments (experiments on different treatment effects, or in this case approaches to GOTV, that happen in a natural setting). The results of the research on the efficacy of different types of GOTV efforts are mixed, depending in large on the conditions under which they are deployed. There is less reliable research about the efficacy of a particular organization's GOTV efforts.

With respect to specific GOTV tactics, the extant research shows that some are better than others, under certain conditions. For example, we know that there is an increase in Independent voter turnout from nonpartisan election reminders in the form of postcards (Gerber and Green 2000) as well as from door-to-door reminders (Gerber and Green 2008). When materials are provided in native languages to Asian voters, GOTV efforts increase turnout (Wong 2005). An increase in turnout when text messages are sent has also been found (Dale and Strauss 2009). GOTV efforts that include active vote planning (the canvasser works with the potential voter to plan when they will go to vote or mail in a ballot, how will he or she get there, what needs to be done to make sure that happens) have also been shown to increase turnout (Nickerson and Rogers 2010). However, other research has shown no effect from direct mail, robocalls, and e-mail GOTV efforts (Green, McGrath, and Aronow 2013). These studies were based on nonpartisan GOTV efforts; other research suggests that partisan approaches should work in the same ways (Nickerson, Friedrichs, and King 2006).

The timing and targeting of GOTV efforts also influence their efficacy. Off-cycle elections with low turnout display greater effects of GOTV efforts on election results (Anzia 2011). Minority voters tend to be contacted less often by political parties, so GOTV efforts by third party groups fill the gap in outreach designed to increase voter participation in this group. Related, another study demonstrated increases in turnout among unlikely Latino/a voters from third party group GOTV efforts (Matland and Murray 2012). Although contact by third party groups can be effective, research also shows that third party efforts are not as effective as party GOTV efforts directed toward white voters (Stevens and Bishin 2011).

In sum, voter mobilization efforts by third party groups emerged in the 1920s and over time have become a ubiquitous part of contemporary American politics. A wide variety of organizations are involved in these efforts, from party and candidate-centered groups to nonpartisan organizations, some focused on the general voting public and others focused specifically on mobilizing subgroups within the country. Although there is no specific formula for how to successfully engage in voter mobilization, some approaches have been shown to be more successful than others.

FURTHER READING

Anzia, Sara F. 2011. "Election Timing and the Electoral Influence of Interest Groups." *The Journal of Politics* 73: 412–427.

Baker, Susan G. 1996. "Su Voto Es Su Voz: Latino Political Empowerment and the Immigration Challenge." *PS: Political Science and Politics* 29: 465–468.

Brown, Mitchell. 2005. "Has Hope Died? The Successes of Social Movement and Advocacy Organizations in the Post-Civil Rights Era." College Park: University of Maryland.

Cain, Bruce E., and Ken McCue. 1985. "The Efficacy of Registration Drives." *The Journal of Politics* 47: 1221–1230.

Dahl, Robert. 1961. *Who Governs? Democracy and Power in an American City.* New Haven, CT: Yale University Press.

Dale, Allison, and Aaron Strauss. 2009. "Don't Forget to Vote: Text Message Reminders as a Mobilization Tool." *American Journal of Political Science* 53: 737–804.

Gerber, Alan S., and Donald P. Green. 2000. "The Effect of a Nonpartisan Get-Out-the-Vote Drive: An Experimental Study of Leafletting." *The Journal of Politics* 62: 3.

Gerber, Alan S., and Donald P. Green. 2008. *Get Out the Vote: How to Increase Voter Turnout* (2nd ed.). Washington, DC: Brookings Institution Press.

Gidlow, Liette. 2002. "Delegitimizing Democracy: 'Civic Slackers,' the Cultural Turn, and the Possibilities of Politics." *Journal of American History* 89: 922–957.

Green, Donald P., McGrath, Mary C., and Peter M. Aronow. 2013. "Field Experiments and the Study of Voter Turnout." *Journal of Elections, Public Opinion and Parties* 23: 27–48.

Hale, Kathleen, and Mitchell Brown. 2016. "Inter-Local Diffusion and Difference: How Networks Are Transforming Public Service." In *Transforming*

Government Organizations: Fresh Ideas and Examples from the Field, edited
by Floyd Dewey, William Sauser, Sheri Bias, 333–353. Charlotte, NC:
Information Age Publishing.

Hale, Kathleen, Montjoy, Robert, and Mitchell Brown. 2015. *Administering
Elections: How American Elections Work*. New York, NY: Palgrave Macmillan.

Harris, Joseph P. 1928. "The Progress of Permanent Registration of Voters."
The American Political Science Association 23: 908–914.

Harris, Joseph P. 1929. "Permanent Registration of Voters." *The American Political
Science Review* 22: 349–353.

Loomis, Burdett, and Allan Cigler. 2016. "The Changing Nature of Interest Group
Politics." In *Interest Group Politics* (9th ed.), edited by Allan Cigler, Burdett
Loomis, and Anthony Nownes, 1–36. Washington, DC: CQ Press.

Matland, Richard E., and Gregg R. Murray. 2012. "An Experimental Test of
Mobilization Effects in a Latino Community." *Political Research Quarterly*
65: 192–205.

Nickerson, David W., Friedrichs, Ryan D., and David C. King. 2006. "Partisan
Mobilization Campaigns in the Field: Results from a Statewide Turnout
Experiment in Michigan." *Political Research Quarterly* 59: 85–97.

Nickerson, David W., and Todd Rogers. 2010. "Do You Have a Voting Plan?
Implementation Intention, Voter Turnout, and Organic Plan-Making."
Psychological Sciences 21: 194–199.

Stevens, Daniel, and Benjamin G. Bishin. 2011. "Getting Out the Vote: Minority
Mobilization in a Presidential Election." *Political Behavior* 33: 113–138.

Tocqueville, Alexis de. 1839. *Democracy in America*. New York, NY: Scathered and
Adams.

Ulbig, Stacy G., and Tamara Waggener. 2011. "Getting Registered and Getting
to the Polls: The Impact of Voter Registration Strategy and Information
Provision on Turnout of College Students." *PS: Political Science and Politics*
44: 544–551.

Vanderleeu, James, Liu, Baodong, and Erica Williams. 2008. "The 2006 New
Orleans Mayoral Election: The Political Ramifications of a Large-Scale
Natural Disaster." *PS: Political Science and Politics* 47: 643–651.

Vedlitz, Arnold. 1985. "Voter Registration Drives and Black Voting in the South."
The Journal of Politics 47: 643–651.

Wong, Janelle S. 2005. "Mobilizing Asian American Votes: A Field Experiment."
The Annals of the American Academy of Political and Social Science 601: 102–114.

Who Will Vote? The Election Administration Landscape in 2016 and Beyond

Kathleen Hale

The chapters in this volume explore who votes in America and important factors that contribute to participation or constrain it. Authors have explored a wide range of topics that reflect individual motivations, demographic characteristics, long-standing institutional arrangements, political decisions, and media and interest group activities. Looking ahead at the overall question of "who votes?" to examine "who will vote?" there are several interrelated considerations that will be influential in shaping this most fundamental aspect of American democracy and politics. These include the systemic nature of American election administration, the role of federal oversight, and the influence of technological change.

THE SYSTEMIC NATURE OF ELECTION ADMINISTRATION

The systemic nature of the American election environment will continue to have consequences for voters and potential voters. Many of the authors in this volume have noted the variation among states. American elections actually operate in and interact through multiple systems, including a national institutional arrangement and 50 separate (and sovereign) state arrangements. These systems function as networks rather than hierarchies, and as a result are increasingly complex and interdependent, such that changes in one part of any one system typically reverberate throughout other systems and, at times, in ways that are unpredictable (see Hale, Montjoy, and Brown 2015 for discussion and analysis of election administration systems). At the national level and across the states,

separate laws, rules, and practices will continue to develop as will the
review and interpretation of these, and challenges to them within the constitutional system of checks and balances that characterizes American
government at all levels.

One illustration of those consequences has been evolving since the
enactment of the 1993 National Voter Registration Act (NVRA). For more
than 20 years, states have been required to provide voter registration in
conjunction with applying for and renewing motor vehicle licenses and
many other public services, including those that reach voters with disabilities. As simple as this concept may seem, successful implementation has
been fraught with difficulty in many states. Some states have embraced
the concept and in others, implementation has reached only a tiny fraction
of the eligible voters. The Presidential Commission on Election
Administration opined in its seminal report issued in early 2014 that this
particular provision of the NVRA was most frequently ignored by states
and localities (Presidential Commission on Election Administration 2014).

State implementation of NVRA has been frustrated by questions about
(and challenges to) how to allocate responsibility among elected constitutional officeholders within state government. For example, secretaries of
state responsible for election administration may lack authority to pre-
scribe procedures for executive branch officers responsible for motor
vehicle registration and other public services; at the least, considerable
effort has been expended to establish procedures, coordinate the flow of
data, and train personnel.

States also vary widely in the way that they implement NVRA requirements. An array of approaches can be found today in the procedures that
states use to integrate voter registration into the driver's license application; some states use a single application, some use two distinct procedures, and others fall somewhere in between. As a consequence, voters
may be required to provide duplicate information. Address changes
for motor vehicle licenses or other public services may not be integrated
(or not integrated well) with voter registration databases. Technology
can assist considerably in integrating election information gathered from
other public offices into existing election office data systems. However,
to the extent that public sector technological advances are without
adequate resources across government agencies, election offices are no
exception.

Despite successful implementation of NVRA in many states, some continue to experience low rates of registration through nonelection public
offices. It is possible that states with low rates of voter registration through
nonelection offices already have very high proportions of registered voters and thus fewer non-voters remaining to be registered. A recent study
suggests that there are at least some states where voter registration is considerably lower than the national average in which nonelection office

registration is also considerably lower than other states; these include California, Connecticut, and New Mexico (Naifeh 2015).

This illustration of a specific aspect of NVRA compliance is only one example of the complexity and interdependence that election officials face in bringing about policy change. Alongside their efforts to implement the "Motor Voter" and public service office provisions of the NVRA, states have also had to contend with, and integrate, changing requirements for voter identification; in some cases, states also rely increasingly on government-issued photo identification such as motor vehicle licenses.

What is clear about the systemic nature of American elections is that the processes and relationships are strongly rooted in constitutional responsibilities for state and national officials and are highly unlikely to change significantly. What this means is that any changes that can be achieved through the art of politics will likely be incremental. What this also means is that any such policy changes will certainly require integration with the existing election administration architecture of federal laws, including the 1965 Voting Rights Act (VRA), NVRA, Help America Vote Act (HAVA), and Uniformed and Overseas Citizens Absentee Voting Act (UOCAVA), as well as the Americans with Disabilities Act (ADA) and the laws of 50 separate states. Not least, new policies will have to survive judicial scrutiny. The federal architecture that governs the conduct of elections is already quite highly articulated; it may be the case that one of the best opportunities for additional gains in voter participation can be realized through increased efforts directed at implementing existing federal requirements. States also continue to lead innovation in a number of directions that influence the act of casting a ballot, including vote-by-mail, vote centers, and periods of early voting to name but a few examples. Considerable attention has been paid to whether these voting reforms enhance turnout and with mixed results. Automatic registration takes a different approach by focusing on the front-end of the election process; automatic registration is quite recent and, thus, relatively understudied but may prove to be a powerful tool in increasing participation. As states develop successful innovations in election administration, these can be expected to diffuse to other states, where these ideas will be modified to fit unique political configurations, cultures, and needs. Given the interrelationships among each state system and the national election system, policymakers would be wise to tread slowly and lightly; even very small changes in one part of any of these systems will certainly ripple across the others.

CONTINUING FEDERAL OVERSIGHT

The American intergovernmental policy conversation is an enduring one. In the election arena in particular, the constitutional allocation of roles and responsibilities to both the national government and the states guarantees a continual tension between national priorities and those of states, and also guarantees differences between states. As in all other areas of intergovernmental policy, federal-state-local policy relationships around the conduct of elections continue to be shaped by judicial decisions that resonate throughout the country, creating a host of policy responses from the states. These policy responses, in turn, press against existing laws, rules, and practice and produce new points of conflict and controversy. This enduring conversation is critical to our understanding of who votes and who does not. As the chapters in this volume illustrate, who votes and who does not are structured at the most fundamental level by these laws, rules, and practices and their inevitable intertwining twists and turns,

Thus, what we observe today in the election policy arena is, in all respects, one point in time along a continuum in which the national government and states continue to govern. That said, there are several key judicial developments that are shaping the federal-state election administration landscape and that will shape the answer to the question "who votes?" in the years to come.

Notably, 2016 will be the first time in more than 50 years that voters will elect a president without the protection of federal preclearance under the coverage formula of the VRA. Federal preclearance under the 1965 VRA was found to be unconstitutional in 2013 with the U.S. Supreme Court decision in *Shelby County v. Holder*. Federal preclearance was established as a special provision that applied to election jurisdictions (states and localities) with a history of discriminatory voting practices. If subject to federal preclearance, election jurisdictions were required to obtain federal review and approval of all changes to election law and practice before implementation. In general terms, election jurisdictions were "covered" if they met certain threshold conditions for low voter participation and had historically used discriminatory practices (tests or devices) in conducting elections. Voter participation thresholds were initially pegged to the 1964 presidential election and in subsequent reauthorizations of the 1965 VRA, and were updated as far as the 1972 presidential election. Although the VRA was reauthorized multiple times, and most recently in 2006, the participation aspect of the so-called coverage formula was not updated beyond 1972 or changed otherwise. As applied after the 2000 census, federal preclearance review was increasingly concerned with preventing minority vote dilution and so focused extensively on redistricting boundaries and representational arrangements rather than on barriers to registration or casting ballots.

In *Shelby County v. Holder*, the U.S. Supreme Court invalidated the coverage formula as an unconstitutional intrusion of federal power over the states because it was no longer responsive to current state election conditions. The implication of this decision for voter participation would seem to be negative overall. Some states moved to enact more stringent voter identification laws following the decision, for example. Although the national ban on discriminatory election practices remains in effect (Section 2), litigation will be the primary remedy and plaintiffs will be seeking a required finding of intentional discrimination. The right case(s) could present evidence of intentional discrimination that would be either struck down or require federal oversight through the "bail-in" provisions. Although this is a high bar to meet, election officials and policy makers would do well to remember that it is not impossible to meet and that typical political decisions such as protecting boundaries for incumbents may have consequences that could be discriminatory under the law (see *Garza v. Los Angeles County* 1990).

Of course, Congress could craft a new coverage formula for federal oversight. Two proposals have been introduced since the *Shelby County* decision. One proposal—the Voting Rights Amendment Act of 2014—was introduced in January 2014; the proposal would touch all states in one way or another. The bill was proposed by a bipartisan team (Sensenbrenner, R-WI; Conyers, D-NY; Leahy, D-VT) and specifically exempted disputes about voter identification from the types of state actions that could be considered in determining whether federal oversight would be required. As proposed, the bill would have automatically covered Georgia, Louisiana, Mississippi, and Texas. House leadership, however, failed to schedule a hearing on the proposal. In June 2015, the Voting Rights Advancement Act was proposed by Leahy (D-VT) and Lewis (D-GA). This bill would automatically cover more states and includes the states covered in the 1965 VRA; states covered include Alabama, Arkansas, Arizona, California, Florida, Georgia, Louisiana, Mississippi, New York, North Carolina, South Carolina, Texas, and Virginia. Total coverage would affect approximately half of the nation's population. Different than the 2014 proposal, this bill would specifically consider voter identification practices along with redistricting and minority language demographics. Minority language groups (Alaskan Native, Asian, American Indian, and Hispanic) are protected by the VRA and are identified under the VRA by sufficient population concentrations where English language proficiency is also low. Although the 2006 reauthorization of the VRA passed overwhelmingly in the House (390-33) and unanimously in the Senate (98-0), bipartisan support has not appeared for the 2015 proposal.

Perhaps the most intriguing recent development is the decision from the U.S. Supreme Court regarding the meaning of "one person, one vote." The phrase is the legacy of *Reynolds v. Sims* (1964) and other apportionment and districting cases of that era and is used widely to mean, in popular terms, that every person should be equally represented by the electoral process and that one person's vote should count as much as another's.

And at heart, the concepts of equal representation and equal voting power may seem to be essentially the same. The distinct difference between them is at the heart of *Evenwel v. Abbott*, argued in December 2015 and decided on April 4, 2016.

The *Evenwel* case originated in Texas. The specific question posed by the case was actually about the math behind apportionment and districting (redistricting, except in the relatively rare case of a new jurisdiction where no districts yet exist). At issue was the denominator used in drawing Texas legislative districts. The rulings that establish the "one person, one vote" principle do not specify how that calculation is made. For decades since the original decision, states have used total state population as the pool to be divided in apportionment and redistricting for both state legislative districts and congressional districts. Conceptually, the process is straightforward: a state's total population is divided by the number of seats available to arrive at districts with equal populations. In practice, a 10 percent variance is typically acceptable to accommodate natural geographic boundaries, existing political subdivision boundaries, and the like. The basis of this approach is that each district should be equal to all others in its strength of representation.

The challengers to the use of total population argued that the correct denominator to be divided among districts was actually the state's voter population. This argument is grounded in the notion of "voter equality," that each voter's ballot should carry equal weight. Under this approach, the voter population of each state would be divided into districts among the seats available. Challengers argued that individual votes carry more weight in districts with larger numbers of non-voters and that the votes of those in districts with larger numbers of voters are therefore disadvantaged. Non-voters reside in all districts and include those not eligible to vote because they are not yet old enough, because they are subject to the collateral consequences of felony conviction, and because they are not citizens. Precedent does exist for this argument; the Court decided a case about Hawaii redistricting to permit this approach (*Burns v. Richardson* 1966), however, the main thrust of the decision was that states could choose and the voter registration denominator was Hawaii's choice.

Various outcomes were possible. One is that the Court would choose to uphold state population (and 10 percent deviation) as the constitutional standard beyond which Texas (and by extension, other states) cannot deviate. Another was that the Court would accept the challengers' argument and establish state voter population as the constitutional standard for Texas along with some permissible range of deviation. A third possibility was that the Court might agree that either approach (or any approach) could pass constitutional muster so long as the deviation across districts does not vary too greatly.

The Court ruled that states or localities could use total population counts for redistricting purposes. Writing for the majority, Ruth Bader Ginsburg noted that "voter-eligible apportionment as a constitutional command would upset a well-functioning approach to districting that all 50 states and countless local jurisdictions have followed for decades, even centuries."

The competing formulas are actually code for a more fundamental argument that goes to the heart of what it means to be a representative democracy. The current practices of apportionment and redistricting rest on a theory of representation under which representatives speak for all in the district, not just those who can vote. Put another way, the overriding question is whether the Fourteenth Amendment mandates representational equality (equal power across districts), electoral equality (equal power across voters), or both. In *Evenwel*, the Court seemed to settle that argument, for the moment, in favor of electoral equality by holding that the Fourteenth Amendment contemplates that "representatives serve all residents, not just those eligible or registered to vote."

Although the particular case has been decided, the dynamics of *Evenwel v. Abbott* also highlight a considerable dilemma facing the election policy community. The dilemma is that, even if it seems appropriate to utilize voter registration data in redistricting calculations, it may not be practical to do so. First, the states vary widely in their approaches to voter registration. Eligibility rules differ from state to state, as several authors of this volume have detailed. Related, the administrative practices for maintaining voter rolls also vary by state, and all states that require voter registration have programs in place to remove voters. The Presidential Commission on Election Administration (2014) reported an inaccuracy rate in state voter rolls of 8–15 percent, depending on the reason (died, moved, etc.).

Census data do not present a practical solution. The combination of U.S. census data and geospatial analysis now make it possible to achieve considerable precision in the redistricting process based on population, but do not achieve this accuracy when based on voter registration using census data. Districts can be drawn based on population data that are exactly equal, or nearly so. The collection of decennial census data on population, race, and age (from which voting age can be determined) is mandated by law and grounded in the U.S. Constitution (see also, PL 94-73). In between decades, population demographics are also estimated at various intervals using the American Community Survey (ACS), which is conducted by sampling the population and is the source of citizenship data. It might seem appropriate to base districting calculations on the ACS as the most recent data available; however, the ACS data are estimates that illustrate broad trends (within a margin of error) and may not be representative of any particular district.

States may well prefer to use population data because these are actually readily available. Should voter registration data be used, or required, the net effect could be to call greater attention to registration, which might encourage an increase in it. Focusing on registration as the basis for representation might also foster more restrictive registration regimes, as has been the case with voter identification methods.

Voters with disabilities will continue to experience renewed efforts to make voting more accessible. One reason for this support is that the federal law in this area is mature and well understood. The Rehabilitation Act (RA; 1973), ADA (1990), and HAVA (2002) combine to require that polling places be accessible (RA, ADA) and that voters have the ability to vote privately and independently, and on accessible equipment (HAVA). It is expensive in some jurisdictions to ensure that all polling places are accessible, particularly where older buildings are involved. However, as a significant proportion of the population ages, the number of voters with disabilities continues to rise. The most common disabilities that interfere with voting, among those who report them, have to do with the inability to walk or stand and the inability to see or hear as acutely as when younger. Election offices do not *own* the locations used as polling places (commonly, schools, churches, recreation centers, and so forth), and so this area of the election administration system presents myriad complexities and requires considerable collaboration across public offices and private enterprises. The intergovernmental tension between states (and localities) and the federal government tends to focus, practically, on the costs associated with making changes rather than on ideological differences. Advocacy groups continue to play an active role in bringing disability access problems to the courts, and voters will be well served by compliance efforts to enforce existing requirements for signage and accessible entrances and equipment.

The experiences of Philadelphia (Pennsylvania) and New York City (New York) are illustrative of both the relatively uncomplicated nature of the concerns raised and the administrative complexity of the efforts required to resolve them. Like many other jurisdictions, these cities entered into consent decrees to resolve issues raised by several disability advocacy groups. Their general concerns are common to these types of actions—polling places were inaccessible, entrances were not clearly marked, accessible voting equipment was either not working correctly or was not set up, and poll workers were inattentive or unhelpful. The decrees are modeled after similar approaches used to resolve polling place operation issues (access to building and equipment) in other large jurisdictions. In New York City, this involved accessibility review of approximately 1,200 poll sites in its five boroughs (the Bronx, Brooklyn, Manhattan, Queens, and Staten Island), each of which operates in relative autonomy and with a distinctive approach. Actions taken citywide included the creation of new computer-aided drawings for building access, equipment placement and travel paths to and through the voting area; accessibility training for the more than 35,000 poll workers; and structured, scheduled monitoring of accessibility status and complaints throughout Election Day. Given the long-standing federal requirements for access and the relatively straightforward (albeit sometimes expensive) solutions to the majority of problems that voters with disabilities encounter, these voters and older voters generally should expect to experience continuous improvement around the country.

CHANGING TECHNOLOGY

Several technology issues will influence "who votes" in the near term and in different ways. First, it is clear that equipment will have to be "rebooted" in some way. It is well documented that voting systems are aging out of their useful lifespan (is any reader using a cell phone that they purchased more than 10 years ago?).

The HAVA funds that states used to make the transition to electronic voting systems from the punch card, lever, and other mechanical systems have been spent. Vendors are challenged to develop new technology that will serve what is essentially a limited market (50 state purchasers) with expanding requirements (numerous ballot styles in multiple and character-based languages) and for which no resources appear to be available; vendor support for hardware and software is dwindling as well and states do not necessarily have the capacity to address these issues (Hale and Brown 2013). The costs for new equipment will be considerable. More than $3.5 billion in HAVA funds were spent by the states and the bulk of that amount was spent on equipment; current voting machines cost $3,000–4,000 apiece and are maintained through equipment contracts that exceed $250,000 annually. Moreover, election officials do not appear content with the options available. The Presidential Commission on Election Administration (2014) reported widespread dissatisfaction among election officials with the technology available to them as they considered replacements; in simple terms, voting systems lag considerably behind the technology that is now common to many consumer products and commercial transactions.

Older or aging equipment can translate indirectly into who votes, or who can register to vote to the extent that equipment issues plague a poll site on Election Day or during the voting period. Voters can be disadvantaged by possible long lines and wait times or by faulty interaction with the voting equipment. Voters who experience difficulty because of equipment may also be less likely to vote in the future. Modernizing the voting experience may make it more appealing to first-time, younger voters; this group is considered most familiar with electronic technology.

On the horizon, at least two large local jurisdictions are experimenting with developing unique voting systems that meet their specific needs. Los Angeles County, California and Travis County, Texas (Austin) are working on unique voting systems that, when operational, should provide insight into what is possible when voting technology is developed at the local government level. Local election officials in these jurisdictions plan to use commercial, off-the-shelf technology such as tablets to operate their voting systems.

The shape of these endeavors will be influential across the country. Travis County will couple tablets with printed paper ballots that voters can verify. Its system utilizes an encryption system, and is named STAR, which stands for Security, Transparency, Auditability, and Reliability. It is expected to be operational by the 2018 gubernatorial election in advance of the 2020 presidential cycle. The project has a reported budget of $8–9 million and will serve approximately 700,000 registered voters.

Los Angeles County has been working on its voting system, which it will own, since 2009. Cost estimates are reported at $13–15 million for the project, which will serve the county's approximately 4.8 million registered voters and will improve the voting experience for voters with disabilities and voters who vote in languages other than English. The system is expected to pilot in 2018 and be fully operational for the 2020 election cycle. If fully implemented, the new touch screen system will include the paper trail required by California law. It will also incorporate voting by smartphone and customizable font sizes and languages other than English. The approach is also expected to incorporate the ability to use interactive preview ballots that can be filled out in advance so that voters can scan their preselected choices at the polls, mirroring the boarding pass method used in air travel.

These may appear to be relatively small-scale efforts within each state; Texas has more than 13 million registered voters and California has more than 17 million. Yet, these projects are much anticipated by election officials and the successes and challenges that these jurisdictions experience will be felt throughout the election administration systems in the states.

The idea of Internet voting has been growing for over a decade (Alvarez and Hall 2004). Internet voting also holds great popular appeal, particularly as the general public increasingly uses (and on personal devices such as smartphones) multiple applications that involve other data that they consider to be important and personal to them—such as bank transactions—and which therefore should be maintained privately and securely. Public officials may also be interested in looking for ways that voters can cast ballots outside the traditional poll place location, which is an expensive one-day operation in many states. Many states use the Internet to accomplish some interactive aspects of voter registration and other voter assistance functions such as polling place lookup and Election Day hours and instructions. Alaska and Arizona permit limited use of the Internet in voting; both allow voters to return ballots via e-mail or upload. In 2015, 10 states considered legislation to permit some form of Internet voting; although these bills were defeated, the activity speaks to the level of interest among the public, which we can only expect to increase (National Conference of State Legislatures 2016).

Questions continue about security, privacy, and transparency. However, a tipping point can certainly be imagined and perhaps in the nearer future than critics predict, given the spread of electronic transactions into essential services. Considerable groundwork has been established by experts in the field. In 2011, the EAC reported on the use of Internet voting systems used around the world from 2000 through 2011; the report examined 31 projects in 13 countries including the United States, Canada, Europe, and Oceania. The purpose was to identify standards used for development and testing, the levels of risk assumed and how these were estimated, and the entity that determined the acceptable level of risk (Election Assistance Commission 2011). The findings indicate that these projects were uncoordinated and that governments—including those in the United States—are proceeding ad hoc to determine risks and standards. Since that time, at least some in the technology community have taken up positions of cooperation instead of opposition, as encryption advancements make possible new levels of security and transparency that will facilitate transparency and auditability (Kiniry and Zimmerman 2015).

There is also one caveat about embracing Internet voting, and particularly about utilizing it as the only means of voting, and that is the lack of Internet access that persists in some parts of the country. Digital access has skyrocketed nationally, but remains sparse in some areas. Important for the discussion of "who votes," this scarcity is not distributed randomly. Latino/as who do not speak English are particularly vulnerable. According to recent survey research, reasons that respondents offer for lack of broadband Internet connection extend beyond cost or lack of connectivity options and include the feelings that respondents do not understand how to use the technology and do not see the relevance to their lives (Pew 2015). The digital divide includes an access divide and a skill divide (Mossberger, Tolbert, and Stansbury 2003). In both, age, education, income, and race/ethnicity are barriers. Older, less educated, and lower-income individuals are less likely to have personal access to technology and more likely to need assistance in using it. Latino/as and African Americans are also less likely to have access and more likely to need assistance. The proliferation of smartphone technology may change both access and ease of use significantly for those who can afford it. However, based on demographic data alone, those most likely *not* to vote are those with less than a high school education, those who have moved within the last few years, those whose household income is in the bottom quintile nationally, and those who are nonwhite, Latino/as in particular. The demographic dynamics here suggest the need for close attention to how new voting systems are designed so that the digital divide is not entrenched as a new voting divide.

SUMMARY/CONCLUSION

This volume has presented considerable discussion of barriers to voting and state and federal solutions to address them. Throughout, the authors have noted the intransigency of state and national institutional architecture and the inability to bring productive reforms to current and prospective voters. The sweet spot in election reforms has been, and continues to be, the compromise that fuels policymaking in American politics.

It is true that if we were to establish a voting system from a blank slate, whether for the nation or for states or for both, we might well construct it (or them) very differently than what we use today. Policy makers are also wise to acknowledge that, because elections measure democracy, elections have to be perceived to be fair in order to continue to warrant public legitimacy; the results of a fair process are therefore fair (Dahl 1961; Hale, Montjoy, and Brown 2015, xiv). To the extent that any election reforms are based even in part on ideological positions—voter identification, voting system security, and redistricting seem to be the most clear examples—policymakers are wise to remember that "one size does not fit all." In fact, one size cannot fit all, unless all states decide to change their election laws to be exactly the same.

To that end, the 50 laboratories of democracy that exist across the states are perhaps the most valuable incubators we could hope for in terms of imaging and testing new ideas. There, we see examples across a continuum of perspectives about early voting, districting, identification, and registration methods, as a few examples. As the federal-state pendulum swings in intergovernmental relations, so does the policy pendulum. As states test new ideas along the continuum of what is politically possible and economically and technologically feasible, ideas at the extremes tend to converge toward the middle. To that end, testing a wide variety of ideas in various contexts and with various demographic groups seems the best way to ensure that the good ideas that work will be identified and implemented as broadly as possible so that everyone votes.

FURTHER READING

Alvarez, Michael, and Thad Hall. 2004. *Point, Click, and Vote: The Future of Internet Voting*. Washington, DC: Brookings Institution Press.

Burns v. Richardson (1966) 384 U.S. 73.

Dahl, Robert A. 1961. *Who Governs? Democracy and Power in an American City.* New Haven, CT: Yale University Press.

Garza v. County of Los Angeles (1990) 918 F. 2d 763 – Court of Appeals, 9th Circuit.

Hale, Kathleen, and Mitchell Brown. 2013. "Adopting, Adapting, and Opting Out: State Response to Federal Voting System Guidelines." *Publius, The Journal of Federalism* 43 (3): 428–451.

Hale, Kathleen, Montjoy, Robert, and Mitchell Brown. 2015. *Administering Elections: How American Elections Work.* New York, NY: Palgrave Macmillan.

Kiniry, Joseph R., and Daniel M. Zimmerman. 2015. *The Future of Voting: End-to-End Verifiable Internet Voting Specifications and Feasibility.* Washington DC: U.S. Vote Foundation.

Mossberger, Karen, Tolbert, Caroline, and Mary Stansbury. 2003. *Virtual Inequality: Beyond the Digital Divide.* Washington, DC: Georgetown University Press.

Naifeh, Stuart. 2015. *Driving the Vote: Are States Complying with the Motor Voter Requirements of the National Voter Registration Act?* New York, NY: Demos. http://www.demos.org/publication/driving-vote-are-states-complying -motor-voter-requirements-national-voter-registration-a.

National Conference of State Legislatures. 2016. "Electronic Transmission of Ballots." Retrieved March 30, 2016 from http://www.ncsl.org/research/ elections-and-campaigns/internet-voting.aspx.

Presidential Commission on Election Administration. 2014. "The American voting Experience: Report and Recommendation of the Presidential Commission on Election Administration." Retrieved on March 30, 2016 from https:// www.supportthevoter.gov/files/2014/01/Amer-Voting-Exper-final-draft -01-09-14-508.pdf.

U.S. Election Assistance Commission. 2011. "A Survey of Internet Voting: Testing and Certification Technical Paper No. 2." Washington, DC: Election Assistance Commission. Retrieved from http://www.eac.gov/assets/1/ Documents/SIV-FINAL.pdf.

Appendix A.1: Voter Turnout in Presidential and Midterm Elections, 1789–2014

Figure A.1.1

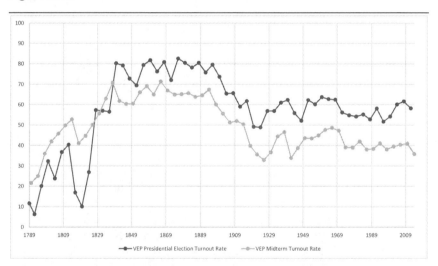

Source: McDonald, Michael P. 2015. "Voter Turnout" United States Elections Project. Retrieved December 18, 2015, from http://www.electproject.org/home/voter-turnout/voter-turnout-data.

Note: There are two ways to measure voter turnout by focusing on the percent of the total Voting Age Population (VAP) that cast a ballot or by focusing on the percent of the Voting Eligible Population (VEP) that cast a ballot. The measure of turnout presented here is based on the turnout of the VEP (McDonald 2015).

Appendix A.2:
Constitutional Amendments

THIRTEENTH AMENDMENT

Section 1

Neither slavery nor involuntary servitude, except as a punishment for crime whereof the party shall have been duly convicted, shall exist within the United States, or any place subject to their jurisdiction.

Section 2

Congress shall have power to enforce this article by appropriate legislation.

FOURTEENTH AMENDMENT

Section 1

All persons born or naturalized in the United States, and subject to the jurisdiction thereof, are citizens of the United States and of the State wherein they reside. No State shall make or enforce any law which shall abridge the privileges or immunities of citizens of the United States; nor shall any State deprive any person of life, liberty, or property, without due process of law; nor deny to any person within its jurisdiction the equal protection of the laws.

Section 2

Representatives shall be apportioned among the several States according to their respective numbers, counting the whole number of persons in each State, excluding Indians not taxed. But when the right to vote at any election for the choice of electors for President and Vice President of the United States, Representatives in Congress, the Executive and Judicial officers of a State, or the members of the Legislature thereof, is denied to any of the male inhabitants of such State, being twenty-one years of age, and citizens of the United States, or in any way abridged, except for participation in rebellion, or other crime, the basis of representation therein shall be reduced in the proportion which the number of such male citizens shall bear to the whole number of male citizens twenty-one years of age in such State.

Section 3

No person shall be a Senator or Representative in Congress, or elector of President and Vice President, or hold any office, civil or military, under the United States, or under any State, who, having previously taken an oath, as a member of Congress, or as an officer of the United States, or as a member of any State legislature, or as an executive or judicial officer of any State, to support the Constitution of the United States, shall have engaged in insurrection or rebellion against the same, or given aid or comfort to the enemies thereof. But Congress may by a vote of two-thirds of each House, remove such disability.

Section 4

The validity of the public debt of the United States, authorized by law, including debts incurred for payment of pensions and bounties for services in suppressing insurrection or rebellion, shall not be questioned. But neither the United States nor any State shall assume or pay any debt or obligation incurred in aid of insurrection or rebellion against the United States, or any claim for the loss or emancipation of any slave; but all such debts, obligations and claims shall be held illegal and void.

Section 5

The Congress shall have power to enforce, by appropriate legislation, the provisions of this article.

FIFTEENTH AMENDMENT

Section 1

The right of citizens of the United States to vote shall not be denied or abridged by the United States or by any State on account of race, color, or previous condition of servitude.

Section 2

The Congress shall have power to enforce this article by appropriate legislation.

TWENTY-FOURTH AMENDMENT

Section 1

The right of citizens of the United States to vote in any primary or other election for President or Vice President, for electors for President or Vice President, or for Senator or Representative in Congress, shall not be denied or abridged by the United States or any State by reason of failure to pay any poll tax or other tax.

Section 2

The Congress shall have power to enforce this article by appropriate legislation.

TWENTY-SIXTH AMENDMENT

Section 1

The right of citizens of the United States, who are eighteen years of age or older, to vote shall not be denied or abridged by the United States or by any State on account of age.

Section 2

The Congress shall have power to enforce this article by appropriate legislation.

Source: U.S. Government Publishing Office https://www.gpo.gov/fdsys/pkg/CDOC-110hdoc50/pdf/CDOC-110hdoc50.pdf.

Appendix A.3: Probit Regression Model Predicting Voter Apathy Abstention

Variables	Lack of Interest Coefficient Estimates (standard errors)	Did Not Like Candidates Coefficient Estimates (standard errors)
Income	0.007	(0.009)
	(0.004)	(0.002)
Age	−0.005*	0.002*
	(0.001)	(0.001)
Education	−0.076*	−0.030
	(0.018)	(0.019)
White	0.159*	0.439*
	(0.051)	(0.061)
South	−0.013	−0.064
	(0.036)	(0.038)
Female	−0.103*	−0.112*
	(.034)	(0.036)
Constant	−0.812*	−1.559*
	(0.082)	(0.093)
	N = 7,936	N = 7,936
	$\chi^2 = 56.33$	$\chi^2 = 83.70$

*$p < 0.05$.
Source: 2012 Current Population Survey Voter Supplement File.

Appendix A.4: Demographics California VAAC Survey Respondents, 2012 and 2014 (in percentages)

	Category	2012 (percent)	2014 (percent)
Age	18–30	17.5	8
	31–40	14	16
	41–60	47	45
	61 and older	21.5	31
Disability	Mobility	31	27
	Dexterity	12	9
	Mental health	17.5	13
	Developmental	11	8
	Vision	19	21
	Hearing	15	5
	No disability	12	6
Income	Less than $11,000	30	26
	$12–32,000	28	35
	$33–53,000	17	17
	$54–74,000	12	6
	$75–95,000	7	5
	Greater than $95,000	7	10
Ethnicity/race	White	67	63
	African American	4	7
	American Indian or Alaskan Native	3	1

(Continued)

	Chinese	0.7	1
	Filipino	1	–
	Korean	–	1
	Other Asian	1	1
	Hispanic	15	18
Survey respondents		336	193

Source: California Secretary of State's Office.

Appendix A.5: California VAAC Respondent Voting Preferences, 2012 and 2014: Habits and Preferences (in percentages)*

	Category	2012 (percent)	2014 (percent)
Voting habits	Always	64.5	81
	Vote in most	27	16
	Seldom	5	3
	Never	3	1
Voting preference	By mail	52	53
	Polling place	40	40
	Early voting site	2	4
	Election office	1	0
If VBM, why?	Convenient	75	43
	Can take my time	51	38
	Cannot leave home unassisted	14	5
	Polling place not accessible	12	6
	Other	20	7
Election material preference	Paper	62	56
	E-mailed	14	13
	Access online	13	12
	CD	4	6
	Audio cassette	2	1
	Large print braille	–	5
	Other	0	5

(Continued)

Registered		90.5	94
Knowledge to find polling	Yes	78.4	91
place?	No	21.6	9
Knowledge of polling place	Yes	52.3	66
accessibility?	No	47.7	34
Knowledge of federal law	Yes	81.9	90
requiring accessible	No	18.1	10
polling places?			
Knowledge of federal law	Yes	70.8	81
requiring accessible voting	No	29.2	19
machines?			
Past use of machine designed	Yes	75.3	60
for accessibility?	No	24.7	40
Accessible voting machine	Touchscreen	57.3	50
used?	Paper-marking	42.7	50
Voting machine experience	Convenient and useful	47.3	24
	Private	32.7	18
	Independent	36.7	19
	Slow and cumbersome	13.3	9
	Poll workers did not know	14.7	8
	how to use it		
	Machine was not working	6	5
	Did not know how to use	10	2
Registered		90.5	94

*The percentages exceed 100 percent because respondents were allowed more than one answer selection.

Note: The percentages exceed 100 percent because respondents were allowed more than one answer selection.

Source: California Secretary of State's Office.

Appendix A.6: Alienation Survey Questions

Powerlessness

1. People like me do not have any say about what the government does. (Agree/Disagree)

2. I do not think public officials care much what people like me think. (Agree/Disagree)

Cynicism

1. How much of the time do you think you can trust the government in Washington to do what is right—just about always, most of the time, or only some of the time?

2. Would you say the government is pretty much run by a few big interests looking out for themselves, or that it is run for the benefit of all the people? (Yes/No)

Appendix A.7: Binary Logistic Analysis of Voter Turnout, 2008 and 2012

Variable	2008 Voter Turnout Coefficient (standard error)	2012 Voter Turnout Coefficient (standard error)
Education	0.447***	0.476***
	(0.075)	(0.040)
Age	0.050***	0.314***
	(0.005)	(0.024)
Black	0.216	0.486***
	(0.296)	(0.126)
Latino	−0.080	0.192
	(0.299)	(0.104)
Other nonwhite race	−0.552	0.619**
	(0.304)	(0.243)
Female	0.068	0.013
	(0.146)	(0.079)
Strength of partisanship	0.640***	0.661***
	(0.089)	(0.049)
Income	0.081***	0.182***
	(0.017)	(0.026)
Powerlessness	−0.368***	−0.191***
	(0.099)	(0.051)
Cynicism	−0.130	−0.125**
	(0.134)	(0.052)
Constant	−1.533**	−2.577

(continued)

(Continued)

	2008 Voter Turnout	2012 Voter Turnout
N	2,655	5,914
Cox and Snell R Square	0.131	0.157
Nagelkerke R Square	0.271	0.251
Correctly predicted	90.4 percent	82.2 percent

**p < 0.01.
***p < 0.001.
Source: American National Election Studies, 2008–2009, Wave 11; American National Election Studies, Evaluations of Government and Society Study, 2010–2012.

Appendix A.8: Models of Voter Registration and Turnout

	Registration	Turnout
Online voter registration	0.17*	0.03
	(0.08)	(0.08)
Demographic variables		
Age	0.29***	0.32***
	(0.01)	(0.01)
Household income	0.13***	0.13***
	(0.01)	(0.01)
Residential mobility	−0.31***	−0.35***
	(0.01)	(0.01)
Home ownership	0.36***	0.41***
	(0.01)	(0.01)
Gender (male)	−0.21***	−0.13***
	(0.01)	(0.01)
Unemployed	−0.15***	−0.17***
	(0.02)	(0.02)
Not in labor force	−0.29***	−0.24***
	(0.01)	(0.01)
Education	0.59***	0.55***
	(0.01)	(0.01)
White	0.14***	0.18***
	(0.03)	(0.03)
Black	0.63***	0.81***
	(0.04)	(0.03)
Asian	−0.71***	−0.66***
	(0.04)	(0.04)
Hispanic	−0.19***	−0.18***
	(0.02)	(0.02)

(*continued*)

(Continued)

	Registration	Turnout
Interaction terms (online voter registration X demographics)		
Age	−0.01	0.01
	(0.01)	(0.01)
Household income	−0.02**	−0.03***
	(0.01)	(0.01)
Residential mobility	0.01	−0.01
	(0.03)	(0.02)
Home ownership	0.04	0.04
	(0.03)	(0.01)
Gender (male)	−0.04^	0.01
	(0.02)	(0.02)
Unemployed	0.06	0.07
	(0.05)	(0.05)
Not in labor force	−0.06*	0.01
	(0.03)	(0.02)
Education	−0.05***	−0.06***
	(0.01)	(0.01)
White	0.08	0.08
	(0.07)	(0.07)
Black	0.01	−0.09
	(0.08)	(0.07)
Asian	−0.01	−0.01
	(0.08)	(0.08)
Hispanic	−0.02	−0.02
	(0.03)	(0.03)
Electoral conditions		
Election Day Voter	0.03	0.07^
Registration	(0.04)	(0.03)
No-excuse absentee		0.30***
voting		(0.09)
Vote-by-mail		0.46***
		(0.07)
Early voting		−0.36***
		(.05)
Constant	−1.30***	−2.22***
	(0.06)	(0.05)
Pseudo R^2	0.15	0.18
N	324,683	324,683

*$p < 0.05$.
**$p < 0.01$.
***$p < 0.001$.
^$p < 0.10$.
Coefficients for the state and year indicators are not shown.
Note: Entries are logistic regression coefficients with standard errors in parentheses.

About the Editors and Contributors

EDITORS

BRIDGETT A. KING, PhD, is assistant professor of political science at Auburn University and a regular contributor to the Certified Elections/Registration Administrator (CERA) Program, a partnership between the Election Center and the Auburn University MPA Program. Her scholarship focuses on the political behavior of marginalized populations, state voting regulations, and election administration. Prior to joining the faculty at Auburn University, Dr. King was a voting rights researcher in the Democracy Program at the Brennan Center for Justice at New York University School of Law.

KATHLEEN HALE, JD, PhD, is associate professor of political science and director of the MPA Program and Graduate Certificate in Election Administration at Auburn University. Her scholarship focuses on intergovernmental relations, election administration, and the role of professional associations. She chairs the Election Administration and Leadership Section of the Network of Schools of Public Administration and Affairs (NASPAA), serves on the Election Center's Board of Directors, and directs the Auburn University faculty in the CERA Program.

CONTRIBUTORS

Gayle Alberda, PhD, Drake University

Leah Alley, BA, Fors Marsh Group

Jodi Benenson, PhD, Tufts University Institute for Democracy and Higher Education

Elizabeth Bergman, PhD, California State University-East Bay

Margaret Brower, MA, Tufts University Institute for Democracy and Higher Education

Mitchell Brown, PhD, Auburn University

Robert C. Chalwell Jr., PhD, Broward College-South Campus

Anne M. Cizmar, PhD, Eastern Kentucky University

Benjamin W. Cole, MPA, Auburn University

Krysha Gregorowicz, PhD, Fors Marsh Group

Thad E. Hall, PhD, Fors Marsh Group

Kelly Krawczyk, PhD, Auburn University

Christopher N. Lawrence, PhD, Middle Georgia State University

Robert Postic, PhD, The University of Findlay

Megan M. Ruxton, doctoral candidate, Colorado State University

Kyle L. Saunders, PhD, Colorado State University

Keith Smith, PhD, University of the Pacific

Priscilla L. Southwell, PhD, University of Oregon

Dari Sylvester-Tran, PhD, University of the Pacific

Nancy L. Thomas, EdD, Tufts University Institute for Democracy and Higher Education

Linda M. Trautman, PhD, Ohio University-Lancaster

Ryan Voris, doctoral candidate, University of Kentucky

Dominic D. Wells, doctoral candidate, Kent State University

Index

The Case of the Missing Kittens

Mark Taylor

illustrated by

Graham Booth

ATHENEUM · *1979* · NEW YORK

LIBRARY OF CONGRESS CATALOGING IN PUBLICATION DATA

Taylor, Mark.
The case of the missing kittens.

SUMMARY: Angus the dog does some detective work
to locate Mrs. Friday's missing kittens.
[1. Dogs—Fiction.   2. Cats—Fiction]   I. Booth,
Graham.   II. Title.
PZ7.T2172Cas   [E]   78-4908
ISBN 0-689-30627-X

Published simultaneously in Canada by
McClelland & Stewart, Ltd.
Printed in the United States of America by
A. Hoen & Company Incorporated, Baltimore, Maryland
First Printing August 1978
Second Printing September 1979

Angus hurried from room to room . . . .

Everybody was talking.

Angus listened with both ears.

"Poor Mrs. Friday," said Henry. "What will she do with two broken legs?"

"She won't walk for a while," said Henry's father. "She is lucky the car that hit her didn't kill her."

"She won't be able to go to her kittens," said Henry's mother. "Henry, where are her kittens?"

"I don't know," said Henry. "Mrs. Friday hid them somewhere, and I can't find them. I'm afraid they'll starve to death."

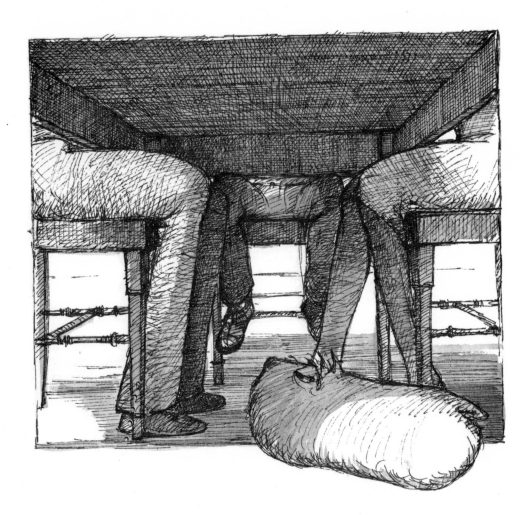

Someone had to find the missing kittens.
Angus knew what he must do. He went
to work on the case at once.

First Angus checked the places where Mrs. Friday often liked to go. He investigated the hens' house, but all he found were eggs and feathers. No kittens.

So Detective Angus went on.

Next Angus checked the old bridge. Mrs. Friday often went to the river to fish. Of course, the kittens wouldn't be on the bridge. Maybe they were under it.

Angus would have to go down and investigate.

It was wet and muddy under the bridge and not a very good place for kittens.

Angus found a cave in the river bank. It might be a place for hiding kittens. Mrs. Friday was very clever. She knew how to hide kittens. And who would ever think to look for kittens in a muddy cave?

Detective Angus would.

There were no kittens in the cave. But Angus did find a very unfriendly muskrat. Maybe the muskrat knew where the kittens were. But the muskrat only hissed and wouldn't tell him anything.

Angus hurried off. A detective could not waste his time with an unfriendly muskrat. Besides, the muskrat probably didn't even know what a kitten looked like.

Angus kept searching for Mrs. Friday's kittens. There were so many places where kittens might be. It would take lots of detective work to find them.

But Angus had a good nose. He always followed it. And right now his nose told him to run up the hill toward some big bushes.

Aha! It looked as if those bushes might be just the place where Mrs. Friday would hide her kittens.

As Angus looked at the bushes, he saw something dark under them. It had black fur and was moving. It looked pretty big for a kitten, but Angus investigated.

Oh, oh! It was a skunk! Mrs. Friday would never hide her kittens where a skunk could find them. So Angus hurried off. No use wasting time with skunks.

Where would Angus look next? He had to find the kittens soon, because a storm was coming up.

Angus saw a big house. His nose told him to go there. The rain told him to hurry. Detective Angus gave a bark and began to run.

What a big, old house it was! And it was so dark and empty. Could Mrs. Friday have hidden her kittens there?

Angus's nose told him to go inside.

Angus entered the house *gingerly*. He looked around at all the shadows. Was something there—just waiting?

Slowly Angus walked across the old dusty floor. Slowly he sniffed all the strange smells. They were old smells and dry smells and spooky smells.

Angus saw some steep stairs. Slowly he climbed up them. Slowly he turned the corner at the top.

WHAT WAS THAT? It was staring at him!

Angus barked, and it barked. And then he felt better, because it was just a mirror. Sometimes detective work was very scary.

Angus hurried from room to room, sniffing for clues as to where the kittens might be.

But the rooms were empty. Angus ran around each one to make sure he didn't miss something.

Outside the thunder gave a grumble, and the rain went *plip-plop* on the windows.

Angus came to a door. He pushed it, and it opened. He walked into a room that was very big. There were some chairs and a a table by the windows.

Then the lightning flickered, and Angus saw a mouse dart across the floor. Angus barked, but the mouse ran up the wall and disappeared.

When Angus ran to see where the mouse had gone, he found a funny-looking cupboard in the wall. Maybe Mrs. Friday's kittens were in it. Angus followed his nose and jumped in.

All that Angus found in the cupboard was the mouse. And the mouse gave a big squeak and jumped out.

Then the wind rattled the windows and shook the house. And the door of the room banged shut.

Angus looked out of the cupboard. He could see the door was shut. Now what would he do?

All at once the cupboard began to move. It began to go down. It was too late for Angus to jump out.

Detective Angus was trapped. And the trap was as black as the blackest night!

Angus was just getting ready to bark, when the cupboard stopped moving with a bounce. Angus could see again. He had come to another room!

What did he hear? Kittens!
What did he see? Kittens!
There they were on a big old sofa. And there was a huge rat poking at them!

Angus began to bark. He jumped out of the cupboard and ran at the rat. The rat was so surprised it sat up and looked at Angus for a second. But Angus barked again, and the rat scampered off the sofa. It ran into a hole in the brick wall. Angus ran up to the hole and barked some more, just to tell that rat to stay away from Mrs. Friday's kittens.

Angus gave each of the kittens a quick lick to let them know he was their friend. This was certainly no place for kittens, not with rats around. But how would Angus get the kittens home? He saw a window where he could get out. But he couldn't leave the kittens.

There was only one thing Detective Angus could do. He began to howl for help.

Angus grew tired of howling when no one came. He would have to do something else to save Mrs. Friday's kittens, himself.

It had stopped raining. Angus found that he could climb on some boxes and reach the window. There was no glass in the window, so it was easy to get out.

Angus carried each of the kittens, one by one, and put them outside. Then he climbed outside, too. Next he took each of the kittens and put them under some bushes by a big tree. It was warm and dry and away from the rats.

Now what would Angus do? He couldn't carry each kitten home. He couldn't leave them alone.

So Detective Angus barked and howled as loud as he could. He barked and barked, while the kittens crawled next to him to keep warm.

And then he heard Henry calling him. So he kept barking until Henry and his father came along. They were really glad to see Angus with Mrs. Friday's kittens.

Mrs. Friday was a happy cat. She gave each kitten one bath right after the other.

"Isn't it lucky that Angus discovered the kittens?" said Henry's mother. "I'll bet he was surprised to run into them under those bushes by that old house."

"I guess Mrs. Friday hid them under those bushes because it was warm and dry there," said Henry's father.

"Maybe she put them in that house," said Henry.

"Oh, I don't think so," said Henry's father. "How could they have gotten out?"

"I don't know," said Henry, as he looked at Angus. "Maybe Angus knows."

But, of course, Detective Angus didn't say
a word.